# MASTERING THE KNIFE

## SEEKING IDENTITY & FINDING BELONGING

### MICHAEL M. MEGUID MD

20 The new University College Hospital, 1906

ISBN 978-0-9992988-3-1

M3 Scientific Media
Marco Island, Florida 34145, USA
www.michaelmeguid.com

Cover Design
Sketch of University College Hospital by Jonathan Marrow FRCS, FRCEM.

Previous Page
Photograph courtesy of University College London Hospitals Trust

# In Praise of *Mastering the Knife*

Meguid is a masterful storyteller, and the story that he seems to have lighted on is about the peculiar mixture of temperament, intellect, skill, circumstance, discipline and luck that go into the making of a remarkable life. Some powerful forces are arrayed against him, of course: racism and xenophobia as well as parental cruelty, neglect and abandonment. The author gets a lot of narrative momentum from the sense of pushing against the forces—even the ones inside his own head—agitating for defeat and failure.

Scenes capture the drama of a particular moment in very few words. Much of the dialogue is crisp. Sometimes it's laugh-out-loud funny. Whenever the author turns his descriptive powers on a place—whether landscape or structure—the writing turns vivid and evocative. Much of the prose about the practice of medicine or surgery, as seen through the eyes of a student, is precise and memorable. The reader finds herself being educated through Meguid's eyes.

—Jennifer Brice, Associate Professor of English, author of
*Unlearning to Fly*

# ALSO BY MICHAEL M. MEGUID

## Roots & Branches

### A Family Saga *Like No Other*

*Roots & Branches* is rooted in a story of love and longing based on a fatal accident in an upper Egyptian village over a century ago. In this rich and powerful story Meguid explores his remarkable early life based on a journal, letters and photos, which amply illustrate the book.

Born to an Egyptian father and a German mother, his earliest memories of Cairo are idyllic, but his mother's refusal to adapt to Egyptian life results in upheaval. At the age of four, his parents leave him in Hamburg with his German grandparents, where life becomes defined by the rigid rules of his Prussian grandfather. The desertion leaves him with a gaping hole, howling loneliness, and a longing that ripples through him.

When his parents collect him five years later, they take him to England, where once again he has to adapt to being an outsider. When he eventually returns to his beloved Egypt, he was gone so long that he no longer quite fits in. His father's premature death thrusts Meguid into an existential crisis. Facing conscription and an uncertain future, Meguid learns to navigate his own path.

## Making the Cut Podcast

Overcoming a childhood of abandonment and neglect, Dr. Meguid becomes a world-renowned surgeon. But before that he had to learn to become a man. Now, that story is revealed.

makingthecutpodcast.com

*Dedicated with gratitude to:*

*Ray Forbes MD and Rich O'Neill PhD,*
*who started me on the road of seeking identity*

*and*

*In memory of my colleague and friend*
*Jonathan Marrow FRCS, FRCEM (1944–2019)*

To heal we must remember. It's hard sometimes to remember,
but that's how we heal.
—Joe Biden

Have I betrayed them all by telling the story?
Or is it the other way around: would I have
betrayed them if I had not told it?
—Amos Oz

# CONTENTS

# AUTHOR'S NOTE

In the writing process of this book the story took on a life of its own, growing in length and scope. Thus the work morphed from a Surgical Trilogy to a Surgical Quartet. *Mastering the Knife* becomes Volume II following *Roots & Branches.*

The occurrences in the sequence are inspired by factual events and are as I remember them, although creative nonfiction is illiberally used as a literary device in that some characters and scenes are composites, and certain experiences were reordered. The names and identifying characteristics of some individuals have been changed to protect their privacy; as unique individuals, however, they may discover themselves in these pages. In other cases, I used names in accordance with historical facts and records.

Quotes from letters originate from correspondence. Whereas when written over fifty years ago some letters fell into the private domain and were never intended to see the light of day, the beauty, passion and tenderness of their message especially in the era of text messages raises these letters to the realm of poetry and merit sharing with the reader in the relevant context.

The narratives reflect my recollection of events during my medical training in England in the 1960s. I've endeavored to be as authentic as possible, relying on my personal archives, including a journal, letters, photo albums, report cards, and stories from familial verbal history. This account does not attempt to tell the whole story. Others may recall things differently or have their own versions of what transpired.

# British Medical Education in the 1960s

## Requirements
High/Grammar School: 2–3 years (biology, chemistry, physics; Bachelor Medicine) Burnage Grammar School, Manchester $\longrightarrow$ 1st MB

Medical School/College
2 years basic science. University College London $\longrightarrow$ 2nd MB

3 years Clinical Training plus, University College Hospital, London
$\longrightarrow$ MBBS

(MBBS is given by the General Medical Council of the United Kingdom.)

## One-year Compulsory Internship
6 months medicine. House Physician (HP) Bethnal Green Hospital
6 months surgery. House Surgeon (HS) Royal Ear Hospital, UCH

(A student can stand in for Locum HP or Locum HS for HP or HS when they take a compulsory two-week holiday)

Receive a medical license issued by General Medical Council of the United Kingdom to practice as GP or to start specialized training.

## Steps to specialize as a general surgeon in UK in the 1960s
Become a Fellow Royal College Surgeons (FRCS).

Study for 6–12 months. Basic science (anatomy, physiology pathology) *as it applies to the surgical patient.*
Sit and pass primary exam given by Royal College Surgeon
$\longrightarrow$ **Primary FRCS***

3–4 years surgical training as Surgical Registrar (Residency)
Sit and pass final exam given by Royal College Surgeon
$\longrightarrow$ **Final FRCS***

*FRCS is equal to the American College of Surgeon's FACS

# PROLOGUE

*Our bodies are the texts that carry the memories and therefore remembering is no less than reincarnation.*
—Katie Cannon

When I was four and a half in the later summer of 1949, my sister and I were uprooted from a cozy, affectionate Egyptian family life and we were deposited with German grandparents in cold, devastated, postwar Hamburg. I didn't know them, didn't understand German, didn't like the meager, strange food, rations, the austerity of their culture or their paltry financial circumstances. I felt I didn't belong to them. Also, I had no friends, toys or books. Mother left me with a gaping hole, howling loneliness, and a longing that rippled through me. Daddy, who had doted on me, disappeared wordlessly with her. There were no explanations. There was nowhere else for me to go.

Coerced by my Opa via threats, bullying, and fears of corporal punishment, to survive abandonment, since I had no defenses or escape, I transformed into a proud German boy. Five years later when my parents—virtual strangers—reappeared, I was wrenched from the comfortable folds of my nurturing Oma who had become my surrogate trusted mother and the other consoling woman in my life. I was taken to Manchester where we constituted a family. Daddy became my friend. Mother remained an aloof stranger. I learned the Queen's English and became a contented British schoolboy.

Two years later, the family returned to Cairo. The new Republic freed Egypt from colonial rule. The elation of wrestling the Suez Canal from Britain and the victory of the Suez War induced national euphoria. Optimistic pan-Arab nationalism reigned, and foreigners were expelled. I was sent to an Arabic school, even though I didn't speak it, I couldn't make friends, I felt unaccepted and didn't fit in. Profound shame overwhelmed me as I struggled to re-adapt to my Egyptian heritage. My fair complexion and my rusty Arabic accentuated my being a stranger in my own country. Daddy, a renowned Arabic linguist, was embarrassed by me. He ceaselessly badgered me to study Arabic, even though we didn't speak it at home. My inability to learn it resolutely enough marinated me in intense humiliation—of being unworthy and unlovable.

The century-long ties to the cultural norms of British rule in Egypt was weakening. The family settled in Cairo. But before accepting a well-paid overseas job with UNESCO in Beirut, Lebanon, Daddy arranged for me to get a bi-weekly Arabic tutor. My parents then sent me to the renowned English School Cairo—the Eton of the Middle East. Supervision of our education continued via his daily letters to us in Cairo. After I failed a term exam in Arabic, he wrote me a stinging rebuke unjustly claiming: *Life is too easy and too comfortable for you. If you had no father, you'd have to struggle, like I had to. Then you might do better in school and in your life.* He died the next day. I was twelve.

His death left me with an unquenchable thirst for justice, recognition, self-worth and success. It also left me abandoned in a society rapidly transforming from an English to an Egyptian-Arab based culture, one I loved, yet could never fit in. Having no passport, I was unable to get out of Egypt. I feared conscription to become cannon fodder in a looming war with Israel, one of America's staunchest allies. Deliverance lay in Britain, a cultural milieu that might accept me. Two questions remained: Would I ever heal from the lacerating psychic wounds inflicted by my parents? And would I succeed in becoming a surgeon?

# PART I

---

# MANCHESTER 1960 TO 1963

# 1

## PRESENCE OF HER ABSENCE

OCTOBER 1960

*I want to leave behind me the name of a fellow who never bullied a little boy, or turned his back on a big one.*
—Thomas Hughes

We disembarked the *Esperia* in Venice, Italy, at 6 a.m. after crossing the Mediterranean from Alexandria. Mother, fortified by cups of coffee, drove our VW north over the Brenner Pass in the Alps into Austria. Following a well-established family tradition, as soon as she reached an Austrian town she bought a pound of sweet cream butter and a fresh loaf of crusty white bread. We sat by the roadside and devoured it with relish. She then drove nonstop on the Autobahn toward Kassel in Hesse, arriving twelve hours later. Dinner was traditional German fare—food she had missed in Egypt.

We never overnighted in a hotel. Instead, we would go to the cinema. This time the movie starred Marlene Dietrich, which pleased Mother to no end. Reinvigorated by the break and amphetamines she drove all night to Hamburg with the intent to arrive just in time for Opa's and Oma's breakfast. The night driving in the rain at Autobahn speeds in our small, overpacked car left me terrified and exhausted. I stayed awake, chatting to her fearful that she might fall asleep.

After a short visit with my grandparents in Wedel, Mother and I arrived in Manchester from Cairo some six weeks into the autumn term at Burnage Grammar School. I was sixteen. The headmaster's Oxford gown complemented his portly good looks. He asked a few bookish questions in pretentious, cultivated Queen's English, distinct from the charming Lancashire dialect I heard all around me. Since my declared career choice was aeronautical engineering, my A-level majors for the next two years before university were math, physics, and chemistry. He offered Mother a cup of tea and then marched me to my new Lower Sixth Form science classroom, telling me that apart from a Jewish boy in the form below me, I was the school's only other foreigner.

Mother had found me a bedsitter in a semi-detached duplex near the school. The next day, she took me to a cooperative for a school uniform—gray shirt, school tie, flannel trousers, a blazer embossed with the school crest—woolen underwear, and long johns for winter. The sturdy black shoes, unlike my brown Egyptian lace-ups, would not melt in the persistent Mancunian rain.

She opened a joint bank account in our names to deposit funds from Egypt for herself and me. To ensure my healthy relaxation, she bought me season tickets to the Hallé Orchestra, Britain's oldest symphony orchestra. Mother's idea was that attending the Saturday night symphony would prevent me from mixing with the wrong crowd while inculcating me with a classical repertoire and further developing my love for music. For the first time, my school life would not include girls—which was totally unnatural for any adolescent—but was exceptionally hard on me because I had always enjoyed the female companionship of a co-ed school.

Having ensconced me in the bedsitter, Mother returned to sunny Cairo. She had fulfilled her maternal duties in every way except one: giving me her love and emotional support, the thing I needed most.

I could hardly bear to see her go. Her abandonment inflicted the unbearable pain of rejection, as she had done in 1948 when I was four years old, depositing me with despotic war weary German grandparents I had never met before. As I learned later, she joined my father at Manchester University to pursue the promise my father had made to her on their marriage in 1939—a promise to follow her academic career at the university. In Hamburg, she had departed without a word of explanation—age four was too young to understand. Still, she had left me. Just gone. And now, at sixteen, the festering wound reopened and with it reappeared the feeling of vulnerability and impotence. I detested her for deserting me yet again. She was a widow, so what drew her to favor Cairo over providing a home for her son?

I failed to grasp how she could leave me when family-based loyalty and friendships were so much a part of the Egyptian side of my cultural heritage. I wanted to come home to a warm nest, not to a lonely bedsitter. My pleading did not persuade her to stay in England.

After she left, I sat sobbing on the edge of my bed, unable to control my hurt as rain streaked down the windowpanes in sunless, cold, smoggy Manchester. I convinced myself that her repeated abandonment reflected her inability to love me or was some form of punishment for a sin I had committed, for which I had no knowledge.

The landlady of my bedsitter, Mrs. Bagley, was a widow who kept to herself. For four guineas a week, she provided me with a room and a cooked English breakfast. On my return from school at 4 p.m., she served high tea, which in the north of England was the equivalent of a light, hot meal like baked beans on toast. I could only have one or two baths per week.

I ate my meals alone in the front parlor, listening to BBC radio. At the same time, I could hear Mrs. Bagley's TV in the back room. After tea, I retired to my bedroom upstairs and tried to do my homework, but my mind drifted to my school friends in Cairo and our comforting camaraderie. At nine, Mrs. Bagley left me watered cocoa with a dry biscuit in the downstairs parlor.

I was forsaken by friends and family—adrift and alone, with no salvation—and stranded in miserable Manchester. I ached for the warmth of the life my family had in Manchester when I was between the ages of eight and ten and attended Birchfields County Primary School. I had a pretty blonde girl-friend, Janet, and was a member of Roy's tough gang of boys, chasing girls during recess and smoking Woodbines behind the garden shed. I had not met any of the boys, imagining they would have gone from the Primary to the Grammar school. They seemed to have disappeared, and Janet was now in the girl's grammar school miles away.

I liked a British breakfast, particularly when my landlady

substituted back bacon for the bread-filled sausage. Meals were not provided on weekends, so on Saturday mornings, accompanied by loneliness, I sat in front of my books in the Central Library in the heart of Manchester. I read. Nothing seemed to be absorbed, even understandable. I lunched alone at Lyons Corner House and then sat in front of my books in the afternoon, and once again, nothing seemed to stick in my mind. Saturday evenings, I'd forsake dinner to attend every recital, orchestral, operatic, and ballet performance at the Hallé—a welcomed distraction from my gray life. Sir John Barbirolli, the conductor, delighted the audience during performances with gin-enhanced athletics, as rumor had it, which became more enthusiastic as the evening progressed. I sat with people whose faces had become familiar, season ticket holders, strangers yet human company nevertheless. Even though we didn't exchange words or acknowledgments, there was comfort in those strangers.

Music had always been a balm to my soul. Now, it carried me back to happier times when we lived in Cairo, when Mother played Mozart, Bruch, Mendelsohn, Bach—records handed down from departing German ex-pats. They were the background music of stability in our ménage. At school and birthday parties, we danced to lively music from the American and British hit parades, along with the occasional French or Italian songs—romantic songs that stoked my teenage hormonal urges. But my soul was captured by the torturing laments of Egyptian love songs that whined and pined for the love of a woman not yet met, kissed, or even envisioned—the elusive *sehnsucht* of love, the *mirage* of deserts.

# 2

# LETTERS OF COMFORT

## MANCHESTER 1960

Dear Marwan,

We send Mummy and you our best wishes for the big feast which is near. How are you all? I hope you are fine.

We were very pleased to hear that you are going to join London University next year. In fact these are very good news. Our best wishes and congratulations.

Thank you very much for your fine photos. It is very kind of you indeed, to send the

All the family members send their regards to Mummy and you. Sheikh Amin is still ill as he is, we hope to see him better soon.

Sitt Eglal sends her regards and best wishes to you all.

We are very happy to know that you are going to visit us in summer. So we hope to see you in a near time and we wish you a happy journey too.

How is Mummy? We hope she is in a good health. Please, give her our regards

*To write is human, to receive a letter: Devine!*
–Susan Lendroth

I n 1960, the relationship between Britain and Egypt had become strained. The Suez Canal was owned by the United Kingdom and France. In 1956, Gamal Abdel Nasser, Egypt's president, nationalized it, which led to the Suez Crisis and the disgraced resignation of Prime Minister Sir Anthony Eden. The British press hammered Egypt for "stealing" the canal, and a few months later, Israel, Britain, and France invaded Egypt to retake it. The military invasion was opposed by the United States. The crisis led to the closure of the English School Cairo, the eviction of all predominantly English teachers and staff, the evacuation of all Egyptian-born foreign nationals, and the evisceration of the foreign-educated middle class, including Miss Freemantle, my beloved teacher, and many of my school friends. Not only was it an international military crisis, but it was a personal one that translated into a further loss of friends and disruption of budding relationships. In England, among certain classes, *Arabs* became a swear word.

I tried hard to fit in at my new school, struggled to make friends. I was unsuccessful. For England, I was too dark. For Egypt, I was too pale. My classmates called me by the menacing name "gyppo" or "WOG" (Wily Oriental Gentleman—a slur for dark-skinned people from the Middle East). Their attitude toward me reflected the anti-foreign sentiments that had been exacerbated by Enoch Powell's "Rivers of Blood" speech claiming that the immigration of foreigners from the declining British Empire, if unchecked, would result in "the black man ruling over the white British race." Whatever animosity they had toward the foreigners coming from India, Pakistan, and East Africa was being directed at me. My fellow pupils didn't know me or talk to me and didn't understand that Egypt was *not* part of the empire.

Adding to my misery, I suffered beneath the perpetually soggy, overcast sky, enduring the early morning and nighttime smog that engulfed grimy Manchester during my first winter, penetrating my clothes and lungs. I decided Manchester was a temporary hostile way-station, one where I would have to await my return to the hospitable land by the Nile, where my friends, my people, waited.

I hated the disconnect, the wrenching away from my immediate family. Neither my sister nor Mother wrote, although from time to time, my dear German grandmother, my Oma, sent a letter bursting with love and empathy. In the bleak postwar years of 1949 when I had lived with her, and despite her advancing age, she had nurtured me, fed me, sewed my buttons, darned my socks, supervised my grade school homework, and watched my transformation from a bewildered, foreign, Arabic-speaking child of four to a confident young German schoolboy of ten. Opa, pedantic and stolid, never wrote. I often wondered whether the Prussian seaman could write.

I wrote long letters to Mother, begging her—*imploring* her. Come back—take me home. Each day before school, I sought out the early morning postman, hoping to see Mother's handwriting on an envelope, but she never responded. When I returned from school, I asked the landlady if the mid-day mail had brought me a letter. I always hung onto the slim hope she would send something. In my imaginary world, when I returned to my room, Mother would be there waiting for me. Months went by without a word from her.

Occasionally, a letter from my uncles in Cairo arrived. I eagerly tore them open to bathe in the sunlight, love and comfort of my Egyptian family.

The first letter to reach me after Mother's departure was from my Uncle Fareed, a young officer in the Armored Division. He frequently called me brother since we were just six years apart.

```
My dear brother Marwan,
I have missed you so much. In fact, all
Egypt is missing you. I think of you
always. I hope you are well, and I
wonder why you don't send letters. Is it
because you are so busy? Find several
minutes to write. I hope to hear a lot
from you.

I am fine and passed my military college
examinations. I am preparing for a
mission abroad at the beginning of the
New Year. When it is finalized, I will
write and inform you, and maybe, we will
have the opportunity to meet.
All my best regards to you.

Your brother,
Fareed
```

His letter made me feel stranded in Manchester. Members of my Egyptian family, who were the most proficient in English, wrote occasionally. Although I was glad to receive their letters, they heightened my homesickness and compounded my sense of isolation. Was this the reason Mother wrote so infrequently? This was hard to believe for she didn't even send birthday greetings. Why did she not understand that I had the same longings with which she had peppered the many letters she had written to family and friends while she lived with Daddy in Sudan and Egypt during the war years?

In addition to the reminders of their affection, some uncles expressed lofty expectations comparable to my father's achievements; this had the effect of putting enormous pressure on me to succeed, rather than being the compliment they had wished to convey. A letter from my Aunt Sanaa was typical. Apart from the greetings she wanted me to satisfy the family's desires: to live up to my grandfather's ambitions for me, so that one day, I'd be as influential as my father had been. It was an unfair comparison.

At age five, my father was displaced in the family hierarchy by a new baby—a stepbrother. Placed on a train to Cairo a year later, he lived with a distant aunt some four hundred kilometers from his father and younger brothers in Upper Egypt. Unable to handle the responsibility, she apprenticed him to a tailor. Hating the manual labor, he escaped, finding shelter at the madrasa of Al-Azhar Mosque, where he learned the Qur'an and classic Arabic. Convinced that education was the path to betterment, he pursued education until he became a confident, ambitious, salaried employee of the Ministry of Education. Teaching Arabic to first graders in a government-run school, my father's meager salary supported his father, siblings, and stepmother when they migrated to Cairo. Ambition and a constant relentless drive were enshrined in his DNA, increasing his success, yet he failed to recognize that his son grew up in different times under different circumstances, in no way comparable to his hardships.

Did Tante Sanaa or the family know I was struggling? Did they suspect that I felt like a total failure? I did not have the courage to write and recount the drudgery of living in a sunless bedsitter or confess that I missed the comfort of family, that I had no school friends, that I missed co-education, and, above all, that I was unable to learn. I was starting to fail the Lower Sixth and was facing utter shame.

I sought comfort from my English School Cairo friends, most of whom had made their way out of Egypt from under its dictatorial militaristic government. Through letters, I tried to reweave our congenial relationships before they had been shattered and torn apart by the Six-Day War—the Suez Crisis and the sudden Israeli, British, and French invasion of Egypt—scattering us to the various corners of the world.

Out of the blue, She'ham Shaffei, a girl in my Cairo class, wrote several importune letters to me. According to cultural norms, our parents had advocated for a possible marriage match. We were barely twelve, so it was an academic idea. Neither of us shared romantic feelings. Four years later, after the Tawgaheia, she went to medical school at Ein Shams, Cairo University—I landed up in Manchester. Her strident letters alarmed me. My responses were cool. She wrote more forcefully proposing a visit. I panicked. I was not doing well; certainly not in medical school. Alone, I barely could cope. What were her expectations? Where would she stay? Her letters suddenly stopped. Later, I heard that she had a fatal car accident. I felt a pang of immense sorrow at the loss of a school friend—a young physician with such great potential.

I reached out to Miss Freemantle, the Aphrodite of my sexual awakening. Miss Freemantle—the tall, strawberry blonde with her distracting high-rising breasts that jiggled with each movement of her arms. I was thrilled to receive a reply from her. She wrote enthusiastically about her memories of our class, calling that time the happiest she'd spent in any school. It was mine, too. Her letter sent rays of sunshine—she remembered me. I liked to think that Asad, a close friend, and I were among her favorite students. A letter I received from Asad, at Sevenoaks School in Kent, described his own hardships. He also was struggling with academic life, adding that Miss Freemantle "lived *only* five miles away."

Carol, my first girlfriend when I had been in Cairo, was studying at an all-girls boarding school in Arundel, Sussex. She sent monthly letters full of familiar sentiments—loneliness and isolation—yet her letters fostered a feeling of kinship and caring for one another that we kept through life. The memories she recalled, "like the time we dared to dance cheek-to-cheek and felt so grown up," warmed me and momentarily soothed my loneliness. At sixteen, I met Magdalena, a Polish girl who became my serious girlfriend. She had joined our class during my last year at the English School, and now that we lived on different continents, we wrote from time to time. She relived our brief but memorable times together in Cairo. As mature innocent teenagers our interest in one another had reached the point near intimacy before her father, then in the Polish diplomatic corps, was recalled. Shortly thereafter, I too left Cairo for Manchester. In her letters, she also related her difficulties in adjusting to school in Krakow, Poland, and expressed hopes that her father would be posted to Europe so she could freely travel and come visit.

Among the trickle of letters, from friends and family, none were from Mother. She had vanished from my life—leaving a void, a yearning. By early December, I became ashamed of mailing almost weekly entreaties of despair and gave up hope. I felt trapped like a coal miner forgotten underground.

Toward the middle of the first term, it was evident that I would not pass the Lower Sixth. Failing was a profound shame. I did not measure up. I felt my father's disappointment and disapproval with a sense of disgrace. Branded on my forehead for all to see were the letters "F" for failure and "S" for shame, like the stigma of leprosy. With my self-esteem at its lowest, I dropped math and changed my curriculum to include biology, chemistry, and physics, constituting the first MB—the initial step toward a Bachelor of Medicine.

Mother was a prolific letter writer to her friends. She kept carbon copies of the more than 1,500 letters written from 1935 until the mid-1980s. One that I found after her death, dated August 30, 1961, was addressed to my headmaster:

Thank you for your letter. I do appreciate your comments on Marwan's attain-

ment at the end of the last academic
year. I agree he should repeat the
year.

I am sorry I was unable to leave Egypt
as I had initially planned. Now all my
affairs have been settled, and I am
going for Hamburg by long sea route
within a week's time, hoping to be in
Manchester not later than at the very
beginning of October.

Although Marwan was reasonably comfortable in his lodgings, I can see now that
the abrupt change from one country (culture) to another and being left for the
first time to cope entirely on his own
has aroused such anxiety, and most
likely has been magnified by discovering
some weaknesses in basic mathematics. I
am, however, grateful for the considera-
tion you have extended to him. I feel
confident that with a home of his own in
the background, he will have a happier
time ahead of him which should reflect
on his work.

There was a bright side to my failure: Mother finally arrived
in late autumn. Our meeting didn't have a feeling of fuzzy
warmth and unbridled love. I was pleased that she came,
feeling that at last, she was supporting me as a mother should
—still, I was ashamed of my need. When I complained of her
past absence in my life, of the difficult time I had experienced,
of my feelings that she had abandoned me yet again, she

offered no apology, no explanation or remorse. It was as if she had not heard me.

"I'm here now. What can we do to get you through this time in your life? Your father would want to see you go to university and make something of yourself." Her analytical side failed to see that I needed a mother's love, encouragement, and nurturing. She had not changed. She remained emotionally distant. I could not bridge the gap between us.

She brought with her the devastating news that my beloved grandfather, Sheikh Amin, had died six months previously. The family had not shared his loss for fear of distracting me. The news of his death numbed me; I could hardly stand another loss in my life. Without my father and now the loss of the patriarch, my emotional ties to my Egyptian family weakened. My future in Egypt felt tenuous, and the urgency to pass my exams now became my focus.

## 3

# THE CIRCUIT

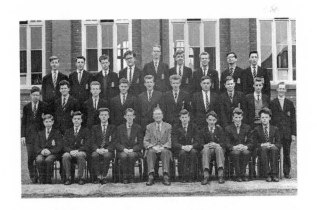

*Our dreams are big—our hopes high—*
*our goals long-term . . . and the path is difficult.*
*But the only failure is not to try.*
—Jimmy Carter

Mother and I moved into a flat at 9A the Circuit, in Didsbury, a short bus ride from Burnage Grammar School. My sense of humiliation and anger slowly dissipated, replaced by the expectation of a fresh beginning. The boys in my new class crowded around me, asking questions. Had I lived in a pyramid? Did I have a pet camel? Is it true every man has a harem? I was inclined to string them along but decided they were probably testing my sense of humor. I made them laugh, which helped them accept me. I felt the better path was to be truthful with them, even if it spoiled their fantasy of life in Egypt.

During the morning assembly, we sang rousing and cheerful hymns, including my favorites, "All Things Bright and Beautiful" and "Morning Has Broken."

With the weight of the assembled staff behind him and the mighty authority of his position, the headmaster proclaimed the general policies, philosophical and moral positions concerning the pupils, and the running of his school and society. When he stood in front of the podium in his flapping Oxford gown, his fly open, it would titillate the older boys, who speculated endlessly about him and the flaming redhead secretary standing close behind. On ending his pronouncements, he'd step back, a cue for the music teacher seated at the upright piano to start the next hymn. We joined in at the top of our voices, venting our pent-up energy.

After school, at 4 p.m., a double-decker bus took me back from Burnage to Didsbury. Walking down the cul-de-sac, I would see that the curtains to Mother's bedroom were drawn. I would let myself in, pick up the mail, and while climbing the stairs, would hear her stir. She would greet me in her dressing gown and make me a cup of tea.

I was always mystified by her Olivetti, which lived forever in the kitchen. It sat on a gray blanket on the corner of the kitchen table. Had she typed a letter? I saw no paper or envelopes, but if she had typed a message, she must have gotten dressed and walked to the post office to mail it. On her return, she must have changed into her nightie and climbed back into bed. This was all very mysterious, particularly when I caught her glancing sideways at the machine. Why the secrecy? When I asked, she'd reply, cagily, that she had typed a short note to Oma.

Each morning, Mother rose, made me breakfast, and sat with me in silence, drinking her German coffee. She apparently spent many days in bed listening to the BBC while I was at school. Perhaps, she was grieving the loss of her husband —grief had its own timeline. We never discussed it, and I didn't want to start a conversation on grief. Especially about my father. I was still angry with him for the unjust accusation in his last letter to me.

He was in Beirut working for UNESCO. I was in Cairo— twelve years old. We were awaiting his imminent arrival with joy. Mother had written: *Your son has done poorly in an Arabic test.* He wrote to me: *Life is too easy and too comfortable for you. If you had no father, you'd have to struggle, like I had to. Then you might do better in school and in your life.* After receiving his rebuke, I'd done well—news that hadn't been received before he died. A day after, I got his note. I was stunned. The next day, his body arrived in a pine coffin. Family in black. A blind Sheikh sat cross-legged chanting Qur'anic verses. Three professional wailing women—all in black—sat barefoot, cross-legged on the sofa—their unison howl filled the air late into the evening.

In the past, when I had expressed my anger, she would always defend my father, minimize the injury and dismiss the topic, accusing me of taking his message too seriously. She left no room to explore my pain, which became a chronic, festering wound of injustice.

A couple of times, we went to the symphony, and she dressed entirely in black. On one occasion, David Oistrakh and his son were playing Bach's Double Violin Concerto in D Minor. This was one of the few records she had in Cairo, one she played several times a day. I grew very fond of this score and could whistle it almost in its entirety. Listening to their performance, accompanied by the Hallé Orchestra, was a nostalgic reminder of home. Throughout its eighteen-minute performance, tears quietly cascaded down her cheeks. We took the bus home in silence. I wanted to comfort her but I could not reach out to her.

*With Prefect Badge*

In the summer of 1962, I was promoted to the Upper Sixth and was given the responsibility of a prefect at the beginning of my last year of grammar school. Mother told me she was returning once more to Cairo: "Your headmaster tells me that you are doing sufficiently well." She expected I would successfully pass my A-level exams at the end of the school year and then enter medical school in the autumn of 1963. "You can fend for yourself since you are a young man of eighteen," she said.

Mother departed. I was left alone once more.

Because of failing, David, the school's "only other foreigner" by virtue of being Jewish, as the headmaster had said, was now in my class. He was a loner, which drew us together, an Arab kid from Egypt and a Hasidic Zionist Jewish immigrant from Central Europe. The differences didn't matter. What mattered was the affinity and friendship that arose between us, driven by our need for human connection and our loneliness.

Being of different faiths, we argued endlessly about various aspects—political, moral, legal—of the Palestinian–Israeli issue. Since David had spent the previous summer in a kibbutz, he was full of enthusiasm and support for the new state, oblivious of politics and their consequences. I held my ground, arguing for the rights of the displaced indigenous inhabitants. Despite our political differences, we remained firm friends.

Friday afternoons were devoted to biology lessons. Our teacher, Mr. C., customarily concluded his class by lecturing us about the dangers of having a wild weekend instead of studying biology. "Remember, boys. It takes *only one* sperm to ruin your life." He repeated this with the fervor of a preacher, a waggling index finger pointing skyward. He became the evangelist of the "Only one," chant—his weekly mantra. The boys chimed in, a chorus of "Only one, only one, only one," as we dispersed through the school corridors.

With the new year, the dynamics of my social life slowly changed, and my chronic anxiety waned. I made friends with other boys in my class, attended their parties, and even met a girl. Kate's fascinating looks drew me to her, and we soon sought understanding and body warmth in the frigid Manchester weather. We joined Saturday night dances, shaking our bodies to the Beatles' refrains. She also lived in Didsbury and took the same public bus to school every morning, getting off a few stops after me—the girl's grammar school was a few kilometers up the road. On weekends, we walked the snow-covered parks or sat chatting in my flat, all the while convincing myself that I loved her.

# 4

# TICKET TO LONDON
## NOVEMBER 1962

*Eat, drink, and be merry for tomorrow we shall die.*
—Imhotep, Ancient Egyptian Physician

I worried I would miss my train. The bus was late. I stood at the stop just before 7 a.m. shivering in an early morning light shrouded by Mancunian smog. I had a noontime admission interview at University College Hospital Medical School, London. Its outcome would determine the course of my life.

During a counseling session in that autumn term, I firmly expressed to the headmaster my desire to go to medical school in London; particularly to University College, an institute founded on science and not on religious conviction. But above all this is where my father had been a successful student. Somehow, I felt I too would be successful there.

My headmaster grudgingly agreed to support my audacious bid, although he could not resist adding in a paternalistic tone, "In my opinion, your chances of admission to a prime institute such as University College are quite low . . . quite low." Then after a pause where he directed his gaze at me, he offered, "The odds of being accepted to the smaller and newer Liverpool medical school are probably more realistic." I despised him for such a prejudicial statement and his lack of faith in me. Was he right? I was a less than stellar pupil, having failed the Lower Sixth form, which I had to repeat. However, my resolve to achieve my aim was firm.

The headlights of the double-decker bus materialized through the swirling fog on Wilmslow Road. It lurched forward, attempting to make up time, lumbering through the snarled traffic toward Piccadilly Station. Approaching the stop, I jumped off the rear platform and ran through the station. I chased the slowly departing intercity train down platform No. 7 and then leaped through the open door of the last carriage. A middle-aged Caribbean conductor had lingered there, weighing my chances of success. In a split second, he stepped aside as I lunged into the moving train. Panting, I dropped to the carriage floor, suit jacket crumpled under my arm. He admonished my recklessness, sold me a ticket and slammed shut the door. The train gathered momentum. It rolled out onto open tracks, through the Lancashire countryside heading south —destination Euston Station, London. I was on my way.

The yellow smog had disappeared and a pale November sun pierced the rising mist. We passed the massive dish of Jodrell Bank, the world's third-largest radio telescope, pointing toward infinity, seeking contact with intelligent life in deep space. The sight left me still yearning to become an engineer or a scientist, despite my headmaster's insistence that my grasp of math was too weak to realize my ambition to design the next generation of fighter planes.

"If you like machines, become an anesthetist," he told me, adding that his brother-in-law was one, and his anesthetic machines had knobs, taps, and levers. I found the comparison of fighter jets to anesthetic machines a ludicrous proposition, particularly since I had learned the intricacies and sophistication of flying a glider in Egypt a few years earlier.

"You need a label . . . some professional title," he mused aloud. "A medical degree is a fine choice. You can become a GP, a surgeon, or even a writer like Somerset Maugham . . . I know you like writing." He paused, then added, "The aircraft industry is shrinking. You will soon be redundant—unemployed and on the dole. Besides, every Irish navvy working on the electrification of the train line between Manchester and Birmingham considers himself an engineer."

I attributed my poor grasp of mathematical concepts to always having to move from country to country, and from school to school. I spent a few months in an Egyptian kindergarten, three years in grade school while living with my grandparents in Germany, two years at Birchfields County Primary School in Manchester, then back to Cairo by age eleven. Within my first year there, I was moved from an Arabic school to a German one and finally to the English School in Cairo. With each school, I was either held back a grade or advanced, repeating or missing a lot of teaching. My last six years in Cairo prepared me for O-levels, or the General Certificate of Secondary Education in Egypt, and led me to a grammar school in Manchester. My inability to conceptualize the simple use of a slide rule would have doomed me to mediocrity and failure.

The London trip felt more like a field outing than an impending interview on which my future hung. I was free from the parochial school environment, the racial slurs, and the constant workload that came with preparing for university entrance exams—the A-levels. The early winter chill had receded, and London was in the midst of a late autumn day with a blue sky and few clouds. Relaxed and at ease, I walked from Euston Station to my interview.

At first sight, University College Hospital resembled a grand Victorian public toilet with Gothic-style turrets. Shimmering in the sun, its red-glazed brick exterior was intended to resist the corrosive effects of coal-burning pollution. Drain and water pipes adorned the outside of the building—plumbing added as an afterthought. The numerous ledges housed a flight of London's pigeons.

The medical school was nearby. A beadle in a mauve coat with tails, top hat, black tie, and white shirt found my name on his clipboard. "How was your trip down from Manchester, sir?" he asked. "Fine mild weather we have today." I felt special—no one in England had ever called me "sir." Changing his tone, he asked me to verify my home address. "The results of today's interview will be mailed to you by week's end," he told me. "Follow me, please, sir."

He led me to a closed oak door with a sign that read: Dean's Office, *Mr. B. Harries.* He swung the door open, ushering me into the sanctum sanctorum.

Two men rose. Dr. James was a warm, convivial man who introduced himself as the Academic Dean. The second, the medical school dean, was a distinguished-looking, white-haired man wearing a clinical coat who emerged from a cloud of pipe smoke. Once we were seated, Dr. James asked me a series of questions that had not appeared on my application form. I had expected these questions, though, and had rehearsed the replies:

"My father was a student at University College."

"He won a scholarship to study in England before the war."

"He did his Ph.D. in pedagogy with Sir Cyril Burt."

"Professor of Arabic and Education at Cairo University."

"In 1949, my dad became a lecturer at Manchester University."

"No. We were . . ." I hesitated, and in a quivering voice said, "My sister and I were left in Germany. We joined them five years later."

"He died in 1957 working with UNESCO, heading up a multinational team focused on an educational program for Arab refugees. I last saw him in Old Jerusalem during the summer of 1955. He died of a pulmonary embolus while in a hospital."

"My mother is a psychiatric social worker. She studied at Manchester University at the time my dad was there in the early 1950s. We joined them after she completed her degree, and we lived in Manchester until 1955 before we all returned to Cairo."

"Yes, she worked for Manchester City Council. She's currently living in Cairo."

They listened intently to my replies and smiled. Dr. James tanned face lit up from time to time.

The dean's window was open. The breeze blew the scent of his apple-flavored tobacco toward me. Dr. James turned to the dean, who proceeded to ask about my interests.

"I am interested in science and curious if it can be applied to patient care."

Throughout, the dean, Mr. B. Harries, eyed me intensely through a cloud of white smoke as he puffed his pipe, sending smoke signals, it seemed, to Dr. James. He asked his last question: "Why do you want to become a doctor?"

I heard myself say, "I'm not sure, sir."

Had I said that to the dean? I could not believe my ears. Of all the questions I had practiced with Ted, this one snuck up on me.

I considered Ted to be my tutor, and he had spent days

preparing me for this interview. Like me, he had once been discouraged from applying to London and was determined to improve my chances of success. A young consultant gastroenterologist at the Manchester Royal Infirmary, Ted lived with his nurse bride, Tessa, in the two-story house we occupied. He had prepared me for everything, from the gray flannel suit, white shirt, and blue tie, to my polished shoes and fresh haircut; finally, he coached me on the appropriate answers to the various probable questions. But this one? This question we never covered.

The dean repeated himself. I gave the same answer. Dr. James jumped into the conversation. In a lively voice, he said, "Surely, you must have some idea why you want to become a doctor?"

Suddenly, the events of the previous night's Q&A session came to mind. Ted and I had sat opposite one another in a late afternoon simulation exercise. An hour later, Tessa walked into the room, signaling that he should wrap up the session. Eager to ask one more question, and without averting his gaze from me, he slipped his arm around her waist, pulling her closer while continuing to interrogate me. I got the message.

Facing the dean, I answered hesitantly, "Because of the nurses..."

A roar of laughter erupted from Dr. James, and a smile exposed the dean's teeth, still clenching his pipe. Both rose and shook my hand. I acknowledged their joviality with a smile, wondering if I had blown it.

The beadle stood outside. The dean deftly passed him a yellow folder. The door shut, and hoots of laughter echoed behind me. We entered the lift. He quickly peeked into the folder and escorted me to the medical school entrance, stating, "Tell me, sir, how you pronounce your surname." He repeated it correctly. "Ah, yes. Where are you from, sir?"

"Egypt."

"I served in El-Alamein." With pride in his voice, he said his goodbyes and added in a barely audible murmur, "Look forward to seeing you in October."

The electrification works repeatedly delayed the mid-afternoon train back to Manchester, giving me plenty of time to rerun the interview over and over in my mind—assigning different interpretations to each word.

"How did the interview go?" asked the headmaster the next day as he passed me on his way to assembly.

"Oh. Quite well." I paused. "I got in."

He was taken aback. "You got in? You got accepted at a prime London medical school?"

"Yes, at University College Hospital."

"How do you know? Did the Dean tell you?"

"No, sir, I just know."

"Did they give you a letter to that effect?"

"No, sir, I just know."

"What do you mean, you *just know*? Who told you what?"

"The beadle told me."

"The beadle? The beadle!" he repeated incredulously, almost in a frenzy, his face red with rage. "You mean the actual doorman? How incredibly naïve you are. So it's come to this: the doorman makes decisions!" He snorted and walked away, farting loudly as his Oxford academic gown flapped behind him.

Had the beadle not peeked into my file? Had he not wanted to know how to pronounce my surname only when I was leaving?

It was lightly drizzling Saturday morning when I awoke at 7 a.m. I lay in bed, listening to the postman working his way down the Circuit.

A dull thud sounded. It was not the gentle swish of a light letter. I lay in bed, afraid—always scared of failure. If it was an acceptance letter, I reasoned, then the stuffed envelope would have an assortment of forms and papers. In the morning light, streaming through the front door's stained-glass window sat a large manila envelope. I ran down and tore it open. I made out "accepted" before tears of joy flooded my eyes. Numerous flyers touting various university clubs and interest groups tumbled to the floor. I reread the word: "accepted."

Accepted!

For a moment, my father's ever-present admonishing spirit receded. In defiant triumph, I yelled out: "Fuck you, Dad! Fuck you, headmaster! *I* did it."

I discovered the reason for Dr. James's question about my nationality. According to the admissions policy at the time, the school officially accepted a limited quota of overseas students and few females.

Overseas students were denoted by the abbreviation OS after their names. Was this a subtle bias against OS, who were expected to pay for their education? To my surprise, I received a generous scholarship from the Manchester City Council, providing me free university education and a £700 living stipend, giving me the sense of acceptance as one of them —British.

Reading my mother's correspondence with the headmaster years later after her death, I found no clues to this mystery. Nevertheless, I would not put it past her to have planted the seed in his ear, for he must have endorsed the scholarship application. Whatever the explanation for my good fortune, I now had my ticket to London—intellectual sophistication and freedom from racism and xenophobia.

# 5

# A CASUALTY OF SUCCESS

*When you get to the end of your rope, tie a knot, and hang on.*
—Franklin Delano Roosevelt

School, too, started to have appeal again. I passed my examinations and was free to enjoy a long summer holiday. Regrettably, Kate had no time off so I went alone, her scent lingering on my fingertips. Crossing the English Channel, I took the train to Göhrde in the Lüneburger Heide, northern Germany, to attend a free two-week youth conference on "The Industrialization of America," arranged by the U.S. Cultural Exchange Program. Afterwards, I was to take a train up to my grandparents for the rest of the summer and spend it alone with them.

I headed to the old monastery set on the fringes of a vast, wooded heath in a dense pine forest. The gentle wind through the trees induced a state of tranquility. I felt very much an adult, full of confidence, about to become a medical student at nineteen. My limited sexual experience—the loss of my virginity to Kate in a one-time bang—was my permit allowing me to join the human race. I missed Kate's presence or, more precisely, the company of a female companion. Thirty young people from many countries gathered at the monastery to learn from a faculty of American scholars. The attendees, along with the instructors, ate in a communal hall. Many of the women— German, French, Senegalese, South Africans—were youthful, attractive. I felt alive and accepted among them. I wanted to wear a badge proclaiming, "I am not a virgin!" We slept on cots in individual cells. I imagined a priest had slept there, praying in his silent isolation for sex.

The early morning sun shone through the surrounding pines as I walked to the amphitheater. Each lecture covered an aspect of the United States Constitution—an astonishingly liberal and enlightening document. The faculty enthusiastically championed the hope, the dynamism, and the future that America held for its citizens as the shining beacon on a hill. The lectures were gripping and entirely different from those doled out in grammar school. Seduced by the lecturers, I wanted America in my future. In the afternoons, there were social events and field trips, including one to the border of Soviet-occupied Germany, a few kilometers up the road toward the Elbe. The watchtowers surrounded by barbed wire emphasized the hard reality of the Cold War and its proximity to the free life I took for granted. It unnerved me to think that the monastery was only a few miles from a potential battle line.

―――――

A few days later the first mail arrived. When I opened Kate's letter, I read that she had met another. My heart beat faster, my stomach tightened, and my sense of helplessness reappeared. Would her passion for her new man dwindle? Would she then want to come back to me? I relived the familiar emotions caused by Mother's repeated desertions. I was four years old again. I wanted Kate at that moment as much as I had wanted Mother back then.

I departed the conference well before learning about the full extent of America's industrialization. With quixotic fervor, I walked with my backpack along the narrow asphalt road that wound through the dim, silent woods, heading west toward Ostend, Belgium, to catch the ferry, determined to cross the channel, go to Manchester, and get Kate back.

The two-way road cut sporadically through open meadows. In the distant woods, I occasionally spied several helmeted crosses marking the graves of German soldiers. For the first hour, the road was eerily quiet. I stewed in the anguish of rejection. Having little money, I preoccupied myself with how I would get to Manchester. A white Mercedes loomed behind me, stopping at my wave. The driver was a contractor in his early forties who looked honest, and I got in. My destination?

Overcome with self-pity, I related my story, weeping. He looked sideways with empathy, keeping one eye on the road.

"I was a soldier on the Russian front when I got a similar letter from my girlfriend back in Germany." He continued to drive slowly through the woods. "The freezing wind blew the letter away. Death was all I wanted. I stepped out of my trench into the deep snow, howling at the Russians, 'Shoot me, shoot me.' My comrades tried to pull me back, but I kept walking forward in the whipping snow, tears freezing on my face, bellowing her name. The Russians stopped shooting, took me prisoner, and offered me hot food. I eventually returned to Luneburg." His unhurried words as he navigated the narrow road, measured in long, drawn-out pauses, suggested that this was probably the first time he had related his story. "I fell in love again. I have two wonderful children and an astonishing wife."

I fell silent, even though my tears resumed. As we drove on, he watched me in pensive stillness, meandering along the road.

"I'm in no hurry. I'll drive you to Ostend. Promise me you will not do anything foolish. You will find a new girlfriend. You'll be very happy. You'll become a famous doctor—a surgeon no less."

When he dropped me off at the ferry, he reached into his wallet and gave me a DM50 note. I hesitated, overwhelmed. I never asked him his name, although to this day, I see his face. He taught me a valuable lesson: the act of random kindness.

Of course, I did not get to see Kate. Her mother was very sympathetic. We sat in the kitchen, and she offered me a cup of tea while I cried, more out of self-pity than love for her daughter.

"You're going to London, starting a new life. You'll be happy; life will be fulfilling," she said.

I went home wondering if Kate had truly loved me or if I even had loved her.

Love? To me, it was a series of clichés—the emotional but nebulous state of mind, a constellation of feelings—ambiguity and turbulence, trust, jealousy, betrayal, contradictions, and uncertainty. How would I know? Mother never loved me. She never said these words to me as I grew up; she never hugged or kissed me. How was I to know what true love was. Presently it represented a source of joy and pain. Driven by the over-whelming power of Eros, tempered by fear of pregnancy, passion and pain, more than casual sex, and, in Kate's case, less than romantic love. I was confused.

Would another girl ever fall in love with me, cherish and hold me? Would I love again?

# 6

# SEX - 101

*Love is a matter of chemistry, but sex is a matter of physics.*
—Unknown

To celebrate the end of the school year, a friend invited a group of us for Chinese downtown. I sat next to Marie, a Swiss au pair about my age, whose last week in Manchester coincided with mine. She was drawn to me, which was consoling; in my state of sorrow and wounded ego, another female found me attractive and exciting. Sitting among our English friends and speaking German with Marie created an air of familiarity, intimacy, and closeness. She had been caring for three small children in relative isolation in the Lancashire countryside, miles away from Manchester. Speaking with a Lancaster lilt, she spoke freely about her experiences, having had limited access to adult conversation for a year.

I could not help but compare her to Kate, who was more reserved. Marie was taller, slimmer, with the soft material of her dress clinging to and accentuating her thighs. I immediately tried to suppress the dormant, provocative, lusty thoughts stirring within me. Now that my exam-related anxieties and stresses were over, there was more room for wondering desire —evocative, licentious thoughts.

"Is your girlfriend going with you to London?"

"I don't have one. Anyway, I'll be too busy for one," I replied. She half smiled and winked at me. *The crafty creature!* She turned away and focused on the food on her plate.

Per European tradition, she gave me a goodbye kiss on each cheek, not needing to stand on her toes. Quite unabashedly, she also gave me her telephone number, stating she wanted to see me two days later when she had the afternoon free.

"I'll be packing—the place will be in a mess," I said, trying to politely discourage her. She did not seem put off. My mind was still on Kate, however much Marie intrigued me.

———

Two days later, Marie knocked on my front door. She greeted me joyously in her enchanting feminine way and with her charming Swiss-German accent, once more with the European kissing routine. Her perfume intoxicated me. She was about to climb the stairs to my room when instead I suggested going for a walk. We strolled through Fog Lane Park, a short distance from the Circuit, in warm sunshine that was unusual for Manchester. Sunbathing couples in various stages of undress lay on the grass, radiating contentment.

She took my hand, expressing regret we had not met earlier, for she had felt cut off, and our friendship would have been "fun-filled." Her enthusiasm for our friendship was evident, puffing up my recently deflated ego. Yet her expectations scared me. I felt uncomfortable with such ardent attention, and I didn't know how to deal with her obsession with sex. And how could anyone love—or even like—me when my father branded me as a lazy failure? And, when I had failed the Lower Sixth and had to repeat it? I told her I was moving to London the following week, a few days ahead of the start of term to find a flat and that I was on the waiting list for Commonwealth Hall, a student residence, thinking this would put distance between us.

"Can I come too?" she asked. Perhaps, she suggested, turning to me, she could stay in the flat. "We can see London's sights together. I have plenty of pocket money to spend before returning to Zurich."

This alarmed me and posed a dilemma. The idea of viewing the unseen sights of London was exciting, but my purpose for going early was to familiarize myself with the work situation, get the first-term books, and prepare myself so that on day one, when the term started, I would be prepared. I did not have a flat, nor money of my own to spend entertaining her, nor the time. My aims focused on my future and conflicted with her plans to be a tourist.

"I'll be busy trying to settle in," I said to her.

"I'll help you."

I meant my statement to convey that I'd be busy, and her intrusion scared me, particularly since I had this sense of inhibition and fear of intimacy and sex with someone I hardly knew. "Nice boys" didn't behave like that.

We returned in contemplative silence to 9A the Circuit for a cup of tea. Was she more than I could deal with? Looking around my flat, she suddenly said she hoped I had brought her back to make love. Was this the beginning of the rumored Swinging Sixties? If so, no one had told me. Seeing my surprise and discomfort, she changed the subject. Although I found her fetching and was more relaxed now that I did not have to study, I was too frightened to jump into bed with a stranger, and I was still grieving for Kate. We parted with her usual flurry of continental kisses. I was relieved to see her go.

In London, the housing department at University College told me that the prospect of getting a room in Commonwealth

Hall was uncertain and instead gave me an address on Baker Street close to the medical school. Two young secretaries had rented a well-appointed five-bedroom flat with a kitchen and two bathrooms. They had sublet one room to an American law student, Harvey, who was very welcoming. I took the furthest room down the hall because it had the most natural light and was the quietest. I had imagined living by myself in a dingy flat in London and hated the idea of being alone; it had never occurred to me that I would be subletting a room. I felt lucky to find accommodations so quickly.

The girls took great pains to inform me which refrigerator shelf was mine—I should not eat other people's food because the kitchen was a common area—and which bathroom I could use. They didn't object when I announced that a friend, a Swiss female tourist, would be visiting for a few days on her way home. When I mentioned that she would not be sharing my bed, they exchanged looks. "She can temporarily have the fifth bedroom," they said. That being settled, I went the following day to meet Marie at the station.

Marie's arrival was an ambivalent distraction. She was not really my type: did not seem studious enough and far too eager about our relationship. Yet I did find her background interesting. She was cultured, and the idea of having a German-speaking female friend with whom I could do some sightseeing was appealing. Her must-see list included the art galleries, Trafalgar Square, St. Martin in the Field's mid-day concerts, the Tower of London, Parliament, and Buckingham Palace. Perhaps we would attend an evening show. She wanted to do some Oxford Street shopping for family presents, and she was not penny pinching. She might even pay for me when we went to the various venues, helping to support a medical student with limited means.

Strolling toward disembarking travelers, I heard a "yoo-hoo" echo over the station's din and slamming of train doors. A hand waved some distance down the platform. From its direction appeared the tall, elegant Marie, wearing a red beret and a white mohair coat, each flapping stride accentuating the curves of her body. Although I always loved women wearing hats, I intensely disliked berets. Or was this dislike of berets irrational based on my ambiguous feelings evoked by her visit—and her expectations? Marie approached me, smiling keenly, dropped the cases, and hugged me too enthusiastically for an English public setting. In the taxi, she said in a soft voice, laying her hand on mine, that she was sorry we had not made love in Manchester. Her unaccustomed frankness embarrassed me. How would I handle these advances?

We arrived at my new abode, and I carried her cases to the unoccupied room. She tossed her coat over the back of the single chair. She wore a cashmere sweater and a closely tailored woolen skirt ending above the knees, once again emphasizing her appealing figure. "How about a cup of tea? I need to do food shopping. Something simple since I hate cooking," I said. She mentioned it had been a long day and that we should have an early night to start our sightseeing first thing in the morning. I planned to show her University College, the mask and figure of Jeremy Bentham, its founder, the medical school, and the iconic University College Hospital.

Later, on saying good night, she asked if I did not want to come to her bed. I felt awkward, yet the physical stirrings were being set into motion. Didn't men make the advances? How could a seemingly nice girl like her make such propositions? I hesitated. Seeing my dithering, she gave me a goodnight peck on both cheeks. Her nearness and faint perfume once again caused a surge of arousal. I was of two minds. I wondered again —sex for the sake of it? Sex without romance or love? Just lust? Would this be taking advantage of a woman? I was confused. To give myself to someone, I needed a sense of emotional worth, of belonging, of being cherished. I stood there torn. She stepped forward to kiss me on the lips—a quick one, which tasted good —then went off to bed.

Relieved, I turned off the light and settled into my bed. A moment later Marie appeared in a silk gown, stepping into my dark room, eerily lit by the streetlight streaming through the bare window. My heart raced and I began to panic, and as the gown slid off Marie, and the chiaroscuro of the dim yellow Baker Street light fell on her pale body, highlighting her stark nakedness and shadowy triangle that crowned her magnificent thighs, I relented.

Marie slid under my blankets and laid her warm body against mine. I could feel her breath. She was in command; seeking my mouth, she gave me a deep lingering kiss with a hint of toothpaste, murmuring something I could not follow. Was it in English? German? French? My reservations and self-control evaporated. She stretched out on top of me, our toes touching. Her breasts softly nestled on my chest, her hips and bottom soft to my touch. It took only a few moments of clinging to each other for a mindless freefall into dark emptiness. The surrender was good, peaceful, and guilt-free, draining away my anxiety. We had made each other feel as alive as two people could.

Exhausted and sweaty, we lay side by side in the narrow bed, her head on my shoulder, long hair plastered to her face. She whispered, "*Bei Mir Bist du Schön.*" How did she know this old Jewish song, or was she gratified following our pleasure? What else didn't I know about her? I did not ask, but I wondered as I stared at the ceiling, marveling at what we had just experienced.

Guilt and apprehension crept over me again. Concerned that someone might knock on my door, I told Marie that my bed was not wide enough for us to get a good night's rest; in reality, I was nervous that my flat mates might discover us together. She left, reluctantly, opening the door without even listening for anyone in the corridor.

The next morning, we walked to the university's accommodation office near Gower Street on our way to the National Gallery. She held my hand, swinging our arms like youngsters. Her caring and genuinely happy disposition was fun to be with. She had an eager, child-like manner that was quite different from Kate's.

"Yes, there may well be a room available at Commonwealth Hall. We will know by tomorrow," said the clerk. The news delighted me. My focus was on the freedom I believed university life would give me, the chance to delve fully into what I liked—medicine, probably surgery—without having to deal with practical considerations such as cleaning and cooking.

"What does it mean," she inquired in German as we headed to the National Gallery in Trafalgar Square, "that there may be a room for you? Will you leave the flat tomorrow?"

"If there is a room, I will move. Commonwealth Hall provides meals."

In the late afternoon, we returned to the flat with aching feet. Following a bath, she suggested we retire to her room ahead of dinner. This time, we invested greater degrees of passion and appreciation for each other's bodies—more brains than brawn. Later, over Chinese, I suggested spending my Christmas holidays with her in Zurich instead of with my grandparents in Wedel. She was less than enthusiastic about me joining her parents' ski holiday; there was a line beyond which I was not welcome. Not good enough. Not wanted. Excluded. That night, she was not as responsive to my kisses. Along with our pleasure, ambiguous tears cascaded in silence down her cheeks. Were these in response to joy or sorrow? Concerned, I lingered in her bed, and without getting a response, I eventually retired to mine.

I moved in the late morning the following day. Commonwealth Hall in Cartwright Gardens was a brisk ten-minute walk from the Anatomy Department on Gower Street, my home for the next eighteen months. Marie helped me pack, in greater silence than I had known from her. In a business-like fashion, she informed me that there was a fast train with a channel ferry connection to Zurich that evening. She insisted on going alone in a taxi to the station. We both had set our priorities.

I forged my student life: new friends, new classmates, and a new medical world. Marie sent picture postcards of the Alps, then weekly, lengthy letters. Curious, I skimmed through them, set them aside, studied anatomy, dissected my cadaver, read the physiology of muscle functions in total wonderment. Further letters began to arrive every day, telling me she missed me, yearned for me, loved me. I was alarmed when she wrote that she was thinking of returning to London. How did this get out of hand so fast? How could she like me that much when I was more enticed by Fred, my cadaver?

Additional letters accumulated, emotionally dripping and weighing me down. They became tiresome, competing with the day to day deluge of medical knowledge. I was consumed by daily quizzes, weekly tests, and preparations for my first big mid-term exam. Barely three weeks after lectures started and Marie had departed, she sent me a thick letter that was addressed to the Department of Anatomy. Standing in the dim and damp basement on my way to the dissection hall, I scanned its many pages hastily. ". . . I have missed my period . . . pregnant . . ." Paralyzed by fear, the ghastly phantom of Mr. C. appeared from the dark and mouthed the curse he sermonized each Friday to our class of twenty-seven virile adolescents: "Only one sperm, boys—it takes only *one* to ruin your life."

My world had ended. My life was pointless. I had sacrificed my entire future for a young woman who had, in passing, comforted me in my haunting loneliness. Letter in hand, I sat down in the middle of the gloomy basement steps, my mind numb, unable to continue to the next lecture.

Rory McCloy, a new friend from a nearby dissecting table, sat down beside me. I was helpless, unable to explain my situation, stuttering in bewilderment. He took the letter, reading aloud: "my belly is enlarging . . . early morning sickness . . . I think I am pregnant." My stomach knotted. "I went to my grandmother in the Cantons, confiding in her. She took me to her elderly family doctor, who appeared like I imagine you'd look in the future. He tested my urine. The result was negative. A few days later, I had my period. He diagnosed pseudocyesis." Had I heard of it? Had I studied it? She wished I'd been there with her. She expressed regret; she'd wanted my baby.

I felt a reprieve and exhaustion, then resentment toward her, then self-directed anger.

What would I have done if the result had been otherwise? As if totally unrelated, Mother's past and vague assertion that she'd once considered an abortion when she had found herself pregnant with me floated nebulously through my mind.

Rory's voice came through: "The result was negative. Marwan, did you hear that? It's nothing. You're all right."

I never read the rest of her letter and never replied.

She never wrote again.

I vowed celibacy forever after.

# PART II

---

# LONDON 1963

# 7

# UNIVERSITY COLLEGE LONDON
### OCTOBER 1963

*Illustration by Jonathan Marrow FRCS, FRCEM*

*Never measure the height of a mountain until you've climbed it,*
*Then you'll see how low it was.*
—Dag Hammarskjöld

F ounded under the auspices of social reformer Jeremy Bentham in 1826, University College became the "Godless institution of Gower Street"—a secular alternative to the religiously affiliated colleges like Oxford, Cambridge, and Edinburgh. The Church of England opposed its founding, preventing it from securing a Royal decree to allow awarding degrees until the acquisition of a charter ten years later.

On a sunny morning in early October 1963, about a hundred medical students started preclinical, basic science studies. The beadle, still looking like a well-dressed, dignified figure out of Dickens' novels, stood in the doorway of the Anatomy Department, greeting each newly arriving student and directing them into the large auditorium for the welcome lecture. I wondered if he remembered me and greeted him warmly.

Most of the students did not know each other. The most enthusiastic ones squeezed together in the front row. The few women generally sat bunched together several rows higher. Latecomers snuck in via the rear stairs, staying at the back. Friends, those with common interests, and burgeoning cliques sat sharing small talk until Professor J.Z. Young started his lecture. I generally sat in the second row. We were a motley group of youngsters in hodgepodge garb, the men sporting varying degrees of facial hair. It was hard to imagine that within two years, we would be clinical students morphing into a uniform dress code and seeking professional affirmation and status.

The first day of classes started at 9 a.m. in the main auditorium. The eminent scientist, Professor Young, a zoologist and head of the Department of Anatomy, flamboyantly delivered our first lecture, *An Introduction to the Study of Man,* to a packed student body.

Professor Young was a charming extrovert, classy in his red

tie and blue velvet dress jacket. Each summer, he took a group of anatomy students to the oceanographic institute in Naples, Italy, where he had discovered the giant squid's neuronal axons with visible synapses.

In contrast, Professor Andrew F. Huxley, who lectured next in his modest gray suit, was a serious introvert, relentlessly absorbed in his work, bringing to mind a gentler, quieter version of my father. He and his faculty delivered the physiology lectures. Each week, a small study group attended the traditional tutorials in his office, everyone huddled about his desk.

Using the Socratic method, he aimed to teach us to think. "You are given a candle of edible wax one inch tall and one inch wide. Would you gain more heat from it if you were to eat it or burn it?" I sat impatiently, not contributing to the general discussion. I hated such ambiguous problems. My goal was to learn enough physiology to pass an exam. I wanted to cross Gower Street, see patients, and become a doctor, not be a pundit or pontificator. Yet wasn't he trying to teach his students to think? Wasn't that the reason one goes to university? And wasn't that the primary declared mission of a university or a sound teacher?

Professor Huxley, with his brilliant collaborator, Alan Hodgkin, was inspired to insert glass probes into the axon to measure the electrical activity of a nerve impulse. They discovered the chemical mechanism of nerve conduction—which stands true to this day. The two shared the Nobel Prize in physiology and medicine in 1963, the year Professor Huxley was teaching us.

At the time, being an impatient and not an altogether mature youngster, I didn't fully acknowledge Professor Huxley's approach to teaching, although it left an indelible impact on my psyche. I would begin to appreciate that clinical teaching was done predominantly by the Socratic method and that eventually, I would use this educational approach as I began to hold senior positions.

After the lectures, I walked over to the student union on Malet Street. Several months ago, in Manchester, flyers promoting A Capella, athletics, debating, and ballroom dancing had fallen out of my acceptance envelope. I had pursued gliding in Egypt as a teenager and was surprised that this activity was not available through the university. As a fall-back physical activity, I would try to join the university rowing team, for the Thames was closer than Biggin Hill in Kent, where there was a gliding club.

I had also received a handbook of the university's societies. Two medically related ones intrigued me: The Medical Society, whose honorary president was Professor Young, and the Physiology Society, whose president was Professor Huxley.

The Medical Society confirmed my desire to move to a more diverse set of peers in London. According to the handbook, "The Medical Society was concerned with the social life of students in the Faculty of Medical Sciences, and provided a liaison between the Faculty Staff and the students at University College Hospital Medical School. It has its own Common Room which provides newspapers and scientific periodicals. Lectures are arranged covering a wide range of topics, and the popular Presidential Address is given in the First Term. Coffee Mornings are organized at which staff and students are able to meet informally. The Senior Social, immediately prior to the second MB examination, is an important event in the year, and there are other socials in each term." The final paragraph stated: "All students of the Faculty of Medical Sciences, and many members of the Faculty staff, normally join the Society, and past students can also belong."

But what intrigued me even more was the Physiology Society. Its aims and goals were stated as follows: "The objects of the Society are to promote and encourage the science of physi-

ology in all its varying aspects by means of lecture and demon-
strations, distribution of relevant periodicals, films, visits to
places of interest, and in any other which may arise. The
Society also arranges social functions, including an annual
dinner. The Society's journal *Potential* is published from time to
time. About five evening meetings are held each term, which
are preceded by an informal tea." This society appealed to me
because it seemed to have more in common with biology, one
of my favorite subjects, than the social events touted by the
Medical Society. And becoming the editor of *Potential—Journal
of the Physiology Society* was an attractive proposition that could
advance my interest in writing.

Interest-group tables were set up around the union room
with their presidents loudly touting their activities. The scene
resembled a country fair—noisy, crowded, and colorful. Curious, I strolled, listening to the pitches and reading the posters.
Which group would provide the most significant distraction
from the opposite sex and would allow me to focus on my
goals?

Returning to the basement common room of the Anatomy
Department, the Medical and Physiology Societies had display
tables and sign-up sheets. It was rumored that membership
lists would be given to the department heads. Hearsay strongly
suggested joining both societies. I did. Hustings in support of
new officers were taking place amid the tumult. This British
tradition of democracy in action was new and unfamiliar and,
in a way, alarming to me. In Nasser's Egypt, and in prewar
Germany, opinions were not freely expressed, and dissent led
to disappearance.

The Medical Society had several candidates for president. I
watched the heckling of the speakers with apprehensive fascination. An older student stepped forward. In his stump speech,
I learned that he had been in the Royal Air Force in Hamburg,
deciding late in life to go to medical school. He was eloquent,

projecting maturity and leadership, representing my image of an archetypical Englishman—quiet, confident, speaking beautifully paced Queen's English in a soft voice. He had the making of a politician. I admired him, wanting to be as British as he was. He got my vote and easily won by a show of hands. A fellow student wearing a distinguishing bow tie stood close by his side. They left together following the election.

The next vote was for chairman of the Physiology Society—a two-year term. Despite the buzz in the room, no one put their name forward. In the excitement of the moment, I stepped up on a soap box. "I'm am all for physiology. P-H-Y-S-I-O-L-O-G-Y. Yes. It is the most exciting topic we will learn in the next two years.

"What is physiology you ask?

"It is the science of life which holds the key to understanding normal body function, questions such as: Why we eat and sleep. Physiology is the very the mechanisms of living things, from molecular cell function to the integrated behavior of our body to the external environment. Once we understand physiology, we can treat patients and develop effective medicines to treat diseases."

Then I briefly introduced myself. My German/Egyptian/Manchester grammar school background.

"I like the challenge of leading the Physiology Society, using the leadership skills groomed at the English School, Cairo, considered the Eton of the Middle East. My proficiency as a glider pilot in the Egyptian Gliding Club is an asset—quick, decisive thinking. I will strive to represent your interest in the physiology department." What was the motive of my impulsive decision to lead a society? Was I attempting to emulate my father, who had been a leader among students?

There was no other contender. After a pause, I was voted in —the first time I ever held formal office. Under Nasser's martial law, we did not congregate nor espouse our opinions in public, afraid of the unwanted attention of the *Mukhabarat*—State Security's Secret Service—whose rumored motto was, "Whosoever is afraid remains unharmed." I had just jumped feet first into democracy. What was I thinking?

I did not know what the job entailed and was new to politics. Perhaps it was a form of rudimentary politics when I was a member of neighborhood street gangs in Wedel and Manchester. On the other hand, I have always enjoyed writing and liked the idea of being the editor of *Potential*. I looked for the past president, seeking some form of handover, but she had disappeared—probably anxious to cross Gower Street and start her clinical life. I had been left high and dry.

Somewhat perturbed, I made my way to the Physiology Department office seeking "light, wisdom, and help." I met Molly, Professor Huxley's secretary, who had striking, close-coiffed white hair and a grandmotherly smile—a reassuring persona for a bewildered young student. Despite the piles of papers around her typewriter, she got up to greet me.

Sheila, her assistant, was in her early twenties, fair-haired, my height, and familiar with the society's activities and account. We became friends as she guided me through the transitional quagmire.

"The first order of business," she said, "is to proof the galleys of five articles for the forthcoming *Potential*. Professor Huxley will approve the line-up prior to publication."

"What do you mean by proof?"

Realizing I had never done this before, she volunteered to do it for me. I was relieved. She informed me that the membership dues in the society's bank account were to be used to print the *Journal*; the rest would come from the department's coffers. "Each student in the first and second year, plus the faculty members, gets a complimentary copy. Make sure you print enough," she said. Her parting words were, "The next issue is due. Think of recruiting a line-up of potential authors."

When I learned that the society had a bank account with less than £10, I wondered what I had gotten myself into. Sheila did not have a membership list, making the collection of dues impossible. The past president had saddled me with a massive responsibility with no effective way of fulfilling it.

My first interaction with Professor Huxley in my new capacity of Chairman of Physiology Society—no doubt something close to his heart—would have to be about money—not a propitious start. Sheila introduced me to the society's vice-chair, the co-editor of *Potential*, and a graduate physiology student.

We agreed to split the duties. He would read the galleys and be the go-between with Professor Huxley. I would plan an event. The £10 would suffice to allow me to arrange to visit the pharmaceutical company Parke-Davis outside London and have a tour of their manufacturing facility. The company would provide dinner with wine.

Soon after classes had started, it became apparent that there was a scheduling conflict between an invited speaker for the Medical Society and the Physiology Society outing to Parke-Davis. The word was that I had to change the date. It seemed that these two different societies had not yet learned to coordinate their events yet were catering to the same medical students. Having gone to great lengths to make the arrangements, I was reluctant to cancel them. After all, people could choose which activity to attend. The demand and subsequent bullying caused a standoff. The student sent by the Medical Society's president to resolve the matter was the young man wearing the bowtie. He and I were young, testosterone-driven, and inexperienced negotiators in working out differences. I would not budge at his demand and badgering, which entered the realm of harassment, and I did not have the foresight to go to Professor Huxley or my vice-president for guidance to resolve the dilemma.

It seemed that the Medical Society took precedence over the Physiology Society. I had to give in. In a pause between lectures, I stood in front of our class. "Good morning. My name is Marwan Meguid, student chairman of the Physiology Society. I arranged for members to visit the Parke-Davis Company on a date that conflicts with a visiting lecturer. At Professor Young's request, the event will be rescheduled. My apologies."

Thinking this issue was behind me, I proceeded to explain the society's long-term fiscal dilemma. "Without additional funds, the society is hindered from arranging further social events. I propose that each student pay £1 per annum. It's the regular fee." I slapped a pound note on the lecturer's desk, hearing groans from the audience. "You will soon get a complimentary copy of *Potential*. My co-editor and I are in the process of soliciting article contributions . . ."

Suddenly, a hail of toilet-roll missiles rained down toward me from the back of the amphitheater, accompanied by ferocious yells of "Go back home, you fucking foreigner!" The choleric and bilious uncivil assault continued, "Go back to Cairo" as more rolls, like streamers, flew from the back of the amphitheater.

The discordant voice trying to bring me down was easily recognizable. Bowtie and some others stood at the back. Allegedly, they had taken a dislike to me when they had learned of my Egyptian roots. This perplexed me. Wasn't I like a zebra with different-colored-stripes? All they chose to see were my black stripes—my Egyptian heritage. They willed not to see my white European stripes—although my half German heritage was even more offensive or more traumatic for them. Either way, they did not know my liberal political views, nor my political propensity. In fact, they did not know *me*. Had they been recruited and manipulated to express venomous hate and fear based on my mere Egyptian claim? Like many others I had encountered at Burnage Grammar, they lived in a xenophobic bubble with a vision of white England threatened by foreigners.

The ambush threw me off balance. I held my ground. I would not be intimidated. After all, I had been hardened in my German Opa's crucible. I dodged the rolls and didn't leave the front of the class, heartened by the horrified glances of most of the students.

Professor Huxley walked in and witnessed the scene. His presence brought the assault to an end. Before he arrived, the class, on a show of hands, decided to pay the Physiology Society's membership dues. Even so, the impromptu meeting ended without my arranging a way to collect the dues.

After class, a few fellow students approached me to express their support. They explained that the strident voice came from a public-school student, from a system that tolerated such behavior under the guise of democracy. My supporters were a handful of overseas students, as well as some of my female colleagues who were shocked by the violence. All of them apologized for the unfortunate behavior.

I was more shaken than I let on, particularly hurt by the name calling, which I had not expected at a higher place of learning. Once again, the assault made me question my identity. I thought medical students had matured, were analytical and unbiased. England called itself a tolerant society, the bastion of democracy, which had accepted foreigners from Europe, its Empire/Commonwealth countries, and the Caribbean. Later, I was summoned to the physiology office. Professor Huxley wanted to know what all the fuss was about. I explained the circumstances and the particular hurt I felt when the comments came from individuals, names not mentioned, who I admired.

Professor Huxley listened with focused disquiet. For a man who was generally considered to be an introspective, bookish individual, his comment struck me to be quite thoughtful and kind. "People are complex. They show different facets of their personality at different times, which can be confusing." He encouraged me to continue my activities on behalf of the society and to plan on the annual dinner.

———

It turned out that Dr. James' question about my nationality was connected to the admissions policy at the time. It enforced a ten percent quota of overseas students, who were identified by the contractions "O.S." next to their names on the notice board. I had to wonder if this designation caused a subtle bias, distinguishing "us" from "them."

The abbreviations "O.S." on the class noticeboard following some of our names perhaps perpetuated subconscious prejudice. I had thought that relative to Egypt, my German stripes and European looks would be an asset in England. I would be invisible. I had expected acceptance, at least at university. Eventually, I would be an English physician. And if I remained and married an English woman, I would be British and hold a British passport. In an idle moment, I fantasized about marrying Princess Anne. Then, my title would be "Surgeon to the Royal Household," not "fucking foreigner." But obviously, I didn't belong; I was merely tolerated.

The subtle discrimination continued. I became alert to the possibility that others might show bias, which heightened my defenses. My detractors did not seem to realize that the bullying behavior hurt me and that it reflected poorly on them; most of the students I mixed with tended to avoid close contact with them. At the time, they failed to recognize that I would never cower. And Bowtie didn't realize that he had some attributes I admired and envied; he was English, tall and handsome —snazzy in his colorful bow ties. He had been educated in a public school near London in the affluent Conservative-leaning south. I had been toughened in a grammar school in Manchester in the wealthy industrial Labor-leaning north.

I called a special meeting between classes to solicit solutions to the fiscal dilemma, not wishing to go hat in hand to Professor Huxley. To my surprise, the small amphitheater was packed. Many of the "overseas students" were present. Bowtie demanded a vote to elect a new society chairman. It made no sense to me: those in the class who had remained in the common room had actively voted and elected me to be the Chairman of the Physiology Society. Was it democracy to insist on changing an election's outcome?

After my election, I had gone and met the administrative staff in Professor Huxley's office. Molly had provided me with the society guidelines, which I had skimmed through that night. Sheila planned to chaperone me through the publication process of *Potential* and so on. They had accepted me as the student president and consented to my ascension to a position they seemed anxious to have filled, thus welcoming me—the imprint of legitimacy.

So how did this cradle of democracy differ from the despotic leaders of the pharaonic days and the current military leadership in Egypt? I had not prevented another candidate from volunteering to compete against me. None did. I was voted in legitimately, accepted as the representative of the student body and leader of the society. My term was clearly two years, following which the next class would vote for their representative.

Was Bowtie objecting to my being a "fucking foreigner?" Was this democracy in Great Britain? I opposed Bowtie' demands. He nevertheless insisted. I took one step to the side of the front, thinking that perhaps I would be relieved of these unwelcome responsibilities.

Students whom I did not know well came forward, saying positive things about me and weighing on my side. Others stood up and made the case that the class had already voted. A general murmur showed agreement with that fact.

My nemesis grew more and more agitated. His co-conspirators at the back were ready with their missiles. I requested a show of hands in my support to prevent the situation from becoming more volatile. A vote of confidence carried the day. The toilet-rolls flew toward me anyway. I dodged them. My detractor walked out. I had to look out for him. He would surely strike again.

# 8

## MEETING FRED

*Alick, Neil, Geoff, Jonathan, Marwan, and Dave*

*Anyone can stop a man's life, but no one his death; a thousand doors*
*open on to it.*
—Lucius Annaeus Seneca

Mornings were devoted to gross anatomy, held in a basement dissection room. White floor tiles swept halfway up the walls of the vast underground hall, starkly lit by bright overhead lights. The acrid formaldehyde smell emanating from the cadavers rose overwhelmingly—sweetness mixed with the smell of decay. Bodies in white coats in motion, pickled bodies lying prone, and articulated skeletons dangling from stands between the tables made for a macabre scene.

First-year students had twenty well-spaced dissecting tables at the front of the hall. Second-year students used the tables toward the back. Six students per cadaver formed a team, grouped by alphabet. My team members were all new to me, and I looked forward to working with them.

We sat around our cadaver. He was—or rather, had been— an elderly man, his body withered, his skin shriveled. He lay naked on a glass-topped metal table, and in reverence, a white sheet covered his nude body. His head was wrapped in gauze to obscure his identity. His torso was exposed, while his legs were wrapped to maintain the moisture of the tissues. The colorless body looked waxen and lacked the animation that evoked life and character. I christened him Fred.

On our first encounter with Fred, we were each lost in our thoughts. Seneca's essay "On the Shortness of Life" came to mind. Fred had once been a living, breathing person. I pondered life's transience, my fear of dying, the finality of death, and the reality of the cadaver lying in front of us. What had been his job, his lot? Had he striven and loved? Did he have a wife, lovers, or perhaps even children? Did he die alone, or was his family with him? Had they wept over his body? Had he been a soldier in WWII or a homeless bum? I saw no signs of surgical scars, no tattoos, and I wondered if he had died of a pulmonary embolus like my father. Was his death an agonizingly slow process? Did he put up a fight? Had he bargained with God, or did he go gentle into that good night?

My new colleagues, too, sat in silence, gaping at the corpse. We did not know each other well enough to share experiences of death or the dead. Memories of death passed fleetingly through my brain: hurrying through the morgue when I was three, holding Bakhita's hand as we went to play in the Papaioannou Hospital's garden; a funeral cortege when I was four; and at five, hearing my grandmother's melancholic lullaby, "Tomorrow morning, if God wills/You'll awake once again." When I was twelve, I refused to view my father's body as he lay in his simple pine coffin.

I stood up from the table, holding the dissection manual. My pulse raced, and my mouth was dry. I had never been in such proximity to a naked dead person. Jim, the anatomy technician, and his assistant, stopped at our table.

"Years ago, he signed papers donating his body to science," he said. "He died about three years ago, almost four, at this hospital, and they brought the body here. We infused a formaldehyde solution into his veins and placed his body in a formaldehyde tank in the basement. We periodically rotated it to ensure uniform fixing of the tissues."

We listened in silence. He scanned our faces, adding to reassure us, "In the twenty years I've worked here, no cadaver has ever been recognized." He avoided using words like "pickled." It was a dignified death, not a stolen corpse. I was thankful to Fred and wondered if, like him, I would have the courage to donate my body to science.

Staring at the naked chest, the wrapped arms and legs, the scaphoid or hollow abdomen, the circumcised penis shriveled between the top of his thighs, I learned my first medical lesson: disassociate emotion from reality. I had suffered so much pain in my short life that to deal with Fred and to function as a surgeon I must from now onwards shut down my feelings—suppress all emotions. Bury emotion. Do not be sentimental nor register passion. Be numb to all stimuli.

"Think of him as a mannequin," I said aloud to reassure and shield myself. Cautiously, I poked his skin. Unlike Magdalena's, Kate's, or Marie's, whose flesh I had caressed and tasted, Fred's was not warm or pleasantly moist. It was oily, cold, and tough, and it did not respond to my touch. Fred was indeed dead. And yet I sensed Fred's soul hovering benevolently above us, allowing us to dismember him. He had sacrificed his body so that we might learn. I took up the scalpel.

With my teammate, Jonathan Marrow, reading the anatomy instruction manual and the others watching, all the while imagining my future as a surgeon, I made the first cut—a midline incision from the xiphoid notch at the top of the chest to the sternum above the stomach. The skin parted, revealing globules of bloodless, yellow fat. This cut elevated my sense of being, my essence of control over a wound that would have inflicted pain—a sensation of self-empathy and empowerment. Yet it felt strange, for it was the first and only cut I made on a dead person. Surgeons deal with the living.

We started the first term with the chest and arms and moved to his abdomen and pelvis in the second term. We covered the intricacies of the head and neck in the third, and during the last term, we were to dissect Fred's legs and feet.

There was no escaping the smell of formaldehyde; it invaded our nostrils and hair, clung to our hands, permeated our clothes, and sank into our anatomy books. Each person and each group came to terms with the dead differently. Some students smoked to mask the formaldehyde smell. One group had to uncover the face and head to see the person. Another used the ear or the belly button as an ashtray—in contempt of death, they said, not the person. Jim quietly disdained such behavior, prohibiting the practice. I too disapproved. It smacked of an insult to the sanctity of life. Yet I never came to terms with death.

At the table, I read the dissection manual aloud as Jonathan dissected Fred's chest, his arms, hands, and skinny fingers—the other four students looked on. The intricate structure of the hand muscles fascinated me. In the chest, we observed the intercostal muscles, the diaphragm, the pleura—the lining of the lungs—blood vessels, heart chambers, and nerves. During the second term, I watched Jonathan dissect the abdomen—my favorite domain. I hoped that one day, I'd be operating in this realm; I eagerly touched the liver, stomach, guts, and the appendix, bringing to mind my own emergency appendectomy at age eleven, when I awoke from anesthesia to see a saline-filled glass bottle on the counter beside my bed containing my gangrenous appendix. I had marveled at it in my post-operative misery. How wonderful it would be, I had thought, to help sick people become better. The more anatomy that I learned, the greater my conviction grew that I wanted to be a surgeon.

Fred's abdominal organs were matted together, fixed by formaldehyde. Jim came over to assist in removing the inflexible knotted guts to permit us to view the kidneys at the back of the abdomen. When Jonathan could not find the bladder, we borrowed a huge syringe and filled it with water. I held Fred's penis while Jonathan placed the tip of the syringe into its opening. He blasted the water in to fill the bladder. Water copiously sprayed us as we attempted to dodge it, laughing at our failure, realizing that the bladder was, of course, formaldehyde-fixed and would not expand. We never located it. We examined the testicles in their "wrinkled retainer," as the scrotum was termed. I furtively felt my own for comparison. I never took the opportunity to see the pelvic anatomy of the female cadaver on the next table. Was I not curious to view part of life's origins, the uterus, fallopian tubes, and ovaries? I might have been a little gun-shy from my recent scare. The figures in the book sufficed—in addition to the knowledge acquired with a friend as we lay on the floor of his bedroom in Cairo with an anatomy book during my odd puberty years.

From time to time, members of our dissecting table who were not leaning toward surgery in their future would drift into the dissecting hall to catch up on Jonathan's progress. For their benefit, Jonathan gave elegant, enlightened, and convincing summaries—mini-seminars to bring us up to speed, the most memorable being "The Bones of the Penis." We stood around him, listening in awe to the revelations, as he pontificated the articulation of the six bones that produced an erection—

"Hence the boner," he said, looking around at us in earnest. After a cliffhanging pause, he emphasized, "It's bound to appear in the examination." The fidelity of his conviction was credible. How had I missed reading this in anatomy? We looked about our huddled group, and for a brief moment, we believed him before laughter broke out among us.

Once a week, we had a *viva voce*—an oral exam—given by an anatomy demonstrator to ensure we kept pace with the increasing workload and memorizing of the body's anatomy. Completing our daily dissections, we respectfully covered Fred. Jim removed the superfluous tissues for cremation, and I thanked Fred for his courage to impart the wisdom of his body to me.

# 9

# DIVINE STROKES

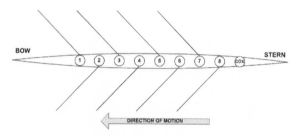

*Illustration by Freshness2go*

*It's a great art, is rowing. It's the finest there is. It's a symphony of
motion. And when you're rowing well, why it's nearing perfection.
And when you near perfection, you're touching the Divine. It touches
the you of yous. Which is your soul.*
—George Youman Pocock

Midway into the term, we started neuroanatomy.
Using preserved whole brains, we studied the
coverings—the three meninges, the major blood
vessels, and the gross areas that they controlled. From pickled
brain slices, we learned the nuclei—clusters of neurons—and
their known specific functions. We traced the connections as

they weaved through the brain from the convoluted outer cortex that controlled willful body functions to the medulla that controlled unconscious activities such as breathing, heartbeat, and appetite. I was absorbed, wanting to understand how this gelatinous mass created the beauty of poetry, the ingenuity of flight, the majesty of music, the devastation of the atomic bomb—the pains of abandonment and those of love. I was also intrigued as to the area in the brain responsible for the magnificent experience of an orgasm.

The physiology lectures dovetailed with courses on histology, embryology, and biochemistry, each of a different duration and each terminating with a test. Apart from the weekly *viva voce* in gross anatomy, we had quizzes in neuroanatomy. There were almost monthly written tests in various subjects such as histology and embryology. I began living from exam to exam. None of the material I was cramming into my brain, which was at the point of explosion, was related to ailing human beings —patients.

The amount of reading I had to do and the quantity of material that needed to be understood consumed my weekends. I was a slow reader, and my notes were useless. I decided instead to read selected texts on the topic, reading the bare minimum to attain a working knowledge. Given the ceaseless workload, I found myself becoming a dull person with a faltering enthusiasm for medicine—more precisely, for the study of medicine. I had thought that going to medical school had something exciting to do with sick humans or their diseases, but so far, I was wrong.

Stimulated by Professor Young's lectures on "An Introduction to the Study of Man," I wondered if I should switch to studying anthropology, thinking that might be more exhilarating and require less reading. Other medical students shared my profound academic boredom, and I watched as one dropped out, another quietly signed up at law school, and a third committed suicide. Sensing our frustration, the science faculty repeatedly assured us that we would draw heavily on pre-clinical knowledge when we eventually examined patients. The hospital on the opposite side of Gower Street seemed like a distant vision, a mirage across a bottomless chasm.

Rory suggested that it would be a welcome diversion from our endless studies if we joined the University College London's rowing team. We would get out onto the Thames and get some exercise. He was handsome, 6'2", four inches taller than me, and with broader shoulders. Furthermore, he was more muscular and had been a competitive rower. I had never done anything like this, but I needed an outlet, so I agreed. He became the captain and I became one of the oarsmen.

We were eight strapping fellows, and in unison, we lowered the 62-foot, highly polished racing shell into the brown, fast-moving water of the Thames. We clambered into the perilously rocking boat at our assigned positions, fearful of falling into the water. Each man grasped one oar. We sat facing the stern on a seat that slid back and forth inside the boat, and each of us fixed our single oar. I placed my feet on inclined footplates and dipped my scooped blade into the Thames as we gently pushed off into the ebbing tide.

Rory, the stroke, sat close to the stern of the boat and set the pace. He faced our puny coxswain, who steered and gave commands in his castrato voice. I was the seventh oarsman, sitting behind Rory, for each rower is numbered by boat position in ascending order from the bow to the stern.

Like everyone else, I followed the stroke's timing, rhythmically placing my blade into the chilly water, fingers from both hands wrapped tightly about the oar shaft. With each drive stroke, I pushed my legs against the footboard, providing the power to the drive, and after my legs were straight, leaned back and pulled the oar to my chest—one smooth fluid movement that drove the boat forward. Finishing the drive, I lifted the blade out of the water and feathered the oar in one continuous, flowing, rhythmic move as it skimmed an inch or so above the surface of the water. The distances between the puddles that my oar left hinted at our speed.

We started at ten to fifteen strokes per minute, a comfortable and easy pace. We were eight sets of coiling muscles hunched gracefully and low against the elements, suddenly and uniformly uncoiling our joint strengths. We closed our anal and laryngeal sphincters to generate a force, subconsciously building up these two vital muscles—no diapers for grunting, grown men.

Breathing rhythmically, we leaned back at the end of the drive and straightened out our torsos. Gathering our energy, we slid forward on our seats once more, tensing our muscles and striking the water again, uncoiling our kinetic power to slice forcefully through the water. This rhythmic pattern placed me in a trance-like state, leaving behind my thoughts, worries, and surrounding awareness.

To mold ourselves into a competitive crew, we rowed the four and a quarter mile course, varying the stroking pace. We started easy, carried along with the flow of the ebbing river. After ten minutes, we doubled our speed. Once we had settled into this faster, more strenuous rhythm for ten to fifteen minutes, we fell back to our comfortable pace to recuperate and prevent ourselves from becoming fatigued too early. The next set of strokes were hard and fast, almost lifting us off our seats —full force racing pace, heaving at our oars, hearing team members grunt at the burst of energy and gasping for breath, giving it all we could—teeth clenched and almost cracking— one stroke after another, over and over again. Gasping as muscle aches set in, the icy air burned our windpipes as it bypassed the warmth and moisture of the nose. After another vigorous period, limited by the onset of fatigue and careless or sloppy strokes, we fell back once more.

As the winter weather became inclement, icy rain often beat down, numbing our hands and nearly freezing them to the oars. One day, hail drove against our forward efforts, pelting my face and melting into my sweat-soaked clothes. I forced myself to focus on the next stroke—numb body, empty mind, rhythmic agony. It was exhausting, physical work in often-rough water that was whipped up by the harsh wind, our feathered blades cutting through whitecaps and water splashing over our frozen legs. As winter progressed, the choppiness of the water and the freezing headwind became even greater.

The other eights from different London colleges and medical schools often rowed nearby. We eyed them up, weighing our chances of beating them in competitive races from Chiswick to Putney Bridge. The winner would compete in the eliminating races a week before the main Henley Royal Regatta by the town of Henley-on-Thames in July.

The end of our Saturday ordeal required supreme effort: after our row, we lifted our boat out of the water, hosed it down, and stacked it with the other boats. The deck was always busy as we hustled among the other crews who had also finished for the day. By three in the afternoon, we sat in silence, often dozing as we were bused back to our dorms. Once in my room, I'd fall asleep and frequently miss dinner.

On Tuesday and Thursday evenings, the crew met at the gym and worked to exhaustion. My weight dropped to 148 pounds, and my trousers were in danger of sliding off. My pulse lowered to forty-eight beats per minute as I became fitter—the heart's stroke-volume increasing with maximum efficiency. The whole grueling business was very different from the intoxicating glide aloft in hot, dry Egyptian skies, the sun beating down, the pyramids on the horizon, and the rush of wind past my open cockpit as the thermals uplifted me.

Why was I punishing myself like this? Painfully, I liked rowing for the instant community and shared goals of a group of like-minded blokes. I enjoyed the company of men, as well as being a member of the prestigious University College London's eight. I felt a deep sense of belonging, of being part of a family. In addition, concentrating on each stroke was akin to meditation; I forgot about my fear of failure, of being judged, and the complex and contradictory outside world. Not only was rowing invigorating, but in a perverse way, I felt alive. Rowing taught me to once more associate sensations with feelings—connecting to myself.

When we won races against other colleges, we celebrated at Ye Olde Cheshire Cheese in Fleet Street, rebuilt after the Great Fire of 1666. We bowed our heads to descend a narrow staircase with low ceilings and no banister. Posted signs warned "Watch your feet" and "Mind your head." We crowded together at a long, well-worn oak table eating shepherd's pie, drinking ale, and singing bawdy songs led by Shawn, a fellow student, who stuttered when he spoke but sang eloquently like an Irish tenor, drawing on a vast repertoire of dirty ditties.

Other songs followed, usually rugby songs, as we became rowdier. We raucously imagined we were drunken sailors immersed in our seafaring world; a band of collegiate mariners joined in song. There were dozens of verses to some songs, and as we sang, we forged a bond that melded us into a team—energy that we drew on to win another race. I felt a sense of communion.

Physically, I was too tired to study regularly and began to fall behind. I saved Sundays to review the week's lectures, thinking I could cover the necessary material in several hours, synthesizing information we had learned from Fred plus other topics. During the week, we sat in our white-tiled dungeon among the dead and the living, comparing pickled slices of human brains—white and gray matter in formaldehyde solution sloshing about open containers—with comparable images in our dissecting manuals that explained their functions.

However, by the weekend, I found reading neuroanatomy dry and boring—though, despite my fatigue, I had no problem remembering the paragraph concerning penile erection: nerves from the spinal cord at the level of the pelvis innervate the penile vessels to fill the gland with blood, making it turgid. Emotions send nerve signals from the brain down the spinal cord to facilitate, modulate, or inhibit the erection. I felt sure this neuroanatomy function would interest Professor James, the charismatic preclinical academic dean who would supervise the upcoming end-of-term written and oral mid-December exams that were ominously close. They loomed like Putney Bridge out of the fog. After all, had he not laughed with delight at my answer during my interview that I wanted to become a doctor because of the nurses?

I passed the two-day essay exam. I was less confident about the much-dreaded orals on the third day because the examiner could ask a wide range of questions to test the limits of a student's knowledge. During the orals, Professor James projected the benign image of Dr. Jekyll, although without his usual warmth. He was all inquisitor. Standing in front of a well-dissected cadaver chest, he quizzed me, pointing to organs or tissues. Confident, I answered: the aorta, the vena cava, the vagus nerve, and then named the different heart valves—describing each of their functions. Satisfied, he moved to a table with pickled brain slices. My anxiety overwhelmed to the point that my head pounded. Handing me a pointer, he told me to identify a structure called the hypothalamus. Uncertain of its location, I observed faint scratch marks made by preceding students in the light reflected off the slices. Hesitantly, I circled a similar area.

"Show me more precisely." He had noticed my hesitation.

Foolishly, I capitulated. Trying to be honest I said, "I'm sorry. I have not finished reading about this yet."

His face turned purple with rage. "You are here to learn, not play. Take this course seriously, or I'll fail you and throw you out," he thundered as Dr. Jekyll became Mr. Hyde.

Bolts of lightning paralyzed me as he skewered and threatened me. My father's apparition, angry and always disapproving of me when I could not meet his high expectations, rose up before me—a terrifying vision. Perhaps my father was right: maybe I was a failure.

The existential threat made me cancel my five-week Christmas holiday with Oma and Opa in Wedel. I had come too far to be thrown out of medical school. I stayed in my room at Commonwealth Hall, grew a beard to save time in the morning, and studied and studied and studied. Rory kindly invited me to spend Christmas Day with his family. I had two compassionate

*Marwan and Rory*

friends, with the other being David in Manchester, who sent me my only Christmas greetings. Written on the inside of a Burnage Grammar School card, I read: "Best wishes from David at Christmas time. From one brother who has been very busy to another who will also be busy with his studies—G-d be with you for the new English year. Hope to be writing soon."

David's card touched me. During the long period of autumn and winter, I had not received any letters from him, and I feared that we had gone our separate ways. His card became my only remaining connection to Manchester. I received no other Christmas greetings—not from Mother nor Gulnar. To them, I may just have been their son and little brother, who, in their eyes, was a man about to become a physician, in charge of my life and not struggling for the persona that would establish my belonging. How wrong they were.

# 10

# ASSIMILATION

*It is not the strongest or the most intelligent who will survive
but those who can best manage change.*
—Charles Darwin

I n the spring term, the high point of each medical school
society's annual activities was a formal sit-down dinner in
the house officers' quarters of the Doctor's Building at
University College Hospital on the other side of Gower Street.
That evening, wives and girlfriends, who were usually not
permitted in the male domain, were tolerated. The Medical
Society's banquet was an elegant, elaborate affair. Professor
Young, resplendent in black tie, gave a short, witty speech,
followed by one delivered by the student president. The
impressive array of cutlery for the multi-course dinner and the
variously shaped wine glasses that accompanied each dish
intimidated me. I learned which of the multiple knives and
forks to use by observing others and practiced the art of small
talk.

Such dinners in medical school were milestones in my
social development. Raised in a Muslim household, there was

no alcohol. Now in England, I always faced the question of "red or white." Additionally, since Mother hated fish, she never bought, cooked, or ate it, so Gulnar and I adopted this culinary prejudice. I decided that as a potential member of the medical profession, I would learn to eat and drink the same way others did.

I arranged a comparable feast on Friday, April 24, 1964, for the students' Physiology Society, courtesy of the Physiology Department. Professor Huxley, dressed in his gray suit, gave a solemn talk about the significance of his research on nerve conduction. As student chairman, I spoke next. Unaccustomed to public speaking and feeling somewhat embarrassed, I limited my comments to say, "The reason the lion did not eat Androcles after he removed the thorn from its paw is that he promised not to give an after-dinner speech." I sat down to wild applause and cheers that I attributed more to the free-flowing wine than to the eloquence of my comments.

Despite my workload, I resumed rowing, sensitive to the University College's high-ranking position that placed us at the top of the various rowing teams competing for the annual Henley Royal Regatta. Despite my reluctance to jeopardize my academic advancement, I respected that my team members needed my physical strength to help cross the finish line and end the season.

In the spring term, our achievement in beating the other London medical school teams and colleges during the heats and clocking the best time placed us in the top position. We would represent University of London at the annual five-day Henley Royal Regatta held later that spring.

On day one of the races, we suddenly learned that based on our timing during the fall trials, we were placed in the first line-up, head to head with Oxford University's team. In the eliminating races the two boats approached the starting line, and as the clock and race began, we sped forth. With willpower we kept the pressure, keeping pace with Oxford's crew, stroke by stroke. As we came around the bend of the river and the spectator marquee appeared, we entered a manic racing mode, dashing toward the finish. Grunts grew louder, farts flew further, and shit escaped our sphincters as we gave it more than our all.

Then, in a burst of steroid-filled energy, unbelievably, Oxford pulled away and ahead of us—their grunts quieter and their farts fainter, more disciplined as a team bent on victory. Crossing the finish line, each man collapsed over his oar, gasping for breath, and feeling utterly deflated and defeated without a shred of charity toward the victors.

I cursed them.

# FIRST APPENDECTOMY

*And isn't it so, everything we do is done out of fear of loneliness?*
—Pascal Mercier

Having missed my Christmas break to focus on studying because of fear of expulsion, for Easter 1964, I flew to visit Oma and Opa in Wedel and to see Gulnar in Hamburg. Arriving late at the British European Airway terminal at London Heathrow, I got upgraded to first class—a treat I attributed to wearing a suit and tie. On my first evening, Gulnar invited Ingrid, a colleague, to Good Friday dinner. They huddled together in the prolonged northern twilight with a single flickering candle, enveloped in the aroma of fresh coffee. I sat nearby, preoccupied with a puzzle of King Tutt's death mask.

The women's murmured conversation revolved around the fate of Ingrid's husband, who had been teaching German at the Goethe Institute in Nairobi, Kenya. Ingrid had received a telegram with news of her husband's sudden death. His body would arrive the following day on a Lufthansa flight. The cause of death of her healthy, thirty-something husband was unknown. While lecturing, he had developed a severe headache, rapidly lapsed into a coma, and died. The two women asked what "*Herr Doktor*" thought the cause might be. I moved opposite Ingrid. In the fading dusk, she looked older than my sister. I told her I was a first-year medical student, but having studied neuroanatomy, I suspected that the symptoms suggested a berry aneurysm—a small outpouching of blood vessels in the brain that had the propensity to burst and bleed. It was also common in younger males. Due to the closed-spaced bony skull, there was no room for the leaking blood, causing a wicked headache, the rapid onset of coma, and death. Ingrid was not listening to my explanation—she seemed far off.

Gulnar read a bedtime story to my two-year-old niece while Freimut, my brother-in-law, opened a bottle of wine and put on an LP of Bruch's haunting violin concert. Still unaccustomed to alcohol, I sipped the wine slowly. Ingrid drank freely, nibbling on crackers with artichoke dip, talking with Freimut about the sudden loss of her husband.

Finally, the lights were dimmed, the candles lit, and dinner was served. Freimut opened a second bottle of wine, and the conversation ranged along a spectrum of political topics, invariably reverting to the incomprehensible death of Ingrid's husband. Toward the end of dinner, she went to the bathroom. We heard sobbing and exchanged glances in awkward silence.

Gulnar knocked on the bathroom door. "Ingrid? Are you all right?" The sobbing stopped, and Gulnar resumed knocking. "Open the door." Gulnar slipped in.

Freimut and I cleared the table, extinguished the candles, and washed the dishes. The LP stopped playing. The room was eerily quiet.

Gulnar joined us. "Ingrid is frightened to go home and be alone. I told her she could stay." Turning to me, she said, "You will have to share the sofa bed."

I was astonished. "Really?" I said with righteous indignation. "She is a stranger. The sofa is narrow. Don't you have a spare mattress? I don't know her."

Gulnar shook her head. "She's very nice. It's only one night," she said in her big sister, dictatorial voice. Once again, big sister became big sister. She saw me as she had all her life: her younger brother who looked up to her and blindly followed her instructions. She hadn't yet comprehended that I was now a medical student well on my way to becoming a surgeon—my own man. Yet I still lived in her shadow—her younger brother. Despite my reservations, I succumbed. I said, "OK. We could manage *if* we lie head-to-feet."

Gulnar and Freimut went to bed. I turned off the living room lights, donned my PJs, and crawled under the duvet. I maneuvered onto my left side, my back against the wall. As my eyes adjusted to the dark, Ingrid came toward me, wearing a pale borrowed nightie. She slithered under the covers, her head near mine. A few inches separated us. She whispered, "My feet smell terrible." Her breath was of alcohol, mixed with tooth-paste. Her body heat crept across the narrow divide.

The prolonged silence was reassuring. Thinking she had fallen asleep I closed my eyes. It was going to be a difficult night.

She whispered, "Do you say a prayer at night?" In the dark, her voice sounded like that of a much younger woman.

"No. My mother used to say it."

"She did?"

"Yeah. She'd say, 'Thank God he's in bed.'"

Ingrid chuckled. Perhaps fearing the nightmares sleep might bring, she spoke again. "Have you ever done an opera-tion?" I wondered if dissecting Fred counted. She shifted slightly to her right, facing me. "Tell me about an operation you'd like to do."

"An appendectomy."

"Tell me about it," she said, adding, "please."

"The appendix is like a worm, with its base attached to the large bowel, forming a landmark on the skin known as McBurney's Point," I whispered. "If you draw an imaginary line between the prominent hip bone and the belly button and trisect it, the outer spot, near the hip bone, is McBurney's Point. That's usually the site of greatest tenderness in appendicitis."

I paused. She lay motionless, and I could not hear her breathing. "Are you asleep?" I whispered.

She nudged me with an ice-cold foot. I jumped. She murmured, "No, of course not. What do you mean by Mc...Mc-whatever point?"

"Shall I show you?"

"Yes," she said. Turning onto her back, she hitched up her nightie and took my right hand and placed it in the middle of her tummy. "OK, start again."

Her skin was warm and supple, her belly flat and smooth. It rose and fell with each breath. She had placed my hand with the tip of my little finger grazing her pubic hair. It felt coarse and rough, like steel wool. Using my index finger, I traced a line from her umbilicus to the anterior superior iliac spine of the pelvis. I trisected it and indicated McBurney's point, pressing firmly to emphasize the location.

"Ouch, you're hurting me."

"Sorry." Lifting my finger, I proceeded to trace a horizontal skin incision with my fingernail, emphasizing the landmark.

"Oh, I see," she said. Her breathing had become irregular. I described a gridiron incision, whereby the surgeon bluntly splits the underlying three muscle layers in the direction of their muscle fibers, each layer running at ninety degrees to the next. I wondered how to demonstrate this. She suddenly threw back the duvet, swung her legs over the edge of the narrow bed, stood up, whipped off her nightgown, took off her ring, and slid back into bed. She was warm against me.

It was a night of firsts: the first time an older woman had

seduced me; the first time I witnessed an all-encompassing and shuddering orgasm, scaring the hell out of me; the first time I came uncontrollably in a kaleidoscope of confused emotions; the only time I aborted an appendectomy and believed that in the future, the use of a scalpel would give me even greater pleasure.

I believed that we are the roles we play and the mantle that is placed on us by those who surround us. As she projected, Ingrid was a high school teacher, a wife, and a brand-new widow. When she took off her ring, she shed her roles, leaving a woman in need of human contact.

Despite my momentary ambivalence, I had agreed to share the sofa bed with the best and most honorable of intentions, following my sister's instructions. I reasoned that my presence and the warmth of another body would be comforting and reassuring to her. Perhaps Ingrid felt that making love to me, a man she barely knew, could save her from facing the loss of her husband—affirming that despite being a widow, she was still alive.

I met Ingrid forty years later at my sister's birthday party. I felt awkward when she approached me with a drink in hand, second husband in tow. I confessed I had written about our escapade. She smiled and said, "*Es war doch schön*"—"but wasn't it nice?"

Still in a state of awe at being seduced by an older woman, the next night, I took the suburban train to Wedel to spend the rest of my Easter break with Oma and Opa, enjoying their welcoming company and Oma's baked yummies, for she was a baker's daughter. It was Saturday night, I managed to catch the last train from Hamburg, connecting to the last bus that ran past my grandparents' house through the Wedel suburbs. Wedel had become a conurbation of Hamburg. Where once spread the fields and woods of my early childhood, there were rows of townhouses. The car-choked streets reflected Germany's post-war affluence. I boarded the crowded bus, standing toward the front. I looked to the back, past fellow travelers hanging onto straps and sleepy, seated passengers. My gaze rested on a young woman standing in a red coat with nicely styled blonde hair. Our eyes met. Could it be my old childhood friend Renate? I had last seen her ten years ago.

I looked inquisitively into the face I recognized; it was the same smile, the same dimples and the same dancing eyes. We made our way toward each other through the crowded aisle, attracted like opposite magnetic poles. We met in the middle of the bus. Surrounded by strangers, we had found each other. She looked more attractive, which induced a twinge of desire. My urge to kiss her hello was suppressed to a ridiculous handshake, as formal German customs mandated. My uncertain feelings erred on the safe side. We conversed, raising our voices above the general background buzz of fellow passengers. We stood together hanging onto straps. She leaned into me when the bus rounded corners, giving me an impression of welcoming familiarity, mixed with anxiety. My stop was approaching. We had not established definitive contact.

I was curious to know why she was coming home late on a Saturday night. I said that I came from staying at my sister's, expecting her to tell me where she had been; she merely asked how my sister was, remembering that they had met years ago. Where had she been? Did she have a steady boyfriend? I searched for clues, checking her hand for a ring, an amulet about her neck or something indicating she was otherwise "taken." She was shoulder height, standing close to me. I could look her over discreetly. Her lipstick was fresh, she wore no perfume, and her hair was pristine. I felt too awkward to ask her questions that would have assuaged my curiosity. When she spoke, I wondered what my prospects were of seeing her again. Might I finally get to know her?

Renate expressed surprise when I did not get off the bus at the stop near my grandparents'. I rode on further with her until we both got off at her stop. We chatted freely in German as if we had known each other all our lives. I wondered what of my past was relevant to advancing our familiarity. I walked her the few hundred yards to her home and stopped. This was the closest I had ever approached. I wondered why I had never sought her out. Somewhere in the past she had told me that her father was very strict, which brought to mind my authoritarian Opa, the likes of whom I had certainly not relished encountering. She hesitated in the dark, a distance from the path leading to her front door. She gave me a peck on the cheek. To my delight she asked me if I'd like to go walking along the Elbe the next day, a Sunday.

*Marwan and Renate*

I collected her in the early afternoon, very briefly meeting her parents. We ambled together along the Elbe, mingling with the Sunday strollers, admiring the freighters and tankers that were mainly leaving port. She was very formally dressed, wearing a plaid frock with a round collar, three-quarter-length sleeves, with a full skirt that extended below her knees. Her high-heeled shoes seemed somewhat impractical on the dirt path along the banks of the river and through the surrounding woods. Her hair was in a fashionable, modest beehive, still appealingly blonde, stiff with hair spray. I felt very sophisticated, determined to behave like a young doctor. We walked hand in hand. I could not help wonder what she would have felt like if we made love. I dispelled that notion quickly, fearing it might betray my carnal curiosity. I wore an open shirt with gray flannel pants and a woolen herringbone jacket, with a silk handkerchief tucked in my breast pocket. I puffed awkwardly on a cigarette, which burned between my fingers most of the time, helping me project a cool image. I had brought along a camera. We took pictures of each other, intending to share them.

Some distance along the Elbe, near the Wedel yacht club, we stopped at a popular coffee house—Hamburger Fehr Haus. We sat outside watching ships of all types, tonnage, and nationalities go by. She was impressed by my ability to recognize the different national flags, by my recollections of our times together at school, and of my subsequent travels throughout the Middle East. I carefully avoided mentioning the various flames. There was my French girlfriend, Carol, with whom I had first danced cheek to cheek at English School Cairo dances; my Hungarian belle, Kinga, who kissed me passionately, leaving me wandering the streets until dawn; Magdalena, my Polish love who disappeared from Cairo before we could consummate our relationship; my English girlfriend, Kate, with whom I had awkwardly sacrificed my virginity in Manchester. Then there was Ingrid, who had seduced me only the night before. I relived the events of the previous night in my mind.

Renate opened up over a traditional German "coffee and

cake," telling me all about her life in Wedel. As she spoke, she began to morph into the caricature of a small-town girl. This image included one of Mother and my grandparents, a sine qua non for the limited world my mother was raised in, the same one into which she had dumped me with such indifference.

Renate chatted on about herself, about being an only child, getting her way, wrapping her stern father about her little finger. Little did she suspect that this tidbit made me cringe. I did not like the idea of being manipulated. I listened as we drank our coffee, eating a slice of delicious cherry cheesecake. Having finished her Abiture, or high school diploma, the previous year, Renate became an apprentice in an accounting firm in Hamburg. She was studying for her diploma. Her English was passable. She had never been overseas, and had lived her entire life in Wedel. She continued to natter endlessly, making up for the twelve years that we had been apart. She embodied the picture I had constructed in my mind of my mother, who had escaped her narrow upbringing by marrying an exotic foreigner.

I found myself wondering why she was wearing such a conservative dress with its only access to her skin via an endless zipper at the back. Did Renate not know the delightful intimacy of a naked body; the pleasure of exploring and above all the joy of giving, aptly described by e.e.cummings in one of his "may i feel said he," love poems?

She prattled. Her conversational topics became progressively more parochial. She drifted further and further away from the image of Renate I had built up over the years. Occasionally, she would ask me a question. I would realize that my attention had wandered. She would repeat the questions, which were quite mundane, such that I cannot recall them now. As the afternoon wore on, I began to wonder what we presently had in common.

We walked from the yacht harbor toward the railway

station down Main Street, passing ABC Street, recalling our days at school. At first, she evaded my curiosity concerning her behavior when we were young. When I pressed her, she did not have a satisfactory answer. I did not have the courage to tell her that when we were kids, I had missed my mother, and desperately wanted Renate's friendship and love. Given my growing ambivalent feelings toward her, it was probably wise I had not confessed to her. Near the school, past the old chestnut tree, was Wedel's first legal brothel, just announced in the local papers. We could see through the display window to the scantily clad women prancing about to music in the dim red light. We peeked inside, curious and uncomfortable. When they beckoned us to enter, we resumed our walk hand-in-hand, her lacquered beehive hair-do reached my shoulder when she pressed close to me.

She suggested we go dancing, which was a great idea. The Beatles were riding the hit parades, even in Wedel. Dancing apart had become the new fad. When night fell, we headed to a local dance hall. On the crowded Sunday-night dance floor, we danced separately, together. When slow numbers played, she eagerly nudged closer. We danced, masking my waning enthusiasm, while I sweated with discomfort, wondering how I could gracefully end the evening.

Hunger saved the day. We walked to a sausage stand near the station, each eating a Bratwurst with bread, and standing under strings of light bulbs. We rode the bus to her stop in silence. She led me through the shrubbery near her house. We kissed, hesitantly. She took my hand and placed it on her breast, continuing the kiss. I froze and withdrew my hand. She searched my eyes for meaning. It was time to see her home.

My childhood memory of Renate did not match the real young woman before me. Time had moved on. She never personified a sexual Renate during this time. Placing my hand on her breast was a psychological transgression of the persona

Renate represented in my mind. I had wanted a friend; someone I could become close to. Then perhaps it might have developed into an ardent intimate relation where my hand on her breast would have been a meaningful signal.

I never saw her again. Over the years I regretted not meeting her expectations that night. Had she waited and built up to a sexual encounter with me all those years—from age six to age twenty? I always regretted disappointing her. My act of removing her hand, taking her home and never contacting her again was a massive form of rejection. It must have hurt her. I'm so very sorry that was not my intent. I yearned for her as I had yearned for Mother. Intimacy wasn't part of the equation.

———

Before my return to London, Opa surprised me with a small Grundig transistor radio, which was so popular back then. Apart from a boat he made for my fifth birthday, he never gave me a present. Now, with me being a medical student, he looked up to me and expressed his love with this radio. I loved it. With it, I could listen to the BBC news and all the pop music on the hit parade charts, music that would lift my spirits on breaks from my unending studies. Opa's present brought tears to my eyes, even though he pushed me away as I tried to hug him in gratitude.

However, the gift created a problem. Should I declare it at the UK customs after landing in London and pay a hefty import fee for electronic goods, or should I try to smuggle it into the country, hoping to evade detection?

A young customs official pointed to my suitcase. "Anything to declare?"

"I got a birthday present while in Germany," I replied, hoping to engage his sympathy. Before I could say anything else, he commanded me to open my suitcase. On top of my clothes, lying in his direct view, was my precious token of Opa's affection.

He picked it up, fingered it. "You'll have to pay an import tax on this plus a fine since you failed to declare it on the customs form," he said in a very officious tone, weighing the Grundig in his hand. Looking up, he paused, gazed at me, and in a softer tone said, "Is that a Burnage Grammar School tie you're wearing?"

"Yes."

"I went there. It must have been a few years before you. I've never met an old boy on this job." He replaced my transistor radio, dropped the suitcase lid shut, checked off my declaration form, and winked at me. "Good luck," he said as he moved on to pick on someone else's suitcase.

Walking away I felt that the branded "F" for failure and "S" for shame from Burnage Grammar began to fade, and I liked the feeling of being one of the boys.

# 12

# UNIVERSITY TERMS

*Success is not final; failure is not fatal.*
*It is the courage to continue that counts.*
—Winston Churchill

I had thought going to medical school would be an enjoyable interlude in my life, a leisurely time when I would acquire information more or less by osmosis and in a gentlemanly manner—totally different from how schoolboys cram in grammar school to pass exams. Ultimately, as a medical student, I would be exposed to patients and diseases—a romantic idea akin to what I had read in Somerset Maugham's *Of Human Bondage,* A.J. Cronin's *The Citadel,* or *The Adventures of Sherlock Holmes* by Arthur Conan Doyle.

What a misguided notion. I was dead wrong.

In reality, my first four terms of medical school heading toward a second MB were a doctor production line; once I stepped onto that conveyor belt, there was no way for me to get off. I began my introduction to the foundation of basic science knowledge on the east side of Gower Street at University College. The fundamental knowledge base about the human body was poured onto us—anatomy for structure, embryology to understand its origins, histology for cellular structure, physiology for its cohesive function, biochemistry and pharmacology as the currency of functional metabolism, and neuroscience, the master switch that coordinated activity and gave us consciousness and perhaps even our soul and humanity. The Bachelor of Medicine—an intensive and comprehensive written and oral exam worthy of the Spanish Inquisition— would serve to evaluate the efforts of our eighteen months of labor. Only after I passed this crucial second MB exam would the conveyor belt then jolt me from University College to the west side of Gower Street, where I would face clinical obligations at University College Hospital.

While I bashed the books for the second MB exams, I doggedly ignored student activities. I avoided meeting with other classmates, shunned small talk, and did not even seek female companionship. I skipped Saturday night hops, whether at University College or live performances in the basement of Commonwealth Hall. Even though I lived in the heart of London, I passed up the lure of the British Museum, the art galleries, West End movie theaters, plays, musicals, and the classical music proms at Albert Hall. Anyway, I hated going out alone.

Throughout the spring term, I could hear John, my next-door neighbor, playing his guitar and serenading his girlfriend.

I picked up some words of the popular folk songs by Pete Seeger and Peter, Paul, and Mary. Over time, his muffled singing changed to laughter, interspersed with silence, followed by the rhythmic banging of his bed against our dividing wall. I slammed my palms against my ears and read aloud to myself. John subsequently introduced me to the "lucky lady," as he referred to her, adding that they were going to marry after term —his last at the university. I envied his new life. With my long academic road ahead and having avoided the company of females, I was a considerable distance behind John's timeline.

Learning was a slow and deliberate process, for I had difficulty reading, interpreting, and understanding words. At the time, I thought my trouble came from learning too many languages in quick succession—Arabic, German, English, math, music, French—before I had turned eleven. That I had dyslexia was not even considered at that time. It took me three passes through the same material to comprehend and conceptualize my medical texts. Embryology was particularly tricky because the course was short and the material was dense, coming with few visual aids, but I deemed it essential to grasp the role of development in defining body structure and function. I was not a memorizer. I needed to acquire an understanding of the subject so that I could recall it when needed and apply it to practical use when I became a clinician.

Even as I studied, I could hear his commanding voice: *If you had no father, you'd have to struggle, like I had to. Then you might do better in school and in your life.* I became more determined to not only emulate his success, but to exceed it at any cost, at least to do so in my desired field—surgery.

Dr. James' tongue-lashing and threats of dismissal from medical school had put the fear of Allah into me. I resolved to spend my three-month summer break revisiting the previous year's work and preparing for the term to come. I even refused the never-ending invitations from the gregarious and wild

Dotty, the exuberant redhead and buxom art student living next door in the all-girls Canterbury Hall who flaunted conventional social behavior by aggressively pursuing gentlemen of interest, giving her a reputation among the guys as being good in bed. The blokes were probably exaggerating, but their gossip put me on my guard. Knowing about my weakness for baked goods, she showed me the Eccles cakes her mother had sent and suggested we share them in her room. My mouth watered at the sight of them, but I declined. It was the end of her academic year, and while she partied, I studied.

By May, the term was over and I witnessed the exodus of students from Commonwealth Hall. Most headed home for the summer, leaving the vast residence an eerily and empty space —especially on a Saturday night. The handful of remaining inhabitants—graduates, overseas, and medical students—ate in the dining hall in the basement surrounded by deserted tables supporting upside-down chairs. We ate in silence, perhaps thinking of our studies or longing for distant families. I had no family in England into whose folds I could creep.

On the very rare occasion that Mother wrote, her densely typed letters were a mere shopping list of things she wanted me to do, such as write to an uncle who represented the family in the sale of my father's one-hectare plot near the pyramids. Her infrequent lengthy missives from another world drained me. I skimmed through them, feeling unwilling and unable to make a connection in her distant and foreign planet. I wrote to her about my endless studies, my non-stop exams, and my nonexistent social life, hoping she would understand my lack of time to attend to her wishes and to elicit her sympathy. Instead, in a following letter, she would tell me to buck up. Gulnar seldom wrote. Only the regular letters from my Oma comforted me. Her handwritten pages reflected the warmth, caring, and security of the Steinbachs, the bloodline I had come to identify as a loving family. Egypt became ever more distant.

So I bucked up. My home in England was Room 337 in Commonwealth Hall, one of four hundred similar cells set aside solely for men. The space measured about seven by ten feet with a bed, a desk in front of a window next to a radiator, a two-level bookshelf above the bed,  and a small chest of drawers. I used the night table for my kettle, Nescafé, tea and sugar and a grainy picture of Oma next to a provocatively smiling smaller photo of Magdalena, my Cairo girlfriend. She tended to write whenever she planned to come to London. My warm and comforting feelings for her became fuzzy dreams of yearning—*sehnsucht*—for our times together in Egypt.

I became a dull and boorish person with little outside interactions, restricted within my room by my obsession to study. Maybe some social stimulation would have helped my learning, but I was afraid to take the chance of distraction. Isolation and constant study were the punitive remedy that fed my monkey. I would prove to Dr. James, and to the ghost of my father, that I could succeed.

# 13

# LAST SUMMER HOLIDAY
## LONDON 1964

*Solitude, isolation, are painful things and beyond human endurance.*

—Jules Verne

I n the following academic year, after the three-month break, the courses would expand from thirty-six to forty-eight weeks, and there would be no more three-month summer holidays. Despite my resolution to study, I gave in to the temptation to leave London for a brief interlude. I planned to fly to Cairo in early September after finding an inexpensive Marriott promotional travel package. Mother, I imagined, would be pleased with the news of my arrival. I would try once more to establish a meaningful rapport with her, for despite theoretically loving her, a buffer existed between us that neither of us could be rid of. It was as if a powerful electromagnetic shield prevented us from approaching each other. I also longed to reacquaint myself with the kin of my father, move into my old room, sleep in my bed, build model airplanes, and perhaps go gliding.

Mother had maintained our membership at the prestigious Gezira Jockey and Sporting Club in Zamalek. I looked forward to returning to that familiar place, where guests sat about the pool in the afternoon and patio in the shade of umbrellas, drinking and chatting convivially, while waiters scurried about with trays of mint tea held high. I'd sit poolside, sunning myself, at the very spot I met Magdalena. Maybe she would materialize again. More likely, I'd meet some of my old English school friends who lived and studied in Cairo. It would be a warm and relaxing change from my solitary studying in London.

Like the old days, I'd resume my visits to my paternal grandparent's flat in Sayeda Zainab, where two of my aunts remained after my grandfather had died. Just dreaming of it, I could feel the warmth of their embrace, their kindness, love, and acceptance. In the remaining time, I yearned to visit my ancestral home of Beni Harem and my Sa'idi family members, the dark-skinned Nubians of Upper Egypt. It was a small village, a collection of adobe huts clustered about a warren of compacted alluvial mud alleys. I wondered whether, after graduation, I could live in that village and become their physician. Or would I be considered a *khawagah*—a foreigner, a Westerner, a non-Muslim not to be trusted, one who didn't belong?

Excited, I wrote Mother telling her of my Cairo plans. To my utter chagrin, and after I'd made my nonrefundable down payment, she informed me that she would be elsewhere and that she had rented out our flat to the American University for three years. Her news stunned and angered me. The one time I could visit and she'd be away? Exactly where? She did not say. For three years? What had happened to my things, the books that I read during my teenage years, my model airplane collection, my clothes, and trinkets? For a moment, I thought she might surprise me and come to England, but of course, that did not happen. She had virtually disappeared without any explanation once again. I learned years later that Mother had married one of my father's colleagues and had moved to

Damascus, Syria. Did Gulnar know about any of this? I never discovered. Her absence from Cairo did not surprise me, but being made unwelcome in my own home—essentially made homeless—was a shock. Gone was the desire to reconcile with her. I resolved to make the trip anyway, relying totally on myself. As if to heap insult on injury she mentioned that her German friends from Landstuhl, Germany, Tante Trudel and Onkel Hansi, would be visiting London. In her absence, would I take care of her "dear, kind friends." No mention was made of my meager allowance and the cost of dinner in London's expensive City. It was thus no surprise when they turned up at Commonwealth Hall.

I had last seen them almost ten years ago, when our family stayed with them on our way by car from Hamburg to Cairo.

Disinclined to an Indian meal and eager to relish a British one, they invited me to The Guinea and The Piggy restaurant in Lester Square. We could eat as great a variety of cooked meats as I might possibly consume with all the trappings—a piggy indeed. And they tucked in, hungry from their cross-Channel trip, I was delighted the fare was so different to what was dished out nightly at Commonwealth Hall. Naturally we spoke German. To capture the congenial evening, I started to take photographs of our table with heaped plates.

Suddenly there were loud agitated objections in broken English from the foursome who had been seated at a table next to us. We were aware that they spoke a mixture of German and Yiddish. "Stop taking photos of us," they declared. "You can't take photographs of us."

We were surprised for we had no such intent. Yet no matter how much I protested our innocents, and their misunder-standing in English, they became progressively more agitated and confrontational about our activity. The manager appeared. Listening to both sides of the vocal argument, he insisted I stop photographing. He too seemed convinced that because we spoke German our mission was to photograph our Jewish neighbors who were most distressed to the point of being convinced of our malintent.

We abruptly left. In the taxi back to Commonwealth Hall Uncle Hansi, once a prisoner of the Russians for almost seven years and a mis-treated and starved survivor of daily physical threats in the camp, educated me about what is officially defined as post-traumatic stress disorder.

I think I experienced this disorder when Mother's occasional letters arrived. They invoke a physical flashback to the four-year-old helpless boy abandoned in post-war Germany. Over the years, I realized that if I held the scalpel I could overcome the sense of helplessness. The yearning for love and the longing for identity had yet to be fulfilled.

# 14

# ZEBRA COURT

EGYPT, AUGUST 1964

*To see what is in front of one's nose needs a constant struggle.*

—George Orwell

On my arrival at Cairo airport an immigration officer in a standard black uniform stared at the photograph in my Egyptian passport. He opened a huge book, ran his finger down a list of names, and announced, "You are wanted as a deserter."

I was shocked. Deserters faced the stockade or the firing squad. I vehemently denied the charge. I described the recruitment process, including my examination date, Sunday, February 21, 1960, in Heliopolis, north of Cairo. I quoted the law: "'An only son, or the oldest son of a widow, is issued final exemption status.' I am the head of my family, responsible for the care of my mother," and lying, added, "and my unmarried sister. I am an only son. My father, *wallah yarhamu*—God bless his soul—is dead."

He did not flinch. "Where is your certificate?"

"In a bank safe in London. It's a precious document."

"Well you can't leave the country until you produce it," he said.

I, a patriotic Egyptian, was accused of desertion and dereliction of duty? I was incensed.

Indeed, I had not expected to be accused of being a fugitive. To make sense of the situation, I cited my uncle's name, rank, and position in the army's general staff, knowing he was in Russia. I mentioned Mr. Mukhtar's name, the individual working in the *Mukhabarat*—the state security service—who had helped me get a student passport. The immigration officer was unmoved. He dismissed me. I had barely set foot in Egypt, and once more, I was trapped.

For the first week, I moved into the Marriott Zamalek, a former opulent royal palace. Staying in a five-star hotel should have been an exhilarating experience, but tension and worry spoiled my joy. Seeking my family's help, I visited Uncle Saad, one of my father's brothers. Not only had he aged considerably in the four years since I had last seen him, he was teetering on the edge of frailty. He had retired and claimed he no longer had connections—no pull that could help me.

My cousins looked on, observing my dismay without offering suggestions or help. Their response was a stark contrast to the help my father always volunteered to give them. I was angry to the point of dismissing them from my life. I stated my resolution to clear up the accusation myself, and they replied, repeatedly, "*inshallah.*" I understood the phrase and its implication. It reflected a fundamental difference between the Egyptian and German heritages in which I was raised—as distinct as zebra stripes. In Egyptian society—where there is hopelessness and limited upward mobility—invoking *inshallah* was a matter of leaving it to God. My white stripe reflected an active state of mind: self-reliance, or as the common saying goes, "God helps those who help themselves." My German Opa would say, "*Selbst ist der Mann,"* or do it yourself. The two expressions lived simultaneously in my mind. I was a *believer,* and I had *faith.* Those who held faith could act and prevail with God's blessing.

The outcome of my need for a duplicate copy of the military exemption document depended on me being proactive. All government departments were housed in the Mogamma, a monstrous fourteen-story bureaucratic edifice in Midan Tahrir, Cairo's main square. There, some eighteen thousand public servants toiled in offices wrapped inside a labyrinth of dead-end corridors. Most feared of the many government departments was the *Mukhabarat:* the Egyptian secret service. I sought Mr. Mukhtar, a police colonel who, out of kindness, had facilitated my getting a passport and exit visa four years earlier. Without his help, I would have been stranded in Egypt. This time, I could not find his office. No one wanted to acknowledge that they had even heard of him or that he had ever existed. The situation was surreal. I felt like K., the protagonist in Kafka's *The Trial.*

I went to the recruitment center at the end of the Cairo metro line, which at that time was in Heliopolis, about two kilometers from my former school. To my dismay, the sergeant who kept the attendance ledger eyed me with misgivings, despite me falling back to my Egyptian demeanor. He must have wondered if I was indeed an Egyptian, a black-striped *ibn el balad* or a white-striped *khawagah?* When he claimed there was no record of my earlier visit, I insisted on seeing the log. "I saw the scribe write my name," I said adamantly.

He refused, overcome with uncertainty, telling me in an angry and dismissive voice, *"Bukra*—come back tomorrow," the classical move to avoid dealing with difficult issues by deferral. The hope was that the inquirer would abandon the effort and not bother further.

I did return the next morning. And the next and the next and the next. On my fourth appearance, when the sergeant and

I were briefly alone, I slipped him a 20-pound note (equivalent to $120), and he finally let me see the ledger. It was an old British leather-bound book, long and heavy, the pages criss-crossed with rows and columns filled in Arabic with all of the conscripts' information.

"Look," I said. "There, on the third row down. It's my name." The sergeant agreed. The date of my examination corresponded to the date and month I had given him. He agreed again.

Then, he pointed out the date of birth written in the next column. It did not match the date of my birth. "It's incorrect."

I examined the ledger more carefully. "Yes," I said. "The scribe has transposed the dates in the two columns." Such errors frequently occurred in all fields of bureaucracy because the education of the average conscripted military scribe, perhaps once a peasant, was only at the fourth-grade level.

Pointing out the transposition to the sergeant, I argued that if the date of my examination was the date of my birth, I would have been one day old. This was obviously a mistake.

With that, the logbook slammed shut like the crack of a whip. "The army does not make mistakes." In response to my protestations, he refused to issue me another certificate. Once more, I heard, "*Bukra.*"

*Your mother's cunt*, I swore quietly to myself.

I appeared again the next day at around 10 a.m. The sergeant's greeting was formal and cold. I wondered what the problem was as he ushered me into a narrow room that resembled an old barrack.

Five army officers in khaki uniforms sat on a raised platform behind a long table covered in green felt. Two majors and two lieutenants flanked an elderly colonel in the middle. Giant photos of President Gamal Abdel Nasser and Air Marshal Abdel Hakim Amer, both decked out in their military attire, stared down at me. I was facing a military tribunal!

My heart sank. I knew tensions with Israel were rising and that the military would want to conscript every eligible male, particularly those who were educated. I was only twenty and scared stiff, but I was determined to keep my wits about me.

Without introduction, the colonel addressed me, ordering me to step forward. The sergeant stood a few paces behind me to my left. I was surrounded and in some serious trouble. Why had the ante been raised?

I answered the same questions I had been asked at the airport. The grilling seemed endless. Only the colonel spoke, haranguing me. His tone fluctuated between benevolent "fatherly" understanding and harsh authoritarian, with veiled threats for not having such an important document as the final exemption status certificate on me. His fellow officers looked on, entertained by the colonel's show of power. This felt like a circus performance, only with consequences. My uncle, a colonel on the general staff, went unmentioned. When I tried to introduce his name into the conversation, it was ignored.

The finger-jabbing directed at me went on and on. All the while, the colonel glared down at me from his elevated perch. My eyes were riveted to his. When he glanced down at some papers, I caught a glimpse of an old station clock above their heads. Soon, it would be time for the *Zuhr*, noon prayers; surely, he would stop.

While the colonel lectured on with fervor, I realized that when I was in Manchester, I had enthusiastically buoyed the military regime of President Nasser. I was a patriot, not a deserter. In the giant photo on the wall, Nasser's eyes did not focus on one of his ardent supporters, but somehow trailed off into the distance, making me wonder if I did not exist or matter. The colonel and his cronies were part of a totalitarian regime, where unconnected, vulnerable individuals like myself did not matter. Oppression and intimidation were the name of this game, and I was the pawn in their power play. I had lived too long in England to put up with the old bureaucratic ways of Egypt. I no longer belonged here.

Then, the real issue came to light. "Did you bribe the sergeant? Don't you know bribes are punishable in the army?"

One of the junior officers cleared his throat and gently interrupted, saying that I was not in the military. Ignoring the comment and without skipping a beat, the colonel continued his tirade, stating that this was "modern Egypt." Bribes were forbidden.

Had the colonel somehow erroneously surmised that I was part of the old pre-revolution British colonial establishment, probably the son of wealthy landowners or a foreigner who had evaded eviction after Britain's global embarrassment by the failed Suez War? Could he not see that I was a true Egyptian, even if I was attending an English university? Through my veins flowed Upper Egyptian Sa'idi blood. Did he not see that I was an *ibn el balad*—a native son?

In his eyes, I was not one of his Egyptian tribe. He only saw a foreigner, one who didn't belong. He had no idea how I had borne the insults and endured the pain of being one of his tribe when I was in England.

The fear that had me on the knife's edge now gripped me further. I stood silenced and frozen. Either I had given the sergeant an insufficiently substantial *baksheesh,* or someone had seen him accept it and reported it. More than likely, I had simply bribed the wrong person.

Jabbing his finger in my direction again, the colonel repeated his statement that in "modern Egypt," bribes were forbidden.

"It was a present for his children. I swear in Allah's name," I said. As if on cue, the muezzin's call for the *Zuhr* prayers interrupted the charade.

I was dismissed. The frosty sergeant, avoiding eye contact, issued me another final exemption status certificate. I could have kicked him. Acquiring the document had consumed one week of my precious three-week interlude. I stapled that damned certificate into the back of my Egyptian passport, against all bureaucratic rules of defaming government documents. Tough luck!

The episode further quenched my desire to return to Egypt after I completed my studies in England. I didn't want to live in a constant state of chaos under a military regime fearful of its citizens and inflamed with fantasies of greatness. I began to re-evaluate my self-proclaimed identity and ties; I wondered where I truly belonged.

# 15

# BENI HAREM
### SEPTEMBER 1964

*Grain must return to the earth, die, and decompose for new growth to begin.*
Egyptian Proverb

Georgy, my fellow classmate at university, joined me in Cairo. He had hitchhiked from England through Europe, taken a boat across the Mediterranean, and then rode a crowded bus of locals from Alexandria. Before medical school, he had attended Gordonstoun School in Scotland, which was known for its daily morning run, cold showers, and discipline. He was fit, lean, energetic, and a loyal friend who negotiated the world through reason. We both lacked the talent for small talk, which suited me fine.

Since I had resolved the issue with my final exemption status certificate after a frustrating week, I was glad to see George and to begin our travels together. We spent three nights in Sayeda Zeinab, feted by my aunts, Tante Mustakima and Tante Souad. In keeping with Muslim tradition, my grandfather, Sheikh Amin, had been buried within twenty-four hours. He was laid to rest next to his wife, who died a couple of years ago, and my father in our mausoleum in Cairo's City of the Dead. Tante Souad was now the only resident in the flat that had once been home to our large and vibrant family. Tante Mustakima lived with her son nearby. My aunts spent most of the day cooking in preparation for our return after our local sightseeing trips.

In Arab culture, it is customary to leave some food and beverages to signal enjoyment and satiation—indeed, it is impolite to eat everything. George and I had grown up in homes with the ethics of cleaning your plate. Tante Mustakima heaped more food onto George's clean plate, and polite and appreciative, he dutifully consumed the food at a progressively slowing pace. I observed the scenario from the opposite side of the table. He respectfully objected to more food with hand signals. "Tell your aunt I'm full and can't eat any more," George pleaded.

Tante Mustakima, delighted at his ravenous appetite and appreciation of her cooking, piled even more food onto his empty plate, urging him in Arabic to eat, and then resumed circling the lavish display of delicious dishes that covered the dining room table, much as my short, rotund grandmother, Sit Nazifa, used to do. We were the only guests.

"Just leave it," I kept repeating.

"I can't," he protested. "It's so delicious."

The moment she left us alone to go into the kitchen to make Turkish coffee, he stood up, moaning and holding his stomach. "I'm going to burst. I have to lie down on the floor."

"No, George, no. You can't do that here."

"I'm going to vomit," he whimpered, and with that, I managed to steer him to the open window. Leaning out, he let out a huge burp, avoiding a projectile heave into Cairo's night and the Sayeda Zeinab flaneurs in the street below.

We shared Sheikh Amin's large bed. I inhaled the scent lingering in the camel hair blanket, which evoked my deep affection for my grandfather. I missed the warmth and generosity of spirit of that kind and gentle man—his touch, kisses, and blessings lavished munificently upon me, particularly after my father's death.

The open window caught the breeze and brought with it the incessant howling and barking of the wild dog packs that roamed Cairo's surrounding desert, just as they had done in the pharaohs' day. The dogs and the persistent flies prevented us from sleeping soundly until sunrise, when the noise finally ceased and the flies sought relief from the day's coming heat.

George and I saw most of the sights around Cairo: the pyramids, the Christian churches, the ancient mosques, and the Museum of Egyptian Antiquities in Midan Tahrir, a stone's throw from the Mogamma.

I had visited the office of the Minister of State for Youth and Sports at the Mogamma. After paying the appropriate tax stamp, I obtained a letter on their official letterhead authorizing the internal police to facilitate my travels with George, a foreigner, within Egypt.

With our backpacks filled with Tante Mustakima's goodies, we took a bus to its terminus in Helwan, a major industrial city along the Nile, south of Cairo. My overall plan was to visit Beni

Harem and, after a day or so, head further south along the Nile to Luxor. Within minutes of arriving at the checkpoint on the southern edge of the city, George and I were sitting next to a lorry driver who was chugging along at breakneck speed south toward Upper Egypt. The one-lane blacktop shimmered into the distance under eucalyptus and palm trees, past alfalfa fields, with human traffic, donkey-drawn carts, and camels and their herders overflowing onto the center of the road. With the swiftly flowing Nile to our left and the green delta stretching out to the encroaching desert on our right, we barreled along, horn blaring through mud hut villages where life spilled onto the road.

After a couple of hours, the driver pulled over at a road-side tea stop, where villagers with stalls sold food, fruit, and iced Pepsi, and where children and flies gathered in multi-tudes. The sky was clear blue with few clouds. We piled out, seeking fresh air and shade from the high sun. The driver took a few steps off the road and urinated into the alfalfa fields. Before mid-morning prayers, he spread his prayer mat beside the road. Since the custom of touching clean dry soil suffices as a substitute for ablution, we touched the soil and wiped our hands and faces with it. After prayers, we retired to the shade of a huge eucalyptus tree. I bought a round of sweet black tea, which is traditionally served in a glass with a sprig of mint. I made every effort to establish a good rapport with our driver, even offering some of Tante Mustakima's delicacies, all the while including George by translating our conversation.

We watched the dynamic village life around us while George wandered off with his camera. I had warned him about the folkloric belief that to be photographed was to have one's soul stolen, so he might run into objections. George had consumed watermelons voraciously to quench his thirst, thinking the flesh was sterile and safer than tap water, perhaps forgetting that a knife drags bacteria from the skin into the fruit. Refreshed, we resumed our trip. I climbed into the cab. George decided he wanted to sit on the tarpaulin in the back of the lorry, claiming that the engine fumes and the driver continually crashing the lorry's gears were too much for him and that he would have greater latitude to photograph. The driver pulled onto the middle of the asphalt road and blew his horn. Adults with their children and feral dogs in their packs scattered, and we were on our way. We stopped three hours later at the next police checkpoint on the outskirts of Asyut. George hastily climbed down, dragging his backpack. "I have terrible cramps. I need a toilet right away."

The sergeant pointed to a police hut on the side of the road. George rushed off, dropping his backpack at my feet. Ignoring me, the sergeant cleared the driver to continue his journey.

"*Salam Aleikum*," I said, showing him the letter. He nodded as I continued, "How far to Beni Harem?"

He eyed me curiously. "*Beni Harem*?" he questioned in a Sa'idi dialect.

"Yes, I want to visit my family."

He yelled out to his subordinate busily checking north-bound traffic across the street, "Directions to Beni Harem?"

The lanky police officer looked at me incredulously, for I was wearing trousers, an open shirt, and a floppy hat instead of a *galabeya* and a cotton turban wrapped about a skullcap. He waved down the road, saying, "A few kilometers, take a right at the outskirts of the next village. Who is asking?"

"Me! Marwan Abdel Meguid," I said, raising my hand. "Cousin of the *omda*."

I heard him say, "Welcome," as George charged out of the hut.

"We've got to get out of here right now," he gasped out. "I didn't make it, and it's all over their toilet floor."

Fortuitously, a lorry drew up, and we climbed into the cabin while the sergeant instructed the driver to drop us off at the canal some distance along the road. We roared off with the horn blaring as people scattered and music blasted from the radio. The happy driver tapped out the song's beat on his horn, while poor George gripped his abdomen—pharaoh's revenge.

The driver left us at the outskirts of the village, amid a dense growth of sugar cane and date palm forest. We were met by a horde of noisy, barefoot children in *galabeyas*, regaling us with shouts of "Hello" and "How are you?" in Arabic-accented English. When I responded with "*Salam Aleikum*," they approached and touched us as if on a dare.

A smiling young man met us; hand outstretched. "Doctor Marwan, how are you? I am Hakim. Do you remember me? We met before when you were little."

We embraced and exchanged the traditional Arab three-cheek kisses, for Hakim was one of my distant cousins. "How is your father, the *omda*?"

He beamed with delight at the recognition. And just like Sit Nazifa, he repeatedly said the word *Nawartuna*—you light up my day—as we proceeded into the village. George and I frequently heard this affable and welcoming greeting from the growing crowd of relatives and those who claimed to have known Sheikh Amin or my father. I translated the greetings and the general tidings to George, who momentarily cheered up, allaying his anxiety of meeting strangers.

The government had brought electricity to the village. I marveled at the advances that Nasser's government had made —medical clinics and fresh water diesel pumps—although opportunities and jobs were needed to lift people out of poverty. Date palms towered over distant relatives who had matured into sunbaked men with callused hands and lithe bodies. The swarm of excited children and feral dogs outnumbered the few women—the wives in their black *melayas*, the younger ones wearing colorful dresses. We heard the occasional tongue trills, similar vocalizations that almost sixty years ago had reverberated among the cluster of huts, echoed through the narrow alleys, past well sweeps and courtyards to announce the birth of my father. In answer to the questions as to who these strangers were, they whispered, "That's Sheikh Amin's grandson." To those who didn't know the bloodline, we were indeed strangers—European looking and clothed—not belonging to the Delta, Sa'idi, or even showing any connection to the faint Nubian clans.

In a hot melee of humans covered in sweat and dust from the unpaved dirt roads, we arrived outside an octagonal building at the heart of the village, a structure had been hastily converted from a community center into our temporary living quarters. As we settled in the cool building, George rushed to the dry squatting toilet. A knock on the old, majestic door was followed by someone who brought us sulphasomidine antibiotic and anti-diarrhea pills handed out by a pharmacist from the village dispensary. There was no village physician. Despite my earlier misgivings, I mused aloud: Could this be an opening for me?

A cool Pepsi washed down the unleavened bread, feta cheese, and small peeled cucumbers offered to us. A servant took our clothes, and on leaving, locked the door. I lay down on a cotton-filled mattress set on floor matting, fatigued by our travels and overcome by the early afternoon heat. George, showered and wearing fresh clothes, looked through the open windows and reported, with alarm, "We are prisoners here. Look, they've posted a guard with a gun slung over his shoulders. He's pacing about the building."

I looked out. "It's the *raafirr*—the village guard sent to protect us. His gun must be at least fifty years old, and I doubt he has ammunition. It's a show of respect."

"We don't have our clothes. We can't even escape."

"Relax, George. We're among my people—my folks. No harm will come to us." I fell asleep, the serenity of the surrounding silence palpable.

———

We awoke with the muezzin's call for early evening prayers. It came across a loudspeaker—another upgrade. Throwing back the shutters, I saw the red sun nudge its way over the distant furrows of fertile soil that was dotted with white ibises. A murmur of birds swooped over the fields. The evening air felt cool. Soon there was a knock on the door. A young man returned our cleaned clothes. They had even pressed our trousers and polished our shoes.

The *omda*—wearing a clean white *galabeya* over his impressive paunch, amber prayer beads in hand, and accompanied by some of his sons—came to visit. He was a younger and portlier version of Sheikh Amin and was equally tall. Sporting a heavy beard, he had the dark face and broad nose characteristic of sturdy Sa'idi peasant stock. I took an immediate liking to him, for we were kin, and his good nature comforted me.

As the influential village chief, his duties included arbitrating contested water rights and domestic disputes. He held forth in the octagonal building. Sitting cross-legged on a straw mat in his fine *galabeya*, he listened to his constituents, making Solomonic decisions to maintain the peace, even though the decisions were not legally binding.

Following lavish and gracious greetings, hugs and kisses for me, and warm handshakes for George, we sat on floor cushions around a large copper tray laden with a delicious meal of lamb and chicken, rice, *bamia*—okra stew, with side dishes of tahini, and *torshi*—pickled vegetables, and piles of unleavened bread. After the traditional benediction of *Bismillah, ar-Rahman, ar-Rahim*—in the name of Allah, the Compassionate, the Merciful —we dove into the delicious meal specially prepared in our honor. We ate with our hands; etiquette demanded that we use our right hand, scooping up food with the *balady* bread— unleavened country bread—while the left one was reserved for toilet ablution. We quenched our thirst with fresh water filtered from open-necked *ullas*—clay water jars—rounding off the meal with buffalo yogurt and sweet black tea, all accompanied by the constant swatting of ubiquitous, swarming flies.

As George visited the bathroom several times, the *omda* asked about our medical studies and how we knew each other. In turn, I asked questions to confirm what I knew about his brother, Sheikh Amin, about Sit Nazifa, my grandfather's second wife, and why my father had been banished to a distant relation in Cairo when he was six years old. It was less an interrogation than a meandering and clarification of family lore, but he answered hesitantly. Perhaps he was unaccustomed to questions, or maybe, he was more likely searching for diplomatic replies. I could not help wondering if he was scanning for traces of my father in his nephew. I didn't look like the rest of the clan. Was he doubting if I belonged?

Since our conversation was in Arabic, George excused himself and, accompanied by a young man, explored the village, camera in hand, as daylight receded into a soft, warm evening. I took the opportunity to ask the *omda* two more questions that had been on my mind.

"When was Sheikh Amin born?"

He thought for a while. "I was eight years younger. So, he must have been born 1260 *hijra*"—the Islamic calendar—"or there about." He paused, looking up at the wooden ceiling, mumbling to himself and clicking his prayer beads. "Around 1879 to 1882, I think," he added, gazing at me again. "Registering births wasn't customary. You know, at that time, many infants died." I nodded in acknowledgment, trying to calculate how old my grandfather, or Giddi, as I fondly called him in Arabic, would have been at his death.

As we sipped our tea in silence, I wondered how to pose my next question. "What did the family think of my father marrying a foreign woman?"

He nodded his head slowly, shifting his weight on the cushion. "My brother, your Giddi, Allah bless his soul, and I often talked about this matter when he came for his annual summer visit. As long as she was Muslim and lived with the Meguid family, we agreed that Abdel Aziz, God bless his soul, should have his happiness." He went on to say that my father was brilliant, a good judge of character, and somewhat of an idealist, thinking that he and others of his generation could modernize Egypt after the 1952 revolution. "You know, he wrote a biography of Gamal Abdel Nasser, who came from Upper Egypt and was a Sa'idi like us. Your father was very successful in facilitating the development of modern standard Arabic—sad, really, for it minimized the use of the Sa'idi dialect in our schools and for our children."

He paused. "Madame Nadia," referring to Mother by her Muslim name, "I heard, is a good woman." And choosing his words with care, added, "But difficult. She had thick blood, you know, always serious. She was very strict with the young girls we sent as servants to help in the kitchen and care for you." Smiling, he added, "She is not like us. We have thin blood, always joking and laughing." As an afterthought, he said in a quieter tone, "She never came to visit. It would have been helpful had she learned some Arabic, understood our culture better, and mixed more with us, you know, I mean my brother's family in Sayeda." He pointed in the general direction of distant Cairo. After yet another pause as he looked away, he said, "How is Madame Nadia?"

The question hung in the air. I left it unanswered.

After the evening meal, the village men promenaded in the fresh air, sat in coffee houses, smoked their shishas, and generally *shim-el-hawa*—smelled the breeze, recovering from a day's work in the field. Radio music blared from cafes, while in others, men sat about a small black-and-white TV, watching an over-dramatized serial. Women stayed at home, and bands of young children, all boys, still roamed over the silt-compacted mud in the rutted streets.

I felt very comfortable among my folks, the Sa'idi people, who appeared uncomplicated, down-to-earth, hard-working, and trustworthy. They told me anecdotes I had heard in different versions from the Cairo clan. Their generosity in giving me family photographs, particularly of my grandparents and my father, overwhelmed me.

We turned in early, and once more, George expressed his concern. The door was locked from the outside, and the *Raffir* had resumed his patrolling. I, on the other hand, felt cherished and valued. I, the son of Abdel Aziz and grandson of Sheikh Amin—now a "young doctor," whose roots lay in this fertile soil—was protected. As Jesus told his followers and other simple people during the Sermon on the Mount, "Ye are the salt of the Earth," and so too were my Sa'idi relatives whose bloodline and DNA were rooted deep in ancient times. Despite the pride in my heritage and the kindness of my people, I still wondered if I belonged.

———

The next morning, a Friday, the air was pristine. George and I accompanied the *omda* and a horde of curious children for a walk through the community. Curious villagers flooded into the street and crowded about me to shake my hand, repeating again and again, "Doctor Marwan, Doctor Marwan." Some grasped my right hand and kissed it before I could pull it away. This highest mark of respect embarrassed me, for I considered myself one among them. The women who approached greeted me with high-pitched tongue trills, signaling that a native son had returned. Although they recognized me as my father's son, my question of belonging was not answered.

We walked and greeted people among the complex of alleys along clusters of buildings, past the adobe huts like the one in which my father was born, and through the courtyard where a black-horned buffalo at the end of a cross-beam worked the water wheel. It was in a courtyard like this where my four-year-old father and his younger brother were running about when they were chased by their mother, who in a moment of distraction, was struck by the cross-beam, severing her spine and leading to her death.

As we wound through the village, we passed a small adobe Coptic church with a token steeple. Further along the alley, we finally ended up in the village's dispensary. The pharmacist greeted me enthusiastically, having heard from the *omda* that I had floated the idea of setting up a practice after I graduated. The facility was modest: a waiting room, a consulting room, a native toilet with a sink, and a small room serving as the pharmacy, with a meager stock of medications that lay exhibited on three shelves. The pharmacist was apologetic as he showed me around and answered my questions.

"A physician comes from Asyut, the capital of the province, twice a month," he said.

"Urgent cases?"

He took a breath. "Naturally, if it's an emergency, the patient goes to Asyut to see the doctor or his assistant. We can only do simple surgical cases here. Usually, we get antibiotics and other medicine very quickly . . . in two or three days." He smiled, looking at the *omda* for signs that he had his approval.

"*Inshallah*—God willing, when you come, we can get an anesthetic machine."

I responded, "*Inshallah*." With that, we shook hands, and the *omda*, George, and I shuffled out into the morning sun, again followed by our entourage of villagers and curious onlookers.

Following the muezzin's mid-morning call, I joined family members for Friday communal prayers at the small mosque. Unlike my father, who educated himself at the Madrassa of Al-Azhar, the centuries-old Cairo mosque and the premier center of Sunni Islam, I had no formal schooling in religion. After his death, I gravitated toward the faith for comfort. It helped me form a relationship with God, reinforced my faith, and provided a path to God's forgiveness and benevolence. It is stated in the Qur'an: "Prayer keeps one from committing great sins and evil deeds." I also liked praying, particularly at dawn, because I believed in the power of prayer and the way it calmed me down and let serenity wash over me.

I felt close to my kin in Beni Harem. I joined them in this most solemn of the daily prayers. Life in the village came to a stop as ablutions were performed. We lined up shoulder-to-shoulder, barefoot on reed mats facing Mecca, and recited our prayers, facing God and prostrating to Him in humility. At the end of our prayers, while kneeling, I exchanged greetings and shook hands with my grand-uncle and a cousin who flanked me. After this closeness, I had the distinct sense that they viewed me differently—not so much as a *khawagah*, but as family to which I belonged.

At the generous Friday meal at the *omda*'s home, we were overwhelmed with presents. I received a small Qur'an, some amber prayer beads, and a lavishly woven prayer mat. George got a basket of sweet, dried dates. I regretted not having gifts of our own to offer.

After further embraces, kisses, promises to soon return, and wishes of "God take care of you," my cousins accompanied us out of the village, followed by a crowd of curious well-wishers. At the main road, they hailed an intercity bus. We waved our goodbyes through the open window as we headed for Luxor. George, his cramps under control if not exactly cured, was excited that we were going to be tourists.

We checked into the Youth Hostel on the east bank of the Nile. While falling asleep I reflected on the last couple of days, hearing the *omda*'s intimate thoughts about my father: ". . . he was somewhat of an idealist, thinking that he and others of his generation could modernize Egypt." Was I an idealist like my father? If so, where could I best flourish? Perhaps England would be better for me than the land of my father, where I'd be swimming uphill against ingrained conservative cultural norms.

By 6 a.m. we were roused and expected to clear out with the other young men by 8 a.m. when the Youth Hostel's door would be locked until 5 p.m. After renting bicycles, we crossed the Nile in a precarious-looking boat that had seen better days. The oarsman rowed mightily and with great skill, negotiating the swift current, which swept us downstream toward the opposite bank. We wheeled onto the shore then peddled uphill, with the sun beating down as we sweated our way to the Valley of the Kings. George insisted on seeing as many tombs as possible in the free time we had. Halfway through the morning, I wearied, having no historical context for the tombs and the various pharaohs. With the day's heat and dust making things look too much alike, and the ancient stones not revealing their secrets, I sat on a rock waiting for George to visit each tomb and watched the queues of tourists file past me while the colorful hawkers peddled their trinkets and books of the pharaonic dynasties, as the sun beat down and the dust from the shuffling lines of tourists engulfing me.

I felt like a tourist visiting history in Upper Egypt, instead of thinking of myself as an Egyptian in my own land. At the English School Cairo, we were understandably taught English history—the successions of Kings and Queens. No mention was made of our own glorious past—of Egypt's ancient history— and it seemed ironical that I had to go to England only to return to Egypt to learn something about Egyptian history. And, for that I was grateful to George.

Peddling back to the Nile was effortless. The sun set behind the valley and cooled the oppressive heat as we coasted down-hill to a Nile ferry that took us across to the west bank and into the heart of bustling Luxor. During the next few days, we visited several local museums, the great Colossi of Memnon, and the palace of Queen Hatshepsut—the first female pharaoh. Our two main meals of the day were breakfast and an early dinner. We only ate cooked or barbecued street food and bought fruit from time to time.

In the small fishing village of Marsa Alam on the Red Sea there was no Youth Hostel. We settled on the deserted beach. Sweaty from our two-hour mid-morning bus ride from Luxor we quietly changed into our swimsuits and waded into the calm sea—deliciously warm and refreshing. Floating on the surface I admired the colorful tropical fish swimming along the coral reefs, the rays of light glowing playfully on the shallow sea bottom. In the warm afternoon sun, I stepped on a spikey mollusk. I pulled the spike out of my heel and gently placed the mollusk into my backpack. It now adorns my bookshelves, but at that time I saw it as a potential source of infection. None occurred. Nighttime came quickly near the equator. George and I decided to sleep on the uninhabited beach. As we settled into the warm sand, George picked out the Southern Cross from the radiant canopy of stars above us.

"I never imagined I'd see it in Egypt," he said. "We must be quite far south." With that, he drifted off.

In the morning, we dove into the crystal turquoise sea, swam around the coral reefs in the shallow water, spying sea cucumbers and a multitude of amazingly colorful and exotic tropical fish.

Our time was running out since George needed to return to England. We hitched a ride on an ancient rickety old Bedford lorry traveling toward Suez.

The blacktop ribbon stretched north hewn out of desert cliffs that dropped precipitously into boulders of the sea. The engine labored up hills, and the lorry rolled uncontrollably downhill. Fortunately, we were the only vehicle for the distance we saw ahead and behind us. Alarmed at the Nubian driver's lack of skill and the absence of brakes, we calculated our chances of escaping unharmed if he rolled into the sea. We climbed into the back sitting on the tarpaulins in the merciless sun. We reckoned the odds of jumping free might be better. On reaching the outskirts of Suez, we were sunburned, dehydrated, and glad to jump off. We spent the last of our funds riding an air-conditioned express bus back to Cairo—the height of luxury.

The trip with George made me more aware of my family and the tenuousness of my ties in Upper Egypt. I loved meeting and connecting with the members of my father's lineage. I was frustrated by the complacency of my Cairo kin; my helpless uncles, inactive cousins, the constant suspicions and the sense of hopelessness and lassitude. I'd die in Egypt of the inept bureaucracy, which was jokingly called the I.B.M. syndrome: *Inshallah*—God willing, *Bukra*—tomorrow, and *Ma'alesh*—never mind. Most of all, the loss of my home in Zamalek made me feel dispossessed. Again, I thought the odds of returning to Egypt were diminishing.

The strange emotion of not being sure I was one of my clan seeped into my consciousness and surprised me. I wondered if it was more the result of the situations I had encountered on this trip. Despite my abiding affection for my kin, these ambiguous feelings strengthened my emotional ties to England. I had tasted the freedom of an open society despite its many prejudices as compared to spending my life in a small Egyptian village.

———

A week later, at the airport, I emphatically presented the military exemption certificate to the immigration officer. Amazingly he showed no interest. When I complained and told him the litany of my troubles, he said, *Ma'alesh*—never mind. It annoyed me like hell. How could *Ma'alesh* justify all the anxiety that the military tribunal capriciously had imposed and through whose torture I had lived? How could *Ma'alesh* just be dismissed? It had thrown my life into turmoil. Why were my discharge records not clear? What asinine person so callously added my name so very casually to a list without thought? Where was the law and order of the oldest bureaucracy in the world? It's at that moment that I realized I lay personal freedom above autocratic nonsensical laws—at that moment that I valued and fell in love with the freedom of the West and that this constricting feeling of helplessness was less likely to ensure my return to the frustration and confusion which currently imbued my original society.

On my return to London, I found a warm letter from Mr. Mukhtar. He was now the head of the Saudi Arabian Security Services. Someone had alerted him to my inquiries. He had concluded that life overseas offered more financial stability in spite of the loneliness—in Saudi Arabia foreign nationals lived in designated national compounds and could not mix freely with the common Saudi people. There was not as much personal freedom as we had in Egypt. He would earn a substantially higher salary, payed in dollars, which he could send home to support his family, perhaps allowing him to retire earlier to a villa along the Red Sea—for he loved deep-water fishing.

Perhaps we would never meet again.

He never knew that he saved my life.

To liberate myself from the ghost of my father's expectations and the ever-looming threat of conscription, my plan B had been to fly west across the desert in a trainer on my solo flight. I would have flown near the coast over the Bedouin community of Sidi Barani across the sands into Libya hoping to be detected by the radar of the U.S. Wheelus Air Force Base. But for Mr. Mukhtar a more likely end would have been a crash into the sands of Tobruk.

# 16

# TRUE TO HER NAME

## LONDON, OCTOBER 1964

*A' elhoub tisha ayamna. With love, our days will awaken.*
*A' el shouk tnaam layaleina. We spend the nights longing for each*
*other. Enta Omri*
—Ahmad Shafiq Kamil

B y the end of the summer, I was caught up with my studies. I had reached a point in my academic studies where I felt confident in my knowledge. My trip to Egypt had made me understand how difficult it would be to embrace a life there, so with regret, I put Egypt behind me. I faced England. Refreshed and invigorated, I looked forward to the new term.

I watched the new class of medical students' troop into the Department of Anatomy. I was now a second-year medical student—a sophomore. The buzz was that seven to eleven women were among the freshmen of the incoming class. I was determined to enroll all the incoming students into the Physiology Society—at least as many as I could—to increase our operational revenue.

I set up a table in the common room with copies of *Potential* and a sign-up sheet. I watched with interest as the freshmen entered. I knew how they felt. I had been in their position one year ago. I had changed and matured.

A beautiful siren glided into my view. Seeing her, I heard the crescendo of "Ode to Joy."

The world stopped.

Hypnotized by her smile, her porcelain English complexion, and her straight, dark hair, I instantly knew, with crystalline clarity, that this goddess would be my wife.

I fumbled. "Oh, hello! I'm the student president of the Physiology Society. The Nobel Laureate, Professor Huxley is the Chairman of Physiology. It is a 'must-join club.' Only £2 makes you a lifetime member—a bargain." She's nearly hooked. Reel her in, reel her in quickly. "You get this fascinating magazine, *Potential*, with the very latest physiology discoveries. It's a page-turner guaranteed to help you pass any physiology exams —guaranteed."

She paused in animated suspension.

"The society takes you on special tours, to behind-the-scenes visits to pharmaceutical companies where you enjoy drinks and dinner with their CEO, make connections with physicians in industry, and even get free samples."

She took *Potential* from my hand and flicked through it delicately, handling each page between thumb and finger with the gentility of sampling the best silks at a Harrods lady's accessory counter. After a brief pause, I went in for the kill. "All free to members of this elite club. Free for you."

She produced a checkbook—a Barclay's no less. *No student has one.* With casual British upper-class poise, she wrote the check. I studied her; she was more mature than the rest of her group and exuded a sumptuous affluence and sartorial elegance in her pinkish-brown woolen suit, white blouse, leather handbag, and two-inch heels, the essence of sophistica-tion—an English beauty. She handed me the check. I glanced at it. Her signature: Victoria Perfect. Surely not her actual name? It must have been more of an advertisement—of a life-time guarantee—the good housekeeping seal of mature womanhood.

Yes, it was her name. It was a derivative of the French Parfait —sweet, iced dessert.

She later told me that her father was a descendant of a chivalrous French companion to William the Conqueror, the British immigrant of 1066. I, of older pharaonic/Germanic ilk, was an invader to these isles from sometime in 1950. We both held the check for a moment, eyes connected, communicating silently. She lingered, seeming utterly engrossed. The aura was broken when a student stepped into our bubble, approaching the table. For a magical second, she watched me resume my earthly sales pitch before tentatively moving on to the Medical Society display, peering back, sensing my gaze following her. My heart sang in my chest.

Victoria's spell lingered through the evening and the rest of the next day. Thoughts of her invaded my studies, my meals. Unable to concentrate, I held imaginary conversations with her, even finding myself laughing. Pacing about the residence, at dinner, and in the shower, I whistled or sang the Beatles: *I give her all my love/That's all I do/And if you saw my love/You'd love her too.* I could not shake her image or sleep with it—my bed was too narrow. I had to see her, this sweet dessert.

On Sunday, I floated down the five hundred feet to Canterbury Hall. The doorman rang my Venus' room. "There's a young man to see you. Are you available?" He hung up, pointing to a ledger. "Sign here. All guests must leave by 8 p.m." I had six hours.

A few seconds later, she appeared. She wore a light print dress and paused, smiling politely. "Oh. It's you," she said. "I expected someone else." Was she disappointed?

In the tiny lift's cabin, we rose toward the fourth floor in silent close proximity. I inhaled her body scent that was more inviting than her *eau de parfum*, both of us averting our gazes. The silence was killing me.

I blurted out a spontaneous fib. "Your check bounced."

"Bounced?" She looked mortified.

I felt like an idiot and awkwardly apologized. She smiled with relief. "Thank goodness, I wrote several other checks after that."

Victoria looked strikingly appealing, and in my irrational state, she looked even more so. Just seeing her calmed me and brought me down from my high. There she was, a graceful, intelligent beauty.

Although her room looked out onto the same back street as mine, its greater height gave a different perspective of the white-painted houses reflecting the afternoon sun. Fat pigeons strutted on her window ledge, cooing incessantly. It was a tidy room with a potted plant and few books. In the middle of the floor was a magnificent portable LP record player. *My Fair Lady* lay on top of a stack of records that sat next to the player. There were no LPs of the Beatles, classical music, or opera.

Victoria spoke the Queen's English. She had gone to Godolphin, a girl's public school. She told me this sitting on the edge of her bed as I sat on the room's only chair. She offered to make me a cup of Nescafé. I declined.

Somewhat embarrassed, she explained she was expecting

Basil, a friend she had met the previous year when she was an au pair for her cousin. Basil was a colonel stationed with the British Army on the Rhine in Bielefeld, Germany. I wondered what sort of friend. Probably an army sort—a rough, muscular, beer-guzzling type who dropped the vernacular *fucking* numerous times in a sentence. She deserved better—she deserved me. The very thought of Basil made me jealous.

She continued her unnecessary but reassuring explanation. On occasional evenings when she was free from her au pair duty, she and Basil had gone drinking. He was back in England now. By way of clarification she added, "He's a friend . . . a mere friend." After a pause, she asked, "What sort of name is Marwan?"

When I told her, she divulged that her uncle, Dr. John Perfect, had been the physician to the Amir of Bahrain. Dr. Perfect's two children had attended public boarding schools in England. When Uncle John retired, the Amir gave him a pink Pontiac convertible that he drove around Knightsbridge. She giggled at the comical picture this conjured, adding, "The steering wheel was on the wrong side, and parking is a problem. It's so long and wide compared with our cars and relative to the parking spaces"

Her uncle had trained at St. Bartholomew's Hospital, and thinking this would help her, she applied to their medical school. I was astonished. I told her that when I applied, the first question on their application was whether my father had trained at Bart's. I completed the application form, but obviously, I was not invited for an interview, especially given my background—Daddy went to University College. She smiled at my anecdote, not realizing the pain that the rejection had caused at the time. I was pleased that she had persisted in her quest to become a doctor and was full of admiration for her determination. I greatly admired independent women with spirited initiative and resourcefulness. *Good for her.*

She lived with her mother, an immigrant from New Zealand, and with her brother on the Isle of Wight. She would only be at University College for the initial eighteen months of basic science courses, up to the second MB examination, Bachelor of Medicine, and would then do her clinical training at the prestigious Westminster Hospital Medical School. Among its discerning patients were members of Parliament, which rested across the Thames. In contrast, University College Hospital, adjacent to the fringes of Soho, London's red-light district, had pimps and prostitutes among its distinguished patient population.

As she spoke, I watched the light in her pale green eyes sparkle. Her left eyebrow was offset by what looked like a chicken pox scar. She had thin lips, a strong chin, and a long, slim neck. I subtly glanced at her figure, feeling bashful, hoping that I'd have opportunities in the future to admire it sensually —in its totality.

And then, I realized that the pubs had opened. "A drink maybe?"

At the nearest pub, we perched at the corner of a table, sharing space with other patrons. I went to the bar and ordered a Scotch on the rocks and a Babycham. When I returned with our drinks, she eyed my Scotch. "You are not an impecunious student after all. Next time, I'll have a glass of real Champagne."

I smiled.

*Ah, there would be a next time.*

# 17

# SATURDAY NIGHT HOP

*Hand in hand, on the edge of the sand, they danced by the light of the moon . . . the moon.*

—Edward Lear

Victoria was an archetypical first-year medical student, diligently attending the 9 a.m. lecture each morning. By then, I had learned that my ability to focus on and retain material dwindled as the day progressed, so I rose early, a habit from my Cairo days, and studied for two to three hours before breakfast and a couple of hours thereafter. Underlining details and making marginal notes of my own made the information easier to retain than listening to a teacher spout out fact after fact. This schedule mismatch meant that we seldom walked to the department together, but we frequently met during lunch break when I would spy her in the refectory. Her beauty awed me as she sat among her new acquaintances. During the first week, she was constantly in the company of a fellow student, Jane, which stopped me from approaching her. Her gaze followed me as I ambled by, waving slightly. I felt awkward and shy at asking her out, thinking she would decline.

One afternoon, my fortunes changed. Soon after she started to dissect her cadaver on the alphabetical "P" table, conveniently located near the "M," she sought me out. Approaching in her long white coat and carrying the dissection manual—and looking radiantly attractive—she said, "Could you please help me? I have dissected out the left vagus nerve from its exit at the base of the skull through the chest to the heart and beyond. I cannot find the right one."

I accompanied her to her cadaver. She and her team had done a fine dissection of the chest cavity, exposing all the pertinent structures and organs—much more diligently than we had done on Fred a year earlier.

"You see," she said, studiously pointing. "Here is the nerve, but where is the right vagus?"

"Ah," I said, "come with me." I led her around the table to the other side of the cadaver. "See, it's right here. That's why they call it the *right* vagus."

She blushed. Even in her moment of embarrassment, she looked sunny. "Oh goodness."

"Most structures come in twos, right and left," I paused to ease her feelings, "including the eyes, ears, lungs, kidneys, and, to stay clinical, breasts and testicles. The brain and liver have left and right lobes. Does that help?"

She nodded. Taking advantage of the moment, I nervously asked if she would come with me to the hop scheduled the following Saturday night in the central hall of University College under the Octagon dome. It was the first social event of the academic year. A local group was jamming, and we could dance and sing to current hits. She agreed. I was triumphant.

The next couple of days, we walked back to Cartwright Gardens together, lingering before parting. After dinner, we visited in each other's rooms. We explored joint interests and shared our life's stories, becoming more comfortable with each other. Whereas music was my passion, she had an incredible artistic side. She loved to draw anatomical representations of the human form and admired DaVinci's drawings in the books she shared with me.

Fearing the enthusiasm of my growing emotions, I strove to keep my feelings for her at the platonic level. Responding in kind, she treated me like a brother. She spoke often of Massimo, describing him as an oversexed young Italian she had met in Germany, one who tried on numerous times to kiss her and stick his tongue into her mouth. I got the impression that he was particularly insensitive to her conformist upbringing, where her mother's emphasis was on being a "nice girl." Were such anecdotes a form of warning, or was she sufficiently comfortable in sharing these stressful experiences? I was confused, particularly because her beauty, grace, and charm dazzled me, making me fearful of approaching her intimately. I was confused by my intense feelings for this woman and her responses that I could not interpret. I waited for her to move the relationship forward, fearing I might lose her if I pushed too hard. Maybe our relationship would grow with time, security, and comfort.

She was engagingly intelligent, adding a new dimension to

my life. She made me feel like a whole person—one who was important. In a class of one hundred male wolves, just having Victoria Perfect's close friendship was perfection itself. It felt good. When they saw us dance at the hop, they would salivate with jealousy. She was *mine*.

Admission to the hop cost five shillings each, which was collected at the door—quite a tidy sum that I did not readily have. There would also be drinks to purchase. These additional expenses had not been considered when Mother and I worked out my living expenses. Certainly, my Manchester educational grant did not allot for such a budget line item. In Arab culture, men paid, and I knew that was the case in England, too. I did not want to ask Victoria to contribute, certainly not on our first date, even though I knew her scholarship exceeded mine, as she had told me in confidence. A solution had to exist: I did not have the means to entertain this most desirable woman at a level she deserved. What to do? There *must* be a way.

I devised a plan to circumvent the ten shillings admission fee: we would enter the dance hall from an inside door, via a series of corridors, classrooms, connecting halls, and passages through different departments. We would start in the Department of Anatomy and walk north, parallel to Gower Street, toward the music. Victoria expressed no objections.

At six in the evening, the heavy oak door leading from Gower Street to our department gave way to my shoulder, and we entered the dimly lit entrance hall. I closed the door behind us. Victoria looked apprehensive, keeping her distance, particularly since I whispered each anticipated move, not quite knowing the precise pathway to our destination. I had a vague idea of following my instincts, keeping the traffic noise to our left with the music as a beacon.

I had overlooked the fact that on Saturday night, most of the buildings and corridors would be dark. I went ahead, exploring walls, groping for doors, and bumping into furniture.

Victoria lagged behind, and I quietly egged her on. Several times, I thought I heard voices coming from a room we passed. We froze. Were we going to be discovered? To be arrested for trespassing? The voices receded—they were passersby in Gower Street.

I took a deep breath and whispered, "OK, let's go, follow me."

She cautiously followed my voice in the dark until I finally opened a door leading to the dimmed dance hall and the blasting music where the guitars wept, drums thundered, a singer screamed, and a mass of bodies heaved up and down.

Although I was pleased for navigating successfully through the challenging maze, showing ingenuity at beating the system, I also felt cheap. What a jerk I was being.

"I thought you were going to jump me in the dark," she yelled over the noise. I shook my head, acutely embarrassed at my plan's stupidity.

We joined the dancers. Relieved at having achieved the goal of bypassing the gatekeepers, I literally twisted and shouted to the Beatles as the music throbbed from the stereo speakers. Even without the aid of alcohol, I danced without inhibition, joining in the songs. No one cared how I gyrated or what I sounded like. I was just happy that Victoria was with me. To my surprise, her movements were stiff. She expressed her discomfort in dancing, complaining that the music was too loud and that the floor was too crowded. I could see she was too self-conscious to let herself go and enjoy the evening. After dragging her through uncertain darkness, I should have bought her a drink right away.

Some of my classmates saw us together and registered surprise. I might have been a "fucking foreigner," but I had won the prize.

# 18

# PHARMACOLOGY

*Man standing on toilet seat is high on pot.*
—Anonymous

P harmacology was the most important lecture series in the third semester. The professor delivered most of the instructions in an uninspiring drone—a dry monologue delivered in a heavy German accent—as he marched slowly back and forth at the front of the auditorium, head down. He reminded me of my Opa, the autocrat. He peppered his lectures with veiled threats of a tough examination at the end of the term in mid-December, one that we would have to pass if we hoped to cross over to Gower Street. Such comments made me feel that UCH was indeed a mirage and that Gower Street was an impassable moat. Whereas Professor Young imbued his lectures with curiosity and hope, which stimulated our curiosity and the desire to learn, this professor inculcated dry doom. Students scurried away on seeing him in the corridors to avoid his menacing gaze, one that seemed to say: *Why are you not studying pharmacology?*

Below the amphitheater where he lectured were the

stinking male toilets. The glare from the bathroom's single, large window set high on one end reflected off the white-tiled walls. On one side were ten stalls, on the other an equal number of urinals. On the wall of one stall, a student had written some practical advice, "Don't bother standing on the seat, the spirochete can jump six feet." Above a urinal was the historic note, "Custer's Last Stand;" a maxim, "Flies spread diseases, keep your flies closed;" and manly advice, "No matter how hard you shake your peg, the last drop always drops down your leg."

One day, we found large enamel milk urns set in the urinals, with directives taped above that instructed us to urinate into them. The professor's lab had discovered minute amounts of a compound present in men's urine. When injected into mice, it caused hypertension—high blood pressure. Suddenly, he had a gigantic need for piss. His technicians, research fellows, and graduate students schlepped the full jugs to his lab and poured the urine into large boiling vats. The golden liquid bubbled dry to isolate "Compound-H," which was believed to cause high blood pressure in patients, with the goal being to develop an antidote. He persuaded the administration to build, on an almost industrial scale, long distillation columns so he could boil the increasing amounts of urine. Thick glass silos pointed straight upwards toward the sky, passing through several floors of other departments. The air we breathed in the quadrangle behind the medical school's Gower Street façade had a constant, inescapable, uriniferous odor.

Humorous rumors circulated that the underground pipes from the public toilets at the busy Euston and St. Pancreas Stations, a mere couple of miles to the northeast, would be connected to his lab to quench his ferocious appetite for public piss. The idea was analogous to the discovery of urokinase, a protein—and later a lucrative drug—that dissolves life-threatening emboli or blood clots in the heart and lung. Urokinase was first extracted from the urine of Japanese soldiers and then from Japanese public toilets. The idea inspired him, for if the Japanese could do it, then so too could a German or Austrian expat.

The professor's unpopularity among his students during the autumn term led to a furtive campaign to sabotage his project. Students regularly dumped their cigarette butts and any sample medications they had into his urns. The more hostile students knocked over full ones, flooding the men's toilet floor.

Every Friday afternoon, we had a three-hour pharmacology lab after spending time with Fred, our cadaver, in the late morning. When I arrived late in the lab one day, the rest of my group of eleven males, including Rory, had already formed a semi-circle in front of our two instructors—pharmacology graduate students.

"Today, we are going to study the effects of a beta-blocker on our physiological system," the first said enthusiastically.

"Yeah, it's a neat experiment. We'll need a volunteer," chimed in the second.

The first one said, "One of you is going to swallow a 25-milligram Metoprolol pill. It is very likely you will prescribe this medication to your patients with high blood pressure when you are GPs. It's a very mild dose—the usual is four times greater. You'll need to know how it feels and its possible side effects. Its physiological function in the body is described in your lab book, which you should have read in preparation."

I had not.

"So one of you, the druggie," he said with a chuckle, "will swallow the pill. The rest will measure the effects of the drug every fifteen minutes on the volunteer's blood pressure, the degree of lightheadedness or fainting when standing up, together with his pulse. Metoprolol prevents the heart from increasing its beats to compensate for activity. You will measure the degree of blurred vision and length of his stride, along with other side effects. You will chart the various changes that the beta-blocker causes over time. Given this very mild dose, the effects should wear off within three to six hours, and the volunteer will feel perfectly fine."

I suspected it was part of their ongoing research project and that we were their unwitting subjects. The second instructor went on, "To be on the safe side, we'd want the volunteer to go home and stay in bed. You'll need a friend to keep an eye on you. You will not be able to drink, drive, or travel tonight. And by the way, it is difficult to get an erection."

A volunteer?

I avoided their gazes. I could not believe my ears. They were asking someone to be a guinea pig, to "suck and see" the drug's effects. The more these two morons spoke about the study, the more I felt this was some hangover of a WWII medical experiment. Did not the Nuremberg Trial address the ethics of such studies? *Low blood pressure . . . dizziness . . . drowsiness . . . light-headedness . . . pounding heartbeat . . . blurred vision . . . no beer . . . and no erection.*

No erection? On a Friday night? Were they crazy?

Naturally, no one volunteered.

Disappointed, they started going down the line, interrogating each of us about why he could not volunteer. The answers were variations on the same theme: they were driving with their girlfriends to their parents' houses. Most were lying —I knew they did not have cars. I was last in line, with no credible reason to get out of the test. My plan was to visit with my American friend, John Rackey, and listen to his new recording of *Rigoletto*.

John had been a pilot in the United States Air Force, and had been stationed in Mildenhof, Sussex for the past three years. My friend was intrigued by my budding relationship with Victoria, for he'd ask, on a daily basis, about us and

listened with interest to my replies, all the while grinning—
he'd been there once but now was single again.

The instructor stood in front of me. "And you? What are
you doing tonight that would prevent you from volunteering?"

"I'm going with my girlfriend to the Isle of Wight to be with
her family," I said calmly. The surprise on my classmates' faces
nearly gave me away.

The instructor concluded, "Well, I guess we'll have to skip
this experiment. You can all leave." My colleagues' pronounced
glares said it all. *You have a girlfriend, and you are going to the Isle
of Wight? It can only be the incomparable Victoria Perfect.* The less
charitable ones might have contemplated, *an English rose with
this fucking Arab!*

Yes, Victoria was my girlfriend . . . well, sort of. No, we were
not lovers. Yes, she was going to see her mother for the first
time in six weeks. I had learned this over our refectory lunch
before pharmacology lab. I asked her out to dinner Saturday
night at the German Schmidt's Restaurant, a relatively upscale
eatery by student standards, to ensure we would spend part of
the weekend together. I was crestfallen when she told me of her
plans.

"Have a good trip," was all I could muster, still stinging from
the desertion. As we walked out of the refectory, she headed to
the dissection room and I to the pharmacology lab. She looked
back, smiled, and gave me a small wave. My heart sank.

Now, I felt the urgency to get myself invited before the
bastards discovered my lie. I left the lab and found Victoria
departing the anatomy dissection hall.

"I'm coming with you!"

She looked astonished. I explained my dilemma, without
revealing my separation anxiety and fear of loneliness.

"I'll have to call my mother and let her know. Do you have
any coins?"

We crammed into the telephone booth in the dim, damp

basement next to the men's toilet. I held out a palmful of coins. She dialed.

"Hello, Mummy."

"Darling, are you not coming?" I could hear her mother's voice through the receiver.

"Yes, I am. I'm bringing a friend with me."

"A friend? Who is it? Anyone I know? What's her name?"

"No, it's my boyfriend."

"Your boyfriend? Darling, I didn't know you had one. You never told me. What's his name?"

"Marwan."

"Who?"

"Marwan."

"Where's he from?"

"Egypt."

"Good heavens, darling! A WOG." The sound of "WOG" resonated throughout the booth.

Victoria turned away from me in the hopes I had not heard. "Oh, Mummy, he's very nice."

"Where's he going to stay? Your brother's here."

"In the spare bedroom, of course."

We fed more coins into the phone box.

"Oh, darling, how long is he staying? When are you coming?"

"The weekend."

"Tim is driving. We'll meet you at the end of the pier."

I was excited to be going with her, full of curiosity and tense with the mystery of the unknown and vulnerability of new friendships. Victoria, sweet Victoria, had saved me. I felt immensely thankful. I had invited myself to get out of a preposterous experiment rather than face the graduate students and telling them that coercing us to take a high blood pressure drugs bordered on unethical. In any case, I was not going to be alone. Except . . . I hesitated for a minute: What kind of household was I going to where such words were uttered and where racist views were held?

I'd take the risk. Perhaps, her mother had been speaking in hyperbole or was being witty. I was sure that when she met me and got to know me, she would change her mind.

# 19

# ISLE OF SERENITY

*And did those feet in ancient time,*
*Walk upon England's mountains green:*
*And was the holy Lamb of God,*
*On England's pleasant pastures seen!*
—William Blake

A whirlwind transported me into a new and wondrous world of genteel, traditional England, one far removed from the blue-collar air of Manchester and London's international atmosphere. Our fast commuter train from Waterloo surged out of London like a racehorse at the starting gate. It left behind the great pollution-engulfed metropolis, overtook local trains, rattled swiftly through the iconic Clapham Junction, rushed across the green Hampshire countryside, the hedgerows and meadows, past old garden communities, hamlets, and villages, stopping finally at the affluent, conservative, stockbroker enclaves of Woking, Guildford, Haslemere, and Petersfield. Men in suits and bowler hats, with rolled umbrellas and briefcases, disembarked to idling Rovers filled with young families that waited to bring them home for drinks and dinner. They had managed, or speculated with, or made millions in the city on the stock exchange. The train dashed on through Britannia's Surrey countryside.

"Jerusalem," the hymn we sang during assembly in Manchester, singing of "England's mountains green . . . and pleasant pastures" rang true. My week of accumulated tensions ebbed exponentially with our progressive distancing from London. My headmaster's image appeared in the ferry window, angrily mouthing, "Liverpool Medical School." This was the other England, the one I longed to know.

Victoria, sitting opposite me in a summer suit and sensible one-inch heels, belonged to this scene. When we stopped at Haslemere, she told me that her grandmother, Dagmar, from New Zealand, lived there in an old shepherd's cottage, while her Aunt Bunt lived in nearby Petersfield. I liked the idea that I might become part of an established British family and wished I had thought to buy flowers for her mother.

The train briefly stopped in Havant and Portsmouth before finally rolling into Portsmouth Harbour. When the last passengers rushed on board, the ferry pushed off into the Solent, sailing past Royal Navy ships and submarine bases, heading to Ryde on the Isle of Wight—tranquility's base.

When we disembarked, Victoria's mother and brother, Tim, met us at the head of the pier. There was no mistaking Shirley.

She looked just like her daughter, with coiffed hair fluttering in the sea breeze and a slight middle-age spread.

"Darling, it's wonderful to see you." There were smiles all around. No kisses, no hugs.

"You look well. This must be Mawan. Is that how you pronounce it? I was in Egypt years ago."

"It's MaRRRwan, a difficult name."

She told me to call her Shirley and immediately shared the neighborhood news: "Darling, did you know. . ." and "Darling, have you heard . . ." tumbled out of her mouth with the latest gossip, lush with innuendo and scandal. She announced that Tim, home from public school, was taking driving lessons. Tim was a gangly, handsome seventeen-year-old, polite and quiet, with rapidly surveying eyes. Sitting in the front passenger seat, he picked his pimples in the rearview mirror.

I sat in the back with Shirley, absorbing the wonderfully comfortable family environment. In the late daylight, Victoria pointed out various landmarks as she drove the twenty minutes along the coastal road to the village of Seaview. They lived in a semi-detached house, one street from the rolling swell of the Solent. Victoria took my bag up to the front guest bedroom and then showed me her room, Tim's, and Shirley's. She was happy and radiant, beautiful in a red print dress. She gave me a kiss—more like a peck on the cheek. We continued into the front drawing room.

"Would you like a drink?" Shirley asked.

"No thanks, I don't really drink."

"A glass of sherry? A gin and tonic? Vicki is having one."

"A gin and tonic would be fine. Thank you."

"Well, make it yourself, dear boy. I have to go to the kitchen to check on dinner."

Turning to Victoria, she said, "Dinner at eight, darling. We are having leg of lamb, your favorite, darling, and I made a Pavlova for dessert. Darling, *do* change for dinner," she added, disappearing into the kitchen.

At dinner, I wore a shirt, tie, and jacket, which I had never worn to dine in Commonwealth Hall's refectory. Victoria opened a bottle of wine, and Shirley carved the leg of lamb. She was a good cook. The lamb, with roasted potatoes and parsnips, was excellent, but the raspberry Pavlova was exquisite.

Throughout dinner, Shirley monopolized the conversation, chatting enthusiastically about Trevor. How she had gone up to London to be with him, how he might come to the island for a weekend, and so on. This raised questions of "when" and "for how long" from one or the other of her children. The response was always vague. Realizing that I did not know the name, Victoria leaned over when Shirley stepped into the kitchen and said, "Trevor is her on-again, off-again boyfriend." It seemed that my presence had prompted a competition between the two women.

Shirley refused my offer of help to clean up, encouraging us to take a walk as the early autumn darkness was creeping in. The sea breeze was refreshing. A light fog was rolling in from the west. Waves crashed against the seawall, occasionally spraying us as we walked along the narrow path, holding hands. I began to breathe deeply.

"I had to make up your bed and get you some towels. Mummy is hopeless when she's this high."

"What do you mean?"

"She's manic-depressive and on all sorts of medicines. She sees a psychiatrist in London who claims it's a chemical imbalance of the brain, not a mental illness. He put her on lithium.

She's developed a hand tremor. She shouldn't drink, except, she does because she is so very sociable."

This was the first time Victoria had mentioned her mother's ailment although I had observed the tremor at dinner. I sensed the burden of concern that Victoria was quietly carrying, and I wanted to embrace her, to comfort her, to let her know that I cared for her.

"Did she always have this?" I asked, placing my arm around her shoulders.

"The psychiatrist thinks it was brought on by the shock of Daddy's sudden death. You know he designed the Princess, the huge flying boat."

"You mean the one Saunders-Roe built?"

"Yes. And my great uncle, Alliotte Verdon Roe, together with his brother, started the Avro Aircraft Company in the early twentieth century. You know, the one that made the big Lancaster bomber in WWII. They later bought a share in the Saunders Marine Company."

"Really? I dreamed of becoming an aeronautical engineer, but I was lousy at math, so I had to follow my other dream of becoming a surgeon. So here I am, a medical student."

"You're better off becoming a surgeon," she said with a smile. I did not ask her why she thought that. I felt an intense affinity with her and drew her closer as we continued our walk along the seawall in silence.

After a while, she said, "Daddy worked in London and lived at his club during the week. He came home on Friday evenings. When we were young, Mummy would dress Tim and me in nice clothes to greet him. She would tell us to be nice children —no misbehaving. If she thought I did, she would call me "verrucae"—a wart. We were sent to bed early so they could be alone. He returned to London on Monday mornings."

"Sounds like you didn't get to see him much as a small child. That must have been tough." She turned toward me, and for a moment, I thought she was going to embrace me. Her teary eyes did not elude me in the gathering dusk.

I took her hand, and we walked on in silence, listening to the crashing waves and tasting the salty spray that showered us from time to time. I wondered if it was painful for Victoria to dredge up stories about her family. "How old were you when your father died?"

"Eleven."

"Really? My father died when I was around that age too, and my mother hasn't been herself since."

"Mummy was told he was on the Queen's New Year's Honor list. He was scheduled to become a Knight of the British Empire—Sir Robert Perfect. She would have become Lady Perfect. I learned after his death that Daddy had a previous marriage and had a son. I was shocked to discover I wasn't the oldest child. I did find out that Daddy left that son some money in his will."

"My father told me once that when he and my mother lived in Sudan, they thought of adopting a young boy named Ibrahim. Only in Islam, adoption is difficult."

"You'd have had an older, dark-skinned brother."

"Not only that, but after my sister was born, they might not have wanted another child, and I would not be here," I said.

The walk led us to the exclusive Seaview Yacht Club, lit up in the dark like a Christmas tree on a rocky prominence. Sounds of chatter, music, and merriment floated across the water. Beyond the stony shore were mermaid yachts, the ones used in club races. Bobbing up and down on the ocean swells in the moonlight, their mast lights twinkled, and their rigging clanged rhythmically with each incoming wave.

We were both tired and ambled back along the street of semi-detached houses. Passing a house with the drawing room curtains open, we saw an elderly man pulling a younger woman onto the sofa. According to Shirley's earlier chatter, the widower was causing a scandal by running around with all the women in the village. On our return to the house, we found the dishes still on the dining table and others piled up in the sink. We cleared the table; I stacked the dishwasher, and Victoria cleaned up the kitchen.

"Mummy can't manage," was all she said, adding, "It gets worse when she's broody."

In the drawing room, Shirley rose from the sofa, leaving on the TV. "I'm suddenly very tired. I must have nodded off. I'm going to bed." She looked much older than before. "Goodnight. Do tidy up the sofa cushions when you youngsters go to bed. Tim is out, so I'll leave the light on." She walked somewhat unsteadily, closing the door behind her.

"There's no food in the house. We'll have to drive to the shops in the morning. I'll cook dinner or we can go for Chinese. Oh and Mummy arranged to meet friends for drinks at the Yacht Club at eleven. She wants you to meet Mr. Walker, a surgeon on the island. We might lunch at the club, or I'll drive you to the Downs. The view of the sea and the rest of the island to our north is magnificent. On a clear day, we can see the coast of France." Hesitantly, she said, "I'm sorry about Mummy. Her moods are unpredictable. She's fine today, but tomorrow, she may not get out of bed for a week. I hope the lithium will help."

"Who takes care of her when she takes to bed?"

"Various friends in the village look in on her. Occasionally, she has meals on wheels. The nurse across the street telephones me when matters become acute. With my studies, I really have no time to do more for her than worry. Fortunately, our GP knows her well, and one of her friends drives her to see him."

I sensed that Victoria was distancing herself from her mother's illness. I saw no other solution, given the demands of medical school. We kissed and hugged shyly. I felt her body as I rubbed my hand up and down her slim back. We straightened out the sofa cushions, turned off the drawing room lights, and climbed the steps to the landing in semi-darkness. We hugged once more in the dark. She apologized for the situation again, almost beginning to sob. I held her tightly hoping she would sense my loyalty and support.

My bed was comfortable. Exhausted, I was lulled by the rhythmic sounds of a buoy's bell muffled by the thick fog. I slept soundly.

In the village where we shopped, the grocer, the butcher, the newspaper seller, and the postmistress all knew Victoria and asked about her studies and Shirley's health. There was worry on her face when they expressed their concern about Shirley. Victoria avoided questions concerning her mother by introducing me. Walking home in the gloriously sunny morning of the late Indian summer, we could see down the sloping streets to the nanny boat that was taking crews out to the mermaids in preparation for a race. This would be a good day to race since the sea was placid. Victoria shared more stories about how she and Tim had sailed since they were little.

The center of Shirley's social life was the Seaview Yacht Club, festooned with nautical flags flapping in a steady sea breeze that mitigated the heat of the late summer sunshine. Mr. Walker and Shirley sat on the uncovered deck, nursing drinks. He feigned delight at meeting me. He was of Shirley's generation, dressed in a dark blue pinstriped suit with a pale pink tie. I told him about my desire to become a surgeon. As we chatted, I watched the mermaids maneuver into position at the invisible starting line.

On top of the chalk cliffs of Culver Downs, the wind blew steadily across the prominent headland. We sat in the car, where we had a spectacular view of the English Channel, sparkling with a thousand points of diamond sunlight. The area was wild, protected, and pristine with an occasional flock of sheep. Its utter peacefulness was in stark contrast to the hustle and bustle of medical school. I realized I could get used to this. Focusing on Victoria, I fingered her hair and caressed the nape of her neck, telling her I was falling in love with her and thanking her for bringing me to this idyllic place.

———

We returned Monday morning on the first commuter ferry train sliding into Waterloo Station. During our return trip, I was haunted by Shirley's manic depression. Was it hereditary? Would Victoria eventually present with it? I thought about the 9 a.m. pharmacology lecture I gladly missed for the price of tranquility on the Isle of Serenity. My curiosity had been piqued, and my sense of mystery enhanced. I wanted to get to know Victoria better and to explore with her the vulnerability of our new relationship.

I failed my mid-December pharmacology exam; with that, the chasm separating the college and the hospital widened dangerously. Was I going to make it to become a doctor? Failure put a hot pepper up my rectum, as we did in Egypt to motivate a donkey stubbornly stalled in its path. Like the donkey who then takes off, it boosted my determination to focus on the subject. I was successful in passing when the make-up exam was given a month later.

The distilling of urine that fouled our air finally stopped when the precious white powder turned out to be a mundane compound called nicotine.

# 20

# ANATOMICAL TOPOGRAPHY

*I don't have a body; I am a body.*
—Christopher Hitchens

Formaldehyde contracted Fred's tissues and shriveled them up, perhaps into unnatural positions. In anatomy, projecting the thoracic and abdominal organs onto the body's surface was critical for understanding their exact positions.

"Find a partner," our professor charged us. "As your partner reads and describes specific locations and landmarks, you will draw the location of the organs on the skin." Victoria shyly agreed to be my partner on the condition that I would eventually reciprocate when she reached that stage in her studies.

As a future surgeon, knowing the location of organs under the skin, such as McBurney's Point in relation to the appendix, excited me—it was a practical lesson. Saturday morning, Victoria signed into Commonwealth Hall. She shyly asked me to close the curtains. With my eyes averted, she shed her silk blouse and bra in the dim light. She held a towel covering her front. The desk lamp lit her exposed back. I perched on the edge of a chair. She read aloud the anatomical landmarks while I outlined each lung on her lily-white skin from the posterior perspective using a colored pen. We were both amazed at how far down the back the lungs extended, an inch below the belt line of her woolen trousers. I impulsively kissed her back along the lines I had drawn, making her giggle and protest.

Continuing the instructions, I outlined the top of the diaphragm. It separated the lungs from the abdominal cavity and was located at the fourth intercostal space, much higher than I could have imagined. I connected the top of it to the lowest level of the lung line. The three-dimensional effect differed substantially from the image I had obtained from the pickled Fred.

To draw the outline and position of the heart, she had to turn around. She timidly moved the towel, exposing a breath-taking left breast at my eye level. I gazed, mesmerized by her pale, silken skin and the almost saucer-sized, brown areola. She kept her right breast covered. It did not figure into this exercise. I was aroused seeing the nipple of the woman I loved and had wanted to marry since the moment I had first set eyes on her.

She bopped my head with the manual. "Pay attention," she protested at my passionate distraction, insisting I keep to her instructions to locate the heart's landmarks on her skin. She shivered with embarrassment, feigning cold when I touched her. I impulsively placed my lips on her nipple, lingering for a very brief moment until she pushed me away, redoubling her protest. I apologized, quickly stealing a peck from her cheek. Following her directions, I drew the position of the tricuspid valve, the mitral valve, and the apex of the heart, looking through her impressive breast as though it were invisible.

Based on the landmarks she read to me, I outlined the major vessels to and from the heart, the vena cava and aortic arch, negotiating around her towel as she spun around. I sketched in both kidneys on her back and then on her abdomen. When it came to tracing the route of each ureter from the kidneys to the bladder on her abdominal wall, she lay on my narrow bed and stared at the ceiling. The position of the left kidney was high up under the rim of the ribcage, just under the swell of her left breast, which she kept covered; the right was in a similar position, displaced one inch lower by the liver. The ureters' route to the bladder passed closely by her navel and into her lush black forest of straight pubic hair. I kissed her flat abdomen, running my hand tenderly over its softness, sensing every silky cell. My clinical mode snapped from the mounting tension, and I took her into my arms. *Touching your face, your hair, my hands strayed knowing we'll taste ecstasy.*

———

By late afternoon, relaxed and in a lingering aura of love, bliss, and wanting, we resumed the topographic exercise of drawing various abdominal organs on her belly. I drew in the gall-bladder with its characteristic landmark at the tip of the right ninth costal cartilage, the stomach, the spleen on the left, and McBurney's Point in the right lower quadrant of her abdomen.

With the exercise completed, our hunger took us to an Indian restaurant just around the corner. Victoria's cheeks glowed, and her eyes sparkled as she sat opposite me. My heart overflowed with love and bliss while my fingers tingled with the memory of hidden landmarks. She chatted idly. The food arrived, interrupting our conversation, and the waiter filled the distance between us with curry dishes. We served ourselves and shared some dishes, only pausing our conversation to concentrate on our food. The steaming lamb curry, okra, and rice were a treat—so different from the monotonous refectory food at Commonwealth and at Canterbury Halls.

Smiling, she whispered, "I love you."

# 21

# VALENTINE

*One day you will ask me which is more important? My life or yours?*
*I will say mine and you will walk away not knowing that you are*
*my life.*
—Kahlil Gibran

C icero said, "There are proper seasons to life." When I
was a youngster in Manchester, and a teenager in
Cairo, I received invitations to birthday parties. I
rejoiced whenever a friend or I celebrated being one year older.
I remembered living with Opa and Oma between the ages of
four and nine, noting that they read the obituaries in the daily
paper. After a sigh, they would announce to one another in

very few words their need to attend another funeral, never adding what they might have been thinking—that their turn could be next. I wondered if, as they aged, they no longer welcomed their birthdays.

Now, as young twenty-somethings, the season of life was engagements. We were testosterone-driven males with a very small pool of female classmates to vie for. In my initial year of medical school, the first couple in my class announced their engagement. As if triggering the beginning of an avalanche, other coupling announcements followed. I was somewhat distracted by this but was more concerned with pursuing my studies.

We were running a study marathon, and the constant fear of failing the next exam hung over my head. I dared not slack off, having faced the threat of expulsion by Dr. James and the trauma of failing pharmacology. I found the pressure to learn such a tremendous amount of material in a short period was intense: data were conveyed ceaselessly on a never-ending belt of information—data to digest, internalize, and synthesize—all dished out in a solemn voice and with equal importance. Would I know the subject well enough to satisfy an examiner, or was I working this hard to satisfy my father's ghost?

There was barely sufficient time for me to learn. Victoria, too, was swamped with facts. Every free moment when Victoria and I met, our togetherness always led to a tempest of tenderness and an urgency of intimacies. I constantly desired Victoria, her presence and company, and I was assured in our relationship by her need for me, allowing me to focus on my studies.

Yet the burden of time, our different schedules—her thirty-six-week semester and my forty-eight-week one—and the stress of exams caused us to fall into predictably rushed physical routines. We dreamed and longed for leisurely hours together. When we had these during our visits to the Isle of Serenity, we did not find a private space. In our forced environment, there was no opportunity for leisurely exploration of our sexuality or to stage surprise erotic adventures. Hurried intimacy did not guarantee good sex—satisfactory sex. Instead, it became an addictive reliever of stress, albeit a pleasurable one. Defying our attendance at boring lectures, we occasionally snuck off to a matinee at the Piccadilly showing a James Bond movie or *Dr Zhivago*. I was Egyptian like Omar Sharif, and the plot, with its overwhelming emotions, engulfed me. I was totally absorbed by every passionate scene. I imagined that I was the young married physician and that my attraction to Julie Christie had morphed into a full-blown infatuation. I was mesmerized by Julie's face, the way she moved, and when she spoke, it was as if she addressed me personally. Her beguiling looks, mannerisms and speech seduced me—Omar Sharif only loved her—I, on the other hand, made love to her. My love fantasy filled my dreams and helped me escape the drudgery of bookwork.

Victoria, too, was overwhelmed by her studies, although she learned more easily than I did. She was a year behind, so our schedules differed. Whenever possible, she went to the Isle of Wight to spend time with her mother, study, meet childhood friends, and do some sailing. I joined her as often as I could, sneaking away for a regular or extended weekend.

When we were apart, we wrote almost daily. Her comforting letters, written on distinctive blue paper, became addictive, and I wanted one every day. Alone in London, I'd await her letters, disappointed when one did not come in the early morning mail and convinced one would arrive in the mid-day post.

My Darling Marwan,

I love you so very much; it seems you've been away for days, but it's only twelve hours my darling. It was so wonderful of

```
you to come for the weekend and such a
lovely long one. I love you. I do hope
you got to your class at the appointed
time and that your professors are all
nice.

Bahibak, Arabic for "I love you."
```

In her many letters, she always expressed her undying love, even closing with *bahibak*. I wrote back right away or, more frequently, rang her up because I missed her and wanted to hear her voice, which soothed my restless soul. My feelings, like those of a forlorn lover, made me realize that I could not imagine living without her or her words.

Each morning going to the anatomy department, I passed an antique shop in Woburn Place. A diamond ring glittered in the window and caught my attention. "It's a lovely Victorian setting. Platinum no less . . . look how the diamond sparkles. It has great clarity with unique multifaceted cuts. The hint of a yellowish color gives it warmth," said the elderly woman behind the counter, who had a left-side Bell's facial palsy with a weeping eye. "Did you say her name was Victoria?"

"Yes. It's almost as beautiful as she is," I answered, admiring the ring up close.

"Do you want to see it through the loupe? You should bring her in to size it. Nearly half a carat, I'd say. Well worth the price," Mrs. Goldberg persisted. "Have you thought of surprising her for Valentine's Day?"

"It's too soon, I think. Not now. Perhaps in the next few months," I added as I looked at the tag. "Sixty-five pounds! Wow, that *is* expensive. I am a penniless student. Would you take £45?"

"I'll lay it aside for you ducky for when you are ready. Can you get me an appointment with the neurologist at UCH?"

On Saturday, February 10, 1965, Victoria received a Valentine card from an unsigned admirer. There followed a love letter, the next day a box of chocolates, and the following day a single, long stemmed red rose—all anonymous. She showed these to me in the evening, gliding into my dorm room on cloud nine and announcing, "I have a new admirer, someone who wants me."

It seems I had a challenger. I was stunned into muteness, amazed at my apparent insignificance. Didn't she know how much I wanted her? The purportedly lovesick admirer was Tom, a fellow medical student, and Bowtie's friend. Professing his adulation, the admirer invited her for a drink and dinner—"any place in London of your choosing." *What chicanery was this?*

I burned with resentment toward my sudden rival for trying to abduct Victoria's affections. She was only twenty years old; perhaps I had not given her room to breathe, to develop her femininity, or to explore meeting other men. I loved her too much to lose her. I could not release my grip on her, for it would be like inflicting a wound on myself. Yes, that was a selfish thought, but isn't love selfish?

A mature way I might have handled this would have been to agree that she should do what she wanted—her choice. After anguished reflection, I finally said, sternly, "No, you cannot go; it would be the end of us."

I expected her to be indignant and tell me to go fuck myself. It didn't happen. She seemed pleased with my response and came and sat on my lap, and we hugged. She declined his invitation. I did not feel victorious or even happy. It was the very opposite. I felt like a bully. We didn't celebrate our togetherness, and we should have.

At the time, I didn't suspect that Tom was Bowtie's partner in crime who, in turn, may have been put up to this by others as well—part of the ongoing pattern of low-grade harassment against this "fucking foreigner," as he confessed years later in a sorrowful confession when we became friends.

By the end of my second year, Victoria and I were an established couple. I could not imagine life without her. She was the center of my emotional world. With her, I felt safe and whole. Her Britishness minimized my sense of being an outsider. Life together helped decrease the covert social harassment that I perceived and the marginalization I experienced. She understood that my priority was to study so that I could shine academically—we both were ambitious.

I felt euphoric touching her, being with her, and wanted to spend all my time with her, but I worried that being too possessive or jealous would result in losing her love. It was an irrational thought—one that I suspect was caused by my endless wanting of Mother when I was a child and not knowing where she had disappeared to or why. Her rejection caused my anxiety; rejection and hurt were always lurking below the surface of my relationship with Victoria.

In an instant, I had gained a family in Tim, Shirley, her elderly New Zealand grandmother Dagmar, Uncle Dr. John Perfect, and his wife, Aunt Joan, along with Victoria's three cousins from Knightsbridge. They filled the emotional void created by the absence of my distant Egyptian relatives and my loving Oma and Opa so far away in Germany. Gulnar, too, had become distant. Based on comments Mother made to me, she was having trouble reconciling the account they shared in Germany. Maybe she imagined that Mother had confided her financial distress to me. I didn't trust Gulnar, and perhaps she was embezzling Mother's money.

Victoria and I frequently lunched with Uncle John and Aunt Joan, who had lived in Indonesia and Bahrain. Aunt Joan's cuisine was an exotic mix of Indonesian and some delicious Arab dishes. They treated me as a budding physician and saw me as a future in-law. I was pleased that they accepted me on my merits and did not regard me as a WOG.

On one of Mother's infrequent trips from Manchester through London on her way to Germany, I planned for her to meet Victoria. For this happy occasion, I bought tickets to see Dame Margot Fonteyn and Rudolf Nureyev in their premier performance in *Romeo and Juliet* at the Royal Ballet. Mother arrived from Manchester in her VW Beetle and drew up along the pavement outside Commonwealth Hall. I felt confident Mother would approve of Victoria.

"Mother, this is Victoria." Mother looked her up and down. After some social niceties, I said, "We plan to get engaged soon and to marry."

Instead of smiling and congratulating us, Mother proclaimed, "Oh, no. She is not suitable for you. She's not your type."

Victoria and I were totally stunned. I was horrified and embarrassed! Was this the pronouncement of a jealous mother who desperately did not want to lose her son? Still in shock, I didn't have the presence of mind to tell Mother that she was out of line and that she should apologize to Victoria for her very hurtful remark. Mother was wrong. She was a selfish woman who was unable to love her children—to love me even when I was an infant. At that moment, I felt torn between the love for my dearest woman versus the desire of a son for his mother's approval.

Whereas a premier event of Romeo and Juliet with world-class dancers should have been most memorable, the agony of the disparaging remark ruined what was to be a celebratory moment. We sat stonily in the orchestra, neither looking at nor speaking with Mother. I sat as a buffer between the two women, the one who bore me, the other who would bear my children. Victoria and I should have discussed it afterwards, but knowing her reluctance to deal with or discuss emotionally charged matters, I stupidly let the matter drop. Mother's rejection of Victoria made me feel that she was once more rejecting me, that somehow, I didn't matter—another wedge between us.

I realized that Oma's acceptance of Victoria was more important to me, so we planned to go to Wedel to meet her. Oma was my true emotional mother, and I knew this would help counter the effects of Mother's offense. Oma and Victoria instantly loved each other, despite their difficulty in communicating, for Oma spoke no English. Even Gulnar approved of Victoria—not that I cared, but that was saying something. I thoroughly approved of my Victoria, and that is what truly mattered.

# 22

# SECOND MB

## MAY 1965

*Well done is better than well said.*
—Poor Richard's Almanack, 1737

During the term leading up to the exam, Jonathan and some of us at our dissecting table whittled away at Fred's anatomy. The legs attached to the pelvis and torso were Fred's only body parts still in need of dissecting. These lay exposed on our glass table during the day and were reverently covered by a cloth at night. Over eighteen months, Fred had entrusted us with the secrets of his body, hopefully transferring anatomical knowledge to a younger generation learning to heal the sick.

I was most grateful to Jonathan, who diligently and patiently did the major part of the dissection, one body part at a time. If I had invested such time during the four terms—eighteen months—of preclinical studies, I surely would not have needed to read the prerequisite material to pass the milestone of the second MB examination, Bachelor of Medicine exam, in May 1965. My fear of failing the exam prevented me from spending sufficient time in the anatomy dissection hall; indeed, I only attended the essential lectures.

Instead, I cloistered myself in Room 337, bashing the books on every topic and lecture that we had covered during the previous eighteen months. I worked my way down a list of subjects that I needed to grasp. I read and reread the material until I had mastered an issue—how anatomy was connected to its embryological development and how it underpinned its physiological function. It was an ambitious goal but one that allowed me to understand the holistic function of the body. I continued attending specific lectures and revision courses but minimized my dissecting of the legs, leaving it to Jonathan—as most of us did. I even skipped the weekly *viva voce* in gross anatomy.

When some fellow students heard that I wasn't interested in learning the anatomy of the legs, they mocked me. I defended myself, saying that humans didn't really need legs; although I had said it in jest, the statement—"man needs no legs"— became my everlasting tagline, which continued for years during my many medical school reunions. Not being intimately familiar with the anatomy of the leg, its vascular tree, its blood vessels, and its muscles would haunt me in the coming months.

As I studied, I became confident in my understanding of the structure and function of the body, and with minimal distractions, I made good progress. Despite the unavailability of past anatomy exam questions to review, my rationale for not thoroughly studying the legs was weighted on two arguments: first, relative to the rest of the body, the legs were about eighteen percent, or a one in five chance, of being a question. No anatomy faculty member was that interested in these structures compared with the importance of the anal canal—which was emphasized by a don't-miss one-hour lecture. The second reason was that the written exam consisted of essay questions where the candidate chose to answer four out of five questions.

I felt certain that in the written essay exam, I could avoid a question concerning the legs.

I completed the written portion and felt confident that I had done sufficiently well. The nagging anxiety that once more I'd get caught during the orals crept into my subconscious. For this concern, I devised a scheme. The orals occurred over two days following the written exam. My name appeared on the schedule for the second day. The day before, I stood outside the basement where the orals were given and conducted an exit poll. No questions on the legs. Were the examiners holding back? Were they going to ask about the legs on day two of the orals?

That night, I briefly read about the knee and ankle joints, the vascular tree, and main small muscles of the feet and their nerve supplies. To focus the oral examiner on topics I knew well, I bandaged my right wrist and put my arm into a sling. My hope was that the examiner would ask me what happened. "I fell and sustained a green-stick fracture," I'd say sheepishly. The comeback I anticipated would be, "So tell me all about the wrist joint or such similar topic." It never occurred to me that they might see through my devious plot, that they might be familiar with it, or that they'd decide to focus on the opposite end of the body instead.

I entered the anatomy basement and faced a series of oral questions on the cranial nerves, the head and neck, the abdomen, the anal canal, and so on. Nothing about the legs. Phew! Thank God. As soon as I was out of the basement, I unwound my dressing. My fingers were getting blue and cold because I had wrapped my wrist too tightly.

Prior to the second MB, rumors emerged that these were difficult to pass, although my fellow students said the same thing about all exams, and I believed them. To me, it was more important to have a good grasp of knowledge rather than to answer some obscure question about it. My father would have been familiar with the complexities I was facing. I thought of him often, or more precisely, I felt his palpable absence because he too had attended University College. I could imagine him, like me, surrounded by books and studying for his finals. We could have talked of managing the pressures of exams, managing time, and the balance between tests and romance.

Perhaps, he would have counseled me on my cultural differences with Victoria, for he too had wooed and married a "foreign" woman and could have given me advice about the timing of an upcoming marriage. Although I had inherited his spirit to strive and be successful, I lacked his assurance. It would have been nice to have had his support.

I gloriously passed the second MB after all of the book bashing and was on my way to becoming a surgeon. It would have been an occasion to celebrate—one I failed to take. The failure to celebrate any of my achievements, no matter how big or small, was a huge mistake in my life. When I was a child, we did not celebrate birthdays, Easter, or Christmas. Singularly, quietly, and in privacy, Mother celebrated in her German way. She would bake a special cake, light a candle, and have a quiet moment to herself, lost in her thoughts—all without sharing this with anyone.

My father didn't celebrate in an open manner, either. He officially observed the two Muslim feasts—*Eid Al-Fitr* at the end of Ramadan and *Eid Al-Adha*—by taking us to our grandparents, where the family congregated, *sans* Mother, the German outsider. Family gatherings were modest affairs, only an occasion to eat together. My father considered birthdays and the Egyptian national festival, *Sham el Nasim,* which marked the beginning of spring, as days of opportunity to catch up with his work-related projects. I internalized the idea that because failure was not an option for him, there was no need to celebrate success. Only once did I see him smile when he had successfully published another book.

Maybe each of my parents had a different reason for not being openly jubilant. Mother grew up in a very meager household, where the shortages from World War I affected their everyday life in Germany. There was no opportunity for an exuberance of joy or any gift-giving. My father grew up with scarcity in a village in Upper Egypt, where achievement was the only way out of poverty. Once successful, enjoying the moment openly was considered boasting and a concern based in the superstition that "no good deed goes unpunished." The joy of celebrating was unknown in our home. Instead of celebrating, I focused on the next phase of my life—seeing patients and, more importantly, helping them.

One of the greatest emotional benefits I gained from passing the exam was that I could remove my father's specter and the demands he had placed on me. I would be charting my own course, meeting living persons and learning about their illnesses, ministering comfort and mastering a knife to heal their woes. For that, I did not welcome or need my father's ghost.

At least that is what I thought.

By late spring of 1965, I bade farewell to what remained of Fred. My dissecting table colleagues and I passed the exam. We spent little time glancing back at the fate of the five percent of our fellow students, colleagues, and friends held back by the examiners—"There but for the grace of God go I." Most, including my friend John Rackey, succeeded six months later. He and some others followed me across Gower Street in another wave of aspiring physicians. Most of my class would become community general practitioners—the famous British GPs. Others would pursue specialty training in radiology, anesthesiology, pediatrics, surgery, and the subspecialties of internal medicine.

At last, I had jumped that Rubicon—a monumental achievement. I left Commonwealth Hall and moved into a third-floor dormer in UCH's hostel on the west side of Gower Street, fondly referred to as the Annex, down the road from the hospital itself. Victoria remained at Canterbury Hall, embarking on her second year of basic science, preparing to be tested by the fire of the second MB before moving some distance to Westminster Hospital in the heart of London for her clinical training. I realized she would have less time for us while studying and preparing for her second MB, which I was sure she would pass. And with that, I understood we would be geographically further apart and mixing entirely in different clinical circles because her clinical training took her to different Westminster-affiliated hospitals.

In the elation of starting my *true* identity as a medical student, I walked into Marks and Spencer and walked out with gray flannel trousers, a blazer, drip-dry white shirts with essential bland ties, and shiny black shoes. I left behind an indifferent dress code of polo sweaters and pants. A barber neatly trimmed my hair. Also left behind was the burden of the presidency of the Physiology Society.

I was ready for my new profession, at least on the outside.

# PART III

# LONDON 1965

# 23

# 95 GOWER STREET

## MAY 1965

*A man's house is his castle.*
—Edward Coke

My room in the Annex was on the top of the first house overlooking the Anatomy Department, where two years earlier, I had started my life as a student. The doorframe under the rafters was lower than usual. I pushed my narrow bed against the left wall, shoved my desk against it under the window, and moved the bookshelf to its right. A dresser with a mirror stood opposite the bed. On top, next to some loose change, was the only photograph I had of a smiling Victoria. A simple light bulb with a cheap shade hung from the ceiling, while a desk lamp doubled for work and bedtime reading. The wooden floorboards were a deep brown, whether darkened with time or from ingrained dirt, I could never decide. Either way, I took to wearing slippers round the clock, and I bought a carpet, too.

This little room became my home. It was small but cozy, with a character differing from the other rooms in the Annex. Morning sunshine beamed through the window, warming and brightening what was now my new home. The main drawback: three floors below on Gower Street stood a set of traffic lights. It was the custom in the mid-1960s to rev one's engine while waiting for the light to change—particularly with motorcycles. The racket echoed off the high walls of the Anatomy Department's façade, like up a canyon, and the noise carried up past my window and into my room. It was annoying as hell, particularly at night.

The shared toilet on the ground floor was among the tolerable inconveniences. It was the smallest room, with a poorly fitted window that would never close. Without a radiator, it was also the coldest room in winter, where to linger literally risked freezing one's ass off or catching the flu. The only telephone was a coin-fed box that stood on a mantle in the entrance hall by the front door. Everyone in the nearby rooms could hear it ring and overhear conversations. There, too, the mysterious housekeeper would place our mail.

I regularly received letters from Oma, written in German, updating me on family events in Hamburg, the recent activities of my sister and nieces, and, finally, Mother's whereabouts in the world—usually Egypt with occasional visits to Germany. Both Tante Suad and Tante Sanaa, my father's younger sisters, wrote conveying my uncles' greetings for the festive *Eid-el Fitr*

—the feast of breaking—after Ramadan. They expressed their sentiments wishing that I be successful like their elder brother, my father, and that I would soon return to Egypt. These letters were placed on the mantle.

I saw few of the many lodgers including classmates, since our schedules were so different. Each Sunday afternoon, when I studied Barrons, dreaming of making money on the stock exchange one day, I was tortured by hearing someone practicing the bagpipes. It sounded like several tomcats in heat. I traced the noise to a ground-floor room at the back of the second house. I knocked. The squeaking noise stopped and the door opened.

"Oh. Hello. I was wondering what that noise was?" I spoke. "I am new here and curious about what instrument you were playing."

"I'm playing my bagpipes, of course. Tough luck if it's disturbing you. It's my last term before I get the hell out of here."

"Oh no. It's not disturbing me," I said with a big smile on my face. "But why don't you play it in Regent's Park?" He slammed the door in my face and his practice ended. But, in the few moments of our exchange, I saw that he had a large room, with bay windows facing the garden at the back of the house— a quiet room. I left a note to the mystery woman requesting to move into it when he departed.

Sunday was a day of rest, and medical students were not expected to appear on the wards. Although I had plenty of reading to catch up on, I fantasized about Victoria off and on, totally absorbed by thoughts of her and our growing relationship. In my mind's eye, I saw her as Botticelli's Venus, a beautiful face, her naked body, her gorgeous breasts, and the wonder of her dark pubic hair. My nose delighted in the memory of the aroma emitted by her tights when they lay beside me on my chair—the smell of sex. She was so attractive, so intelligent, that I could not believe that she loved me and that I could make love to her.

To keep my mind off her and focus on my studies, I sat on a hard chair at my desk and read aloud, underlining the important facts and repeating the crux of what I had read, yet I could not retain it. It was as if my love for her left no room in my brain to take in vital information. I panicked. How could I pass future exams if I could not remember what I had just read? I slapped myself and yelled, "Concentrate." Other times I would shout, "Focus," and "No," slamming my hand on my desk to banish the fantasy of her from my mind.

On Sundays, Victoria arrived in the early afternoon after finishing with her studies, her laundry, or having talked with her mother. Since I barely could hear her ring on the top floor, I ingeniously finagled another key to the front door. I would hear her footfall on the stairs as she rushed up to the last flight that led only to my room. After a cursory knock, my door flew open. The fears that formed in my younger days when I waited for Mother to return evaporated whenever I held her. I kissed her cheeks and neck, cradling her head in my hands, stroking her straight short hair. I wanted to rip her clothes off and make love to her right then and there.

Instead, inhibited by the thought that this was not how nice men behaved, I sat down across from her as we chatted. She never let me know her desire to be passionate or initiate our intimacies, and I did not want to put her off by coming on too strong. I listened patiently as I heard about Shirley, all while undressing Victoria in my mind, wondering why we were wasting such precious time. Did she not want me?

If it was a sunny day, we postponed our lovemaking. Why did we not have a quickie first and then go for our outing? Instead, we walked hand-in-hand past Oxford Street's closed shops to Hyde Park, where we visited the Speakers' Corner, entertained by would-be politicians and the half-crazed. Then, we would sip a cup of tea at Lyons Corner House before taking the Tube back. If the morning was blustery and gray, we snuggled under the covers and read to each other from the Sunday paper. Our proximity, touches, and caresses eventually led to more fondling, resulting in rapid undressing and rushing to seek the warmth of the covers once more. After our passionate lovemaking, covering ourselves, cuddling close, we drifted into a deep sleep of contentment in my narrow bed.

I would awake an hour or more later and watch how dusk played on her sleeping face, and when I touched it, she would open her eyes, smiling. If she had to pee, it meant getting dressed and walking down three stories, hoping not to meet anyone, for her flushed cheeks and the aroma of sex would tell the tale of our trip to the state of perfect happiness.

Tired of Indian food, we alternated by going to Schmidt's, the German restaurant behind the Goodge Street Tube station or occasionally to the pricier Italian one around the corner. I always insisted on paying the bill, to show Victoria my ability to take care of her. Contented, we returned to my room, and with our bellies full, we resumed reading the Sunday paper, lying on the bed, enjoying each other's company late into the evening, well past the previous Commonwealth Hall curfew hours. I lapped up her love, her embraces, our closeness. I never wanted our evenings to end.

———

During the week, I frequently returned to my room after refectory breakfast to read about conditions, symptoms, diseases, and the treatments for patients I had encountered. My mind was the clearest and least cluttered in the morning, particularly after having lain in Victoria's arms the previous day. By noon, I would make my way downstairs, passing the open door of a classmate. He was usually lying on his bed, throwing a tennis ball against the wall then catching it, over and over. The room was barren, devoid of personal touches—no pictures, books, or photos.

"Aren't you coming to Smith's post-mortem?"

Each time the answer was the same. At first, he claimed to be sick, saying, "I feel grotty."

Not familiar with the word I repeated it, "Grotty?"

"Yeah, you know what it's like." He started to sing, "When you're feeling grotty, stick a finger up your botty and the whole world is a different place." He wailed with laughter, and seeing me smile, he continued singing, "When you're feeling glum, stick a finger up your bum," and again he roared with laughter.

Once more, I smiled, wondering whether he was depressed—my first impression—or if I had made a wrong assumption. Maybe he was gay and trying to deal with his feelings when such behavior wasn't in the open or widely accepted. Maybe he needed a break from school to sort matters out.

Turning solemn, he said that he saw no use in continuing with this "medical stuff." He only did it because his father wanted him to become a doctor, adding, "You know, that whole Jewish thing," mournfully adding, "All these exams."

A few days later, there was my classmate again with his tennis ball. I stopped in the doorway. "Hello, coming?"

"No, I'm not going to lectures or wards anymore." Then a smile crossed his face, and even without a mustache, he had an uncanny resemblance to Groucho Marx. He stopped throwing the ball and turned to me, "When asked to give the etiology of a disease in an exam, I thought of mentioning the first and second causes that come to mind, and adding, 'to name but a few.'" More laughter.

Amused at the absurdity of the reply, I joined in. I walked into his room and sat on the edge of his bed. "You sound depressed."

He resumed throwing his ball and started tearing up. His

lower lip quivered. He rolled toward me, laying his face against my thigh, and began to sob. His whole body shook as I placed my arm around him.

I was in new territory. What should I do? I recognized he needed professional help beyond our potential friendship, and yet, to whom did one go to in this situation? Who was responsible for the health and wellbeing of medical students? I could not come up with a responsible person. "Do you want to join me in the refectory for lunch? We can talk."

"No, I'll be all right."

"Have you spoken to your mother?"

"My mother? No. I'll be alright."

"Do you have a close friend, perhaps a girlfriend or boyfriend I can call who can come and visit you?"

"No. I'll be all right."

I stood and went on my way, alarmed but also baffled. We had academic advisors assigned to us when we crossed Gower Street from University College. I had met mine a few times, and he was my antithesis: an introverted, clinical chemist—very conservative, if not bitter with life. I did not feel he would be sympathetic to my classmate's dilemma, and I failed to ask the beadle, a compassionate and knowledgeable man, who might have had an answer.

The next day, I passed his open door. His room was empty, his mattress rolled up. Had he left? When I inquired among my classmates, I discovered he had committed suicide.

With a knot in my stomach, I retraced my steps to my room and curled up on my bed, my arms wrapped around me. How many times had I nearly given up? How many times had I been despondent? And who had there been to console me?

I could not get his face out of my mind. I remembered him greeting me while we were at University College the year before. Had he been trying to reach out to me then? How was it possible that someone so depressed could joke so much?

I had failed to help a fellow student, a fellow *Beni Adam*—human being. "I'm sorry, my friend. I let you down." I kept repeating to myself aloud, "I'm sorry, so sorry." I did not know him as a person, but would always remember him for his strange humor at a time when he was in need of help. Suffering was part of the human condition, and how people bore their burdens differed. It brought to mind the John Watson quote, "Be kind, for everyone you meet is fighting a hard battle."

# 24

## MY AMERICAN FRIEND

*He was a man who knew a good Stilton cheese and preferred it over*
*ripe.*
—Siegfried Sassoon

I n the summer, I moved to the big, quiet room. I made it
my home by hanging an Egyptian tapestry on the wall,
and setting up the ornamental chair Giddi had given me
to bring to England. I had to persuade the pilot at Cairo airport
that it was safe to carry in the passenger cabin. It went well
with my camel chair. I set my desk in front of the bay window
and did not miss the traffic noise. I loved it when the sun shone
into my windows, flooding the space with warm afternoon
light.

John Rackey, the American fellow "OS" student lodged next
door. He was in his early thirties—a decade older and more
experience in life than me, which I admired. He walked with
military bearing and was of medium height with thinning hair.

When he was demobilized from the United States Air Force
where he was stationed at Mildenhof, Sussex, he successfully

competed for one of the mature student slots at the medial school.

As a college student at Yale, he majored in electronic engineering and then worked at Westinghouse. He and his wife, as he described it to me, enjoyed a suburban life in Connecticut and were proud to become parents. "My life ended when my wife was killed in a car accident. She was expecting twins." The matter-of-fact way he related the event struck me.

"I volunteered for the air force, and trained at the Naval Air Station Pensacola and fell in love with flying and the Florida life style." Smiling, he said playfully, "You Ay-rab you! Some day you should go to Florida." On seeing my surprised change of facial attitude and fearing I might take umbrage, he continued, saying, "It's from a fun song, 'Ahab the Arab.' Have you never heard it?" I shook my head. "Have you seen the musical Oklahoma, or South Pacific?" I once more shook my head. "Wow, you are missing life, my Arab friend. Rodgers and Hammerstein wrote wonderful songs."

It was obvious that our cultural backgrounds were different. This in itself did not bother me. What irritated me was the way he said these things, making me feel like an ignoramus. He did not know of Um Kulthum or the beautiful heart-trembling Qur'an recitation of Sheikh Abdul Basit Abdul Samad. However, I did not challenge him, for I was enchanted by his story. He was slowly seducing me into American culture.

As we became better friends, and knowing of my love for flying, he told me that after advanced training at Pensacola he was posted to Mildenhof where he piloted a plane crammed with electronic gear and equipped with sideways-looking radar. He told me he had gone on twelve-hour missions flying up the Norwegian coast to the Arctic Circle and back. "My co-pilot and I had a crew of ten who spent their time testing the Russian radar system and jamming it."

I interrupted his story by telling him of my crazy plan to get out of Egypt by flying west to Libya. He looked at me skeptically for a minute then nodded, smiling. "You've got balls. I bet you would have gotten there somehow."

He continued his story. "I was among the first in our squadron to take off until one day halfway through a mission I had engine problems and had to ditch in the North Sea. It was freezing and there was blood all around me in the water." He related how scared he had been and how the paralysis of fear had made it hard to haul himself into his rubber dingy. "I had cut my arm with my knife when freeing myself from my parachute." After a silence he added, "Some of my crew did not make it. Thereafter, I was the last to take off, compulsively going over all the items on the checklist—no short cuts."

On the day of his demobilization in 1963, his unit was deployed to Vietnam, where none of his crew survived. He joined our medical school. At first, he had difficulty focusing on book learning, but managed to overcome this problem.

John, like Jonathan, became my close friend during our clinical student days. We shared a passion for classical music. Friday evenings we frequently went out for an early meal and returned to his room to enjoy piano concertos by Arthur Rubinstein. He claimed he was the very best pianist, and I accepted his judgment. John loved Liszt and Rachmaninoff and he told me he had played the piano at concert level while at Yale. Maria Callas and Pavarotti were his favorite opera singers. He had numerous recordings of their work among his large vinyl collection. He was proud of his latest Fisher record player with its stereo sound system. Listening to his records revived my love for opera, connecting me to my Cairo days. He introduced me to Gilbert and Sullivan's operas, and invited Victoria and me to *The Pirates of Penzance* staged at the Tower of London. Despite his room being slightly smaller than mine, and his tendency to play music on the loud side, I seldom heard it coming through our connecting walls.

To John, everything in America was "bigger and better." I teased him by saying I'd heard that even the rain drops in America were bigger and wetter. Some students found his American can-do enthusiastic attitude off-putting and avoided him.

He complained that in England, the sun did not shine, the women were unfathomable, and there were no decent restaurants near UCH. It became clear over our four years at medical school that he was not a happy person. Perhaps his personal burdens were too heavy.

When he returned to America for his holidays, he stayed with close relatives in Naples, Florida. He described Florida by a series of superlatives, indicating he would eventually practice in that beautiful, sunny state, which had acres of orange groves, miles of yellow beaches, and the warm Gulf Stream. His love of America was infectious, such that I was burning to get my BTA —Been To America.

He was not a beer or wine drinker, instead loving cocktails like Manhattans and Old Fashioneds. John's descriptions of an array of drinks was an education; since my parents did not drink, I had zero knowledge of the world of alcohol. For my birthday, he gave me a copy of *old mr. boston deluxe official bartender's guide,* though I never acquired the taste of a regular drinker. Despite this our friendship blossomed.

# 25

# KEYS TO CLINICAL PARADISE

## SUMMER 1965

*The good physician treats the disease; the great physician treats the
patient who has the disease.*
—William Osler

T hat summer, I began my transformation into a young
clinician. The Cruciform Building had a centrally
placed, single-service core providing clean water and
sanitation. From the center, four wings radiated at right angles

from each other. In 1906, when the building was designed, constructed, and opened, the wards were separated because of public health concerns based on the erroneous theory that some putrefaction, a miasma, or pollution of the air was responsible for the spread of illness. Each floor of the five-story building had a series of square windows, apparently left open at all times to provide proper ventilation and light. The interior, too, was designed for practicality. Both the hardwood flooring and glazed red brick walls facilitated easy maintenance. The walls of the hospital's entrance, however, were lined with marble to convey a sense of decorum.

Our non-medical colleagues and those across Gower Street, including Victoria, had their three-month holiday, which Victoria spent sailing at Seaview. We, on the other hand, sat attentively in a Roman-style amphitheater, affirming our eagerness to learn. Professor Bernard Harries, the dean, gave an overview of the introductory course to clinical medicine, explaining that the introductory course was a smorgasbord of presentations that covered every disease except the tropical ones. The heads of the different medical and surgical firms would give lectures intended to familiarize us with their disciplines and their available services. He emphasized that every patient in this hospital was ours to clerk and examine.

Our uniforms were newly starched, short, white coats with name tags that declared our status as novice clinicians. American-style lightweight stethoscopes, neurological hammers, ophthalmoscopes, and pocket-sized emergency medical handbooks—all the trappings of a young physician—impressively adorned our persons.

The faculty wore long coats and trooped through the auditorium to deliver lectures on the Western maladies plaguing humanity, many of which we were likely to encounter in the wards. Their areas of expertise included cardiac, hematological, pulmonary illnesses, neurological conditions, and surgical diseases. We received solid, old-style presentations without audio-visual aids or handouts, and we scribbled down every word, barring the occasional joke made to reinforce a point. To emphasize the connection between smoking, lung cancer, and heart disease, the cardiologist related an anecdote. He asked a patient, "Do you smoke after intercourse?" She replied, "I never looked." The class laughed. The point was that at the time, smoking was pervasive among doctors and some of my fellow medical students, despite solid scientific evidence of the ill effects of smoking accumulated as early as the 1930s, 1940s, and 1950s.

We learned from different specialty heads the process of clerking each type of patient, including how to obtain a medical, family, and social history. We were shown how to perform a physical examination from head to toe. We heard how to determine what factored into a specific diagnosis: the etiologies of particular diseases and their various manifestations, differences between adult and pediatric patients with acute and chronic diseases, and the specific tests to run for each case.

During the summer months we were learning the science of diseases, and we were expected to practice the art of medicine and our newly acquired skills. These included caring for a single patient assigned to us, examining them, and following their hospital course—all through bedside learning. We subtly absorbed the physicians' mannerisms, lingo, and the prevailing medical culture.

At lunchtime on the first day, we crowded about the notice board to see our patient and service assignments. We were expected to clerk and examine the assigned patient and attend rounds with the head of the service when we were not in the introductory course. Lucky me! I was assigned to clerk Professor Max Rosenheim's patient and attend his rounds.

Sir Max, as he was referred to with awe and reverence, was

"the professor" of medicine in the days when a single, all-powerful physician headed each discipline. Not only was he our Caesar—dwarfing the stature of the traditional leader, the professor of surgery—but Sir Max towered over the other professors and department heads by virtue of his presidency of the Royal College of Physicians. From our lowly perch as students, we observed his meteoric rise through the chivalrous ranks of The Most Excellent Order of the British Empire: First from Professor Rosenheim to Sir Max, next to Knight of the British Empire (KBE), and ultimately to The Right Honorable Professor, The Lord Rosenheim KBE FRCP, and a fellow of the highly prestigious Royal Society. And *I* was to clerk one of *his* patients! What an honor, what a humbling task, what an auspicious beginning to my medical career. I was determined to do an excellent job to receive praise from the patient and the notoriously feared ward nurse, Sister W. Rumor had it that she was Sir Max's not-so-secret consort. I believed it to be salacious gossip.

Once a week we were given lectures by esteemed guests. I attended the lecture given by a surgeon, Mr. Dennis Burkitt FRS. He had devoted his medical service to the developing world and moved to Uganda, where he discovered childhood lymphoma. Subsequently it was named after him—Burkitt Lymphoma. This tumor grew at the angle of a child's jaw and only occurred between certain altitudes in the Ugandan mountains. He concluded that the vector was a fly that lived within these elevations. In addition, he discovered that the increased fiber intake in the African diet reduced the chance of colon cancer, introducing an understanding of the need for fiber in Western diets.

I sat at the back of the amphitheater, riveted with fascination. These discoveries gave credence to my dream of connecting science and medicine, as I had told the Dean during my interview. This aspiration, powered by my eternal curiosity, would make the combination of my two interests come to life, but first, I needed to become a surgeon.

Together with six fellow students—again determined by alphabetical order—I would attend an autopsy; the practical application of our afternoon pathology lectures. Having hurriedly wolfed down my refectory lunch, I hastily trailed the others to the morgue. The sweet odor of a freshly deceased body was in stark contrast to Fred's acrid whiff. I had expected a scene resembling Rembrandt's 1632 *The Anatomy Lesson of Dr. Nicolaes Tulp.* Our equivalent was Professor Smith, a tall, lean, handsome man wearing a white shirt and black tie under his long clinical coat. He had a shock of white hair and a down-to-earth medical detective's attitude. These dissections were entirely different from the painting.

The pinkish-gray body lay a few feet in front of me, the scalp drawn over the face, concealing it while exposing the brain. Depending on the diagnosis, the chest or the abdominal cavity was filleted open. The medical history, together with the gross anatomical and histological tissue findings, led to a diagnostic conclusion. Professor Smith held crucial evidence in his hand—the diseased heart or liver, the overlooked perforated appendix, or an obstructed small bowel because of a large gallstone. Pointing to the dissection, he pieced together a story based on his deductions, weaving a narrative of suspense and shock worthy of a prosecutor's summation. By the end of his narration, there was no escaping the truth about the cause of death and the culprit—the negligent physician or surgeon. Mystery solved, *Quod erat demonstrandum*—Q.E.D., "thus it has been demonstrated."

I enjoyed the intellectual exercise and loved the suspenseful account, all the while frantically trying to prevent regurgitating my lunch into a fellow student's beehive hairdo in front of me. At every autopsy, I deliberately stood close behind her, leaning in to inhale the scent of her hairspray to avoid the autopsy smell.

After lunch, the daily pathology lecture brought together the cellular process of disease, making relevant what I had labored to learn in basic science. It vindicated the tortured hours I had spent learning the boring facts. The pathophysiology was dry, but it was the king of knowledge for understanding human maladies.

The last class of the afternoon was clinical pharmacology. I was apprehensive until I discovered that Professor Laurence's lectures, in contrast to basic science, were lively and attention-holding performances peppered with aphorisms, parody, humor, and colorful anecdotes about a drug's discovery—most of which came from precious plants. He discussed patients' psychological attitudes toward taking medication, recommended dosages, and information about the placebo effect. His practical advice proved invaluable. The nature of his delivery ensured my retention of the material, which was helped by reading his heavily illustrated book, *Clinical Pharmacology*. I easily passed my exam and retain the third edition of the book to this day.

After the lectures, I spent hours in the evening randomly clerking medical patients with a myriad of diseases, often at different stages of the same ailment. I learned that each stage was akin to a moment in a continuum of the disease process: presenting with bleeding from gastritis in one patient to a perforated gastric ulcer in a more advanced case of the same condition. I listened to every heart murmur in the cardiac ward and every wheeze in the chest ward, corroborating my findings with the patient's X-rays.

During this period, my bedtime reading was W. Somerset Maugham's *Of Human Bondage*, where I learned the subtleties of human relationships and their quirks. This wonderful novel helped me pay attention to the patients' family histories and their complaints, realizing that the key to diagnostic success lay in hearing how patients related their maladies. If I listened carefully, a patient eventually told me the key feature that would allow me to reach the correct diagnosis. A patient presenting with dull pain between the shoulder blades after eating a fatty meal usually indicated disease of the gall bladder. I learned from each patient I clerked.

The long separation from Victoria during her three-month holiday wore me down from time to time. In her absence, I felt our relationship was being neglected. She was enjoying a summer of sailing and Saturday night parties while I was slogging away. Why was she not by my side? I'd daydream we were together at the Saturday night hop, twisting and shouting to the Beatles and Rolling Stones. My Victoria was a series of thoughts, images, and sensations occurring in my mind; the patients were my reality.

We pined for one another and continued to write almost daily. Occasionally, I'd telephone or visit, too seldom for our liking. Following one of these visits she wrote:

```
Darling,

You have been so wonderful to me while
you were here, my darling; you always
are, but especially this time my sweet—I
do love you so extremely etc. much; I
want to be with you forever and abso-
lutely ever—my own darling. I love you
so much. The neighbors have asked me to
supper, v. nice of them but what a bore!
I love you awi awi awi—a lot.

My love, I don't want to stop writing as
it makes me feel as if I'm almost
```

```
talking to you, darling—my very own
darling, I Love you.

All my love, my darling,
Vicki.
p.s.: Bahibak
```

My response was immediate, pouring out my love and longing for her, describing my thoughts and sensual plans for our next reunion and the enormity of my feelings. Momentarily relieved and reconnected, I could focus on my books again. I summarized the history of each patient I had seen in the margin of my textbooks and read about the conditions associated with their complaints. The symptoms fell into a pattern. I could not memorize the abundance of minutiae, but I could reach a diagnosis based on pattern recognition.

Mysteriously, with each new lecture, I seemed to suffer a new ailment. If I knocked myself, the resulting bruise convinced me I had leukemia. If I had diarrhea, I knew I must be suffering from inflammatory bowel disease. Miraculously, my illnesses were self-curing or replaced by a different neurosis. Was I diabetic? Did I have heart disease, or worse, syphilis?

When I imagined examining a patient, I knew I would not be able to do rectal or breast exams, feeling uncomfortable invading such personal spaces. Further, I had no idea how to make a patient feel at ease to allow me to do these procedures —I'd feel awkward. Two male students, who ultimately became psychiatrists, proposed that the class form a squatting daisy chain to practice rectal exams on each other. This was the humor of the stressed and absurd. In the same vein, some students insensitively floated rumors about doing breast exams on the seven women in our class, who responded with counter-rumors of smashing all the male testicles. We winced.

A consultant urologist, Mr. D.R. Davis, was horrified during a lecture when I confessed to never having done a rectal exam. He instructed me to attend his urology clinic the following morning. I walked into a large examining room, finding a sea of elderly male bottoms sticking up in the air, as the patients knelt on examining stools set in rows, trousers about their knees, awaiting Mr. DRD's finger.

His staff nurse took me aside. Walking among them, she selected a candidate and proceeded to show me how to perform a painless exam. She had me practice all morning until I completed almost sixty rectal exams by noon. When I left, I could distinguish between a normal, an enlarged, and a cancerous prostate and could discriminate among the "Royds" —first, second, and third-degree hemorrhoids. My right index finger ached, and despite wearing a glove, it had a fecal reek no matter how many times I washed my hands. I also learned from the nurse that trumpet players tended to get hemorrhoids since there were no valves in the veins between the liver and the rectum and because the constant blowing pushed the blood into the hemorrhoidal veins. Fascinating stuff.

We learned how to draw blood. We began by examining our own antecubital fossa—the triangular pit of the elbow crease. I identified the three most common veins: the median cubital vein crossing the fossa and connecting the cephalic vein on the outer side of the arm with the basilic vein on the inner side. We were given newly introduced American disposable needles and plastic syringes. Jonathan was agreeable when it came to trying the venipuncture on him, following which he would stick me. When I applied the tourniquet, his veins popped up. Swabbing the area clean with alcohol, I approached him with trepidation, eager not to hurt him. I was fortunate and hit a vein and struck blood—pure beginner's luck. Blood drawing seemed like a piece of cake, making me feel cocky; what else had I expected as an aspiring surgeon other than total success? Jonathan, too, was slick and proficient.

I had never liked needles but learned that the fear of the pinprick was worse than reality.

The first time I made my way to the ward to examine my assigned medical patient, Sister W. challenged me. Standing in the doorway, preventing my advance, she declared, "We are much too busy. Come back later." With that firm statement, she blocked my entry into my patient's room. Sister W. waved a dismissive hand to emphasize the finality of her point, turned on her heels, and with long, efficient strides disappeared into the unusually dim room.

In the few moments of our confrontation, I noted that she was wearing the dark blue uniform and white pinafore that distinguished her rank. Her black belt, with a broad buckle, had the crest of our hospital, and her wonderfully quaint, starched white cap uniquely identified her as a graduate of University College Hospital School of Nursing. The uniform also announced her seniority and authority. We knew of her status as the "queen bee" of Sir Max's medical ward. From the outset, caution was the watchword for what was said in her presence because it was tantamount to whispering into Sir Max's ear, and for the same reason, her word was absolute. Her dismissiveness humiliated me. To clerk my patient and get a good grade, I had to win her over.

With my newfound skill of drawing blood, what better way than to offer my services? I hoped to dazzle her sufficiently to get into her good graces. Perhaps, I might even be chosen as one of the six students assigned to Sir Max's firm at the end of the introductory course for my first clinical rotation in medicine. I felt that a solid grounding in internal medicine was an essential prerequisite to acquiring and mastering the skills of surgery because one operates on a patient, not a body.

One bright summer morning, wearing a freshly laundered white coat, I strode smartly onto the medical ward to offer my blood drawing services. Sister W.'s measured look conveyed an attitude of "you'll do." Her charge nurse, whose diminutive rank dictated she wear a pale blue uniform and a red belt, directed me to the slews/utility room. To my delight, I saw boxes upon boxes of the new disposable needles and syringes recently introduced to the National Health Service. Glass syringes, in use until then, needed constant washing, then sterilizing, with their inner barrels swabbed with sterile oil to minimize the friction between the barrel and plunger. Disposable needles were exquisitely sharp compared with the then-used large-bore recyclable needles that were dull and needed frequent sharpening. Despite steam sterilization, there was no assurance of their absolute sterility, while the new irradiated disposable needles were definitely germ-free and, thus, safe.

As I was reaching for a 20-cc plastic syringe after picking a mid-sized needle in its shining sterile wrapper, Sister W. walked in.

"No, no, no. This will never do. Each needle costs three pence and the syringes at least a shilling. This is much too expensive for a *medical student* to use. Why we have to accept these fandangle American ideas when we've used glass syringes for years, I have no idea. I oppose such extravagance."

With that, she handed me a wrapped 50 cc glass syringe and pointed to a sterile tray of old-fashioned needles that looked more like harpoons. I selected one while she gave me a red rubber catheter to use as tourniquet. Next, Sister W. pointed to an elderly patient at the end of the middle row of beds. When I reached the bed, two student nurses under the tutelage of a charge nurse had just finished making the traditional tuck technique used for flat sheets at the corners of a bed. They beamed with pride at their accomplishment.

The patient, who smiled feebly, sat propped up, encased in pristine, starched, white sheets. After a brief introduction, I surveyed her arms. They were skinny, with pale, soft skin, akin to see-through silk, and her skin appeared to bruise easily. I placed the tourniquet around her right upper arm, resting across the brilliant sheets, and to my utter glee, a gigantic vein bulged up in her antecubital fossa! Even though I was reaching over her from the wrong side of the bed, the harpoon popped in effortlessly and immediately rewarded me by filling the syringe. My success mesmerized me as I watched in awe. Red blood displaced the plunger, filling the large syringe rapidly. Her bright blood, flowing with vitality, looked pretty against the lily-white background. Suddenly, I realized that the plunger had passed the 50-cc mark and was continuing its downward flow. I hastily remembered the next step: undo the tourniquet and promptly withdraw the needle. I was too late. While I was reaching for my sponge to place on the venotomy site, the plunger plopped out onto the bed. To my horror, a tsunami of red cascaded from the draining barrel, spreading in every direction over the sheets—red on white like a gigantic, horrific abstract painting—just as Sister W. appeared.

"You're a silly boy! Get out," was all I heard her yell.

I beat a humiliating retreat, fleeing as fast as I could, but also feeling just a tinge of delight. *Serves you right, you old bitch, for not letting me use the latest technology!* I suspected that Sir Max would hear about it that evening.

On the days that we did not have an afternoon lecture, I and the five other students temporarily assigned to his service attended his medical rounds. Sister W. usually choreographed them through the ward. His impressive team of house officers, registrars, clinical fellows, Sister W.'s staff, and medical students included an entourage of visiting professors and visiting medical students from Germany, Israel, or the United States. They tagged along to observe his care for his patients. Being at the tail end of this snaking assembly and out of hearing range of the discussion, I chatted with the visiting students from America. They were older than me and better read. After rounds, I engaged them further in conversation to learn about surgical training in the United States. John Rackey did not have that type of knowledge to share with me.

Rounds were a show and tell without much clinical teaching. Sister W.'s staff ensured patients sat upright in bed with pillows fluffed, ready for rounds. Sir Max had friendly and reassuring chats with his patients. In serious cases, Sir Max drew the curtain about the patient's bed. Sister W., her house staff, and the patient's medical student joined him. Cocooned within the curtain, they listened to his discussion, and we waited outside, conversing in a low buzz.

When the curtain opened, the team moved to the foot of the next bed. Sister W. made sure the right person in the entourage stood strategically next to Sir Max. The professor would then expound on the previous patient's condition. We huddled around the wise man, trying to catch his pearls of wisdom, while Sister W. intently followed every word, gesture, and movement with profound nods as if lending credence and gravity to his proclamations. Finding myself at the inconsequential periphery of the group I was barely able to pick up a few words or follow the low-tone discussions.

Stopping at the foot of the next patient's bed and chatting about the previous patient led the occupant of that bed to know more about his neighbor's condition than their own. Worse, this led to the alarming conclusion that they suffered from a different illness than what they might have thought. To remedy these misunderstandings, Sister W. would have to return to the worried patients after rounds and straighten out any confusion.

Sir Max randomly quizzed the students. I waited for him to call upon me to answer some arcane or trivial question whose answer I might know and then dazzle him with my reply. I felt ambivalent because I did not want Sir Max to recognize me as the twit who had bloodied the bed. I would not have put it past Sister W. to telegraph him, "This is *the* student." I wanted him to notice my studiousness so that he would remember me at selection time or when assigning a grade or even to consider my future application as his medical house officer. He did not call on me. What a disappointment yet what a great relief.

Toward the end of the introductory course, which spanned the entire summer of 1965, I still had not clerked my assigned patient. My first attempt was aborted. Since then, I had procrastinated in the hope that time would obscure Sister W.'s memory of my bloody ineptitude. Nevertheless, I was determined to clerk this patient and write her up and to do a great job. I wanted to be remembered.

At the time of my dismissal by Sister W., my assigned patient was in a side room at the end of the ward kept for special cases. On a late afternoon, before the last day of the course, thinking it was past Sister W.'s shift, I walked into my patient's room once more. I found the room festooned with flowers, wreaths, potted orchids, plants hanging from intravenous poles, and vases of enormous blooms, including a bouquet in the V-shaped glass containers used to measure a patient's urine. The drawn curtains partially shut out the late afternoon sun, and the humidity in the room mimicked a hothouse. The entire atmosphere was somber, akin to the mood of a chapel or sauna; only the organ music was missing.

The patient, propped up by pillows, wore a green oxygen mask. That was not enough, though, to conceal her face, steroid-bloated from nephrotic syndrome, a chronic kidney condition causing high blood pressure, one of Sir Max's areas of expertise. Her features were distinctly Indian. The humidified oxygen spewing around her mask plastered her long, oily black hair to her face.

Two nurses were fussing about her bed. On seeing me, they shooed me out. "Later, later, can't you see we are busy?" I retreated once more, thoroughly pissed off. I decided to return early the following morning during shift change. I would outmaneuver them to clerk my patient before my time ran out.

By 7 a.m. the next day, our last day of the course, I made my way up the flight of stairs to the medical ward—students were not allowed to use the lift. I marched down the ward, past the length of fifteen beds, running the gauntlet of the nurses gathered about Sister W.'s desk as they were getting their morning reports. I was relieved that she was nowhere in sight. I strode into my patient's room with a sense of purpose. Entering briskly, I bumped into Sister W., who was carrying a bouquet of a dozen long stemmed red roses in their original cellophane.

"What do *you* want?" she barked.

"I want to clerk my patient," I said in a matter-of-fact tone, showing my defiance.

"You're too late. She died." Talking to herself, she said, "More flowers . . . what on earth to do with these?" She shoved them into my hands. "Here, you dispose of them."

---

Victoria had trained up to London to celebrate the end of the summer-long introductory course because the class planned a dance. She glowed in her long, red dress. I presented her with the dozen red roses.

"Oh, darling! They're lovely." She embraced me and kissed me, admiring the bouquet of wilting roses.

"They are gorgeous! Long stemmed, too! You shouldn't have. They must have cost you a fortune."

"I didn't buy them. I got the roses from a dead patient."

She stared at me in disbelief. Her mood abruptly changed; in a falsetto voice, she shrieked, "A dead patient? How could you give me a dead patient's flowers? I don't want them." Flicking her wrist, she tossed the bouquet into the rubbish bin and stormed out.

Surely, flowers were flowers. Common sense dictated that no medical student could afford a dozen long-stemmed roses.

She didn't know that I was saving to buy her the Goldberg diamond.

The introductory course to clinical medicine opened the door to my lifelong obsession to be a doctor. Fortified by my passion to become the best physician I could be, I sought a progressive teacher on whose medical service I could invest my efforts to acquire sound knowledge. It was my conviction that a first-rate surgeon must initially be a well-learned clinician. Thus, I submitted a list of the medical rotations I wanted to attend in the coming six months. First was the neurological services of Drs. Goode and Stern—a well-seasoned clinician and a young, academically oriented neurological consultant, both of whom loved to teach. And for my second choice, I elected to spend the next three months clerking patients on the chest service. I did not include Sir Max's service. After these rotations, I would be ready to do surgical rotations, the dream that had brought me to London.

# 26

## SHOW & TELL

*A righteous man falls down seven times and gets up.*
—King Solomon, Proverbs, 24:16.

Through the luck of the draw, I started at the neurology firm with six other students, where we would clerk for the next months. Three of us clerked for the brilliant and young Dr. Stern. The other three clerked for the more senior and seasoned Dr. Goode, who headed up the neurology firm. After six weeks, we switched, working for the other attending.

Dr. Stern was attuned to the changing demographics in Britain, where students were not solely from prestigious public schools but also from proletarian families and grammar school backgrounds. He was responsive to this new breed of students' educational needs and social backgrounds: he spoke our language. I later discovered that he was the son of Jewish immigrants and that he was raised in the East End of London and had gone to a non-public school. No wonder I felt a connection with him and why he seemed to understand me. His piercing neurological insight, his dignity, and his invincible reserve captured the essence of a man in a time of social transition.

Neurology was an intellectually stimulating field. I saw cases with Dr. Stern in his clinic, watching him as closely as I did his patients to acquire the skills and attitudes of a physician. We saw patients with epilepsy, nerve palsies, and Parkinson's disease, his specialty. A large number of referrals had global deterioration in their intellectual function without specific memory loss, which we called senile dementia. Among them were dietary-related dementias from alcohol, named Wernicke-Korsakoff syndrome; dietary deficiency of Vitamin B1, or hypothyroidism; and dementia from the third stage of syphilis.

I read about these diseases, along with their symptoms and signs. We heard about the patients' social settings and how they and their families coped with personal adversity. I learned how to greet patients professionally, listen to their medical complaints with empathy and erudition, scientifically sort and prioritize their ailments, and then come up with a meaningful working diagnosis that would often lead to a treatment. I read extensively about the subject matter as well, so my knowledge horizons expanded exponentially.

When not in clinic with Dr. Stern, we were assigned to clerk his ward patients. Of the numerous London medical schools, UCH students were the only ones encouraged to write our clerking notes directly into the patient's chart. I inscribed the comprehensive medical history, the results of my examinations, and commented on laboratory tests or X-rays before concluding with my differential diagnosis and proposed treatment plan. I signed my name clearly with great professional satisfaction and then printed "medical student."

I looked forward to reading my attending's critique. Time and again, I looked for marginal remarks. Surely, my notes were not so perfect as to merit no corrections or comments. I began to wonder whether anyone had read them. Annoyed, I scribbled, "Piss! Piss! Piss! Shit! Shit! Shit! Fuck! Fuck! Fuck!" in the middle of my notes, then waited for admonition. None came, proving my theory that our annotations were merely an exercise.

Most of the patients we saw in Dr. Stern's clinic were referred for consultation by GPs whose busy practices were within the geographical vicinity—primarily north London. As I gradually discovered, a percentage of the GPs were UCH graduates. Dr. Stern read aloud their hastily written referral notes, which would elicit a murmured comment as he recalled the impressions that he had formed of them when they were students. After consultation, he returned the patients to their GPs' care, followed by a letter outlining the patient's diagnosis and management.

We saw some remarkably complex and interesting cases. One case exemplified Dr. Stern's superb clinical acumen. A thirty-seven-year-old violinist in the London Philharmonic complained of headaches. When he hit the highest note—the 8C harmonic register, which was bowed on the uppermost rafter of his violin during Paganini's "Fantasy for G String"— the note vibrated and was not clean. Dr. Stern's eyes lit up. He immediately knew that there was a lesion, which he described to us as "likely a tumor," and where it was anatomically located in the brain. Subsequently, he told us that it was indeed a small brain tumor—a low-grade midline chiasmal glial growth—and that the violinist had an excellent prognosis once the tumor was removed. Sure enough, after brain surgery, when the patient resumed his virtuoso performances, he heard and played the note with absolute clarity.

Although Dr. Stern was reserved, there were humorous moments when we accompanied him on bedside rounds or in-house consultations. To test the integrity of the seventh cranial nerve that alters the muscles of facial expression, he asked a patient, "Show me your teeth." The puzzled elderly man pointed to a glass of water beside his bed containing his dentures. Another time, while taking a general history, he asked a patient, "How are your waterworks?" meaning his urinary tract system. The obligingly talkative patient suddenly hesitated and looked at him blankly. It turned out that he was the inspector at the local waterworks.

I found myself drawn to Dr. Stern. I admired his composure, his mannerisms, and his approach toward patients. He was charming, and his patients seemed to worship him and hang on his every word. I emulated him and sensed a hint of mutual liking —approval so vital to young medical students in the throes of metamorphosing into physicians. Years later, when I was an attending physician, sometimes, I swear, I heard his voice in mine.

There was a striking difference between the teaching style of Drs. Goode and Stern. The former seemed worldlier, with a broader knowledge of the literature and history of neurological diseases. For example, he received a letter asking him to see a patient by the name of Bellringer, who had developed muscle weakness and paralysis in his hands. He asked us if we knew what caused these symptoms. Did the patient's name perhaps suggest a diagnosis?

We did not know. He began to relate the history of leprosy, a disease affecting the skin and nerves and that was caused by infection of the indolent and slow-growing mycobacterium leprae, a close cousin of mycobacterium tuberculosis. This organism attacks the nerves of the extremities, leading to loss of sensation and making the patient more prone to injury of the fingers and toes. It also attacks the mucous membranes, resulting in deformity from tissue loss to the nose and mouth, causing hideous facial distortions. In past centuries, leprosy was thought to be highly infectious, and lepers were forced to ring a bell that they held in front of themselves to warn others as they walked toward them. Although we never saw the patient, who did indeed have leprosy, I well recalled this lesson when presented with a patient suffering from leprosy when I visited India several years later.

Halfway through the three-month rotation, Professor Goode invited me to attend Thursday's clinical pathological conference at London's premier neurological establishment: the Institute of Neurology in Queen's Square. I was pleased that Dr. Goode had invited me to accompany him to this weekly clinical pathological conference. He sat in the first row of the semi-circular amphitheater among his gray-haired peers, and I took a seat with the post-graduate students, many of them Americans, toward the back. The smoothly worn oak seats reflected their time-honored use, while the various initials carved into the desktops revealed the self-importance or boredom of a past generation of aspiring neurologists.

On this occasion, the patient was an American college student who was wheeled into the packed auditorium; he was seated upright on a gurney, gazing about and facing a sea of inquisitive, murmuring faces. His neurologist stood slightly behind him and began to present his case in a monotonous on-and-on drone, barely audible in the hushed and airless room. While mumbling, he slowly produced a starter's pistol, pointed it into the air, and fired it. The patient slumped backward onto the gurney, fast asleep. The drowsy audience was jolted.

The diagnosis of narcolepsy was apparent to the clamorous house. A person with narcolepsy has the propensity to fall asleep, particularly when startled suddenly. The gurney was rolled out as the audience settled down. The dilemma presented to the experts was as follows: the college student's driving license had been revoked in the United States based on the neurological diagnosis of narcolepsy, and he was seeking their weighty opinions in his effort to overturn that decision.

The issue was debated with great passion and at some length. I became lost in some of the arguments that followed— erudite views mainly expressed by the senior faculty seated in the front rows. I was still disturbed by the crassness used to dramatize the diagnosis and wondered whether the patient had been forewarned.

On the way back to UCH, Dr. Goode mentioned that this extreme form of showmanship was not unusual at Queen's Square and that this particular trick had been used several times before, perhaps justified by its didactic value. I was not sure I agreed with his ethical point. Was I just young, uninitiated, and naïve? I did not voice my opinion, grateful that he had taken me along, and mindful of his final evaluation of my activities at his firm. However, he asked me if the young man should have his driving license reinstated.

"That's a complex question. It depends on where the patient lives, where he will be driving—in a rural or city environment—who will be sitting with him, and if he is expected to encounter an intense stimulus, like gunshots, on a regular basis. It's like drivers with epilepsy or diabetes, wouldn't you say?" He looked over, smiled, and nodded.

In neurology, we solved medical mysteries based on the neurological symptoms and signs that patients presented. They were fun, intellectual, and detective exercises. Apart from prescribing medicines to some patients, it was disappointing not to see quantum improvements in their conditions. This left me with a sense of frustration, and although I briefly flirted with the idea of specializing in this field, it would have conflicted with my personality. The immediate results of surgery were more appealing to me.

I realized then that most students go through the various

medical disciplines, rejecting the fields that least appeal to them. Medical school was the acquisition of general medical knowledge that led, by the process of elimination, to a physician's specialized career path. At the end of four or five clinical years, most students knew what they liked and wanted to do when becoming a doctor. At the time, internal medicine was a show-and-tell discipline—one limited by the most modern medication to alter a patient's disease or even save their life.

In contrast, even in the 1960s, surgery was a field where the surgeon directly intervened to enact a cure. I yearned for action.

# 27

# NIGHTS IN CASUALTY

*A bellyful is a bellyful.*
—Francois Rabelais

W ith Victoria overwhelmed with her own studies and her evenings tied up preparing for her exams, I found action in the Casualty/Emergency Department dealing with emergencies of every kind. Every free evening and on weekends, I would show up after dinner. Shirley was the senior house officer in charge. She recognized that Casualty was not a rotation for students but tolerated my presence, maybe because she had been the previous student president of the Physiology Society when I appeared on the scene and took over her responsibilities. My regular appearance gradually made me an unquestioned fixture.

In examining surgically sick patients, primarily those complaining of abdominal pain, I began to formulate my identity by putting on a surgeon's mantle. The head nurse, with Shirley's nod, allowed me to do this while awaiting the surgical house officer, who was proverbially "on my way down from the ward." I realized that the mysteries of the abdomen held greater enjoyment for me than watching a 12-inch black-and-white TV in a smoky, stuffy students' common room at the Annex. At the time, most medical students smoked as they watched a series or sport programs. Neither smoking nor passively sitting and watching TV interested me.

I considered the abdomen the most exciting domain in the body. At the time, most patients were not obese. I would examine the patient's belly with great care, imagining with delight that I could feel the stomach, liver, spleen, colon, appendix, and perhaps even the ovaries. As I mapped out during my topography adventure with Victoria, the abdomen is a substantial three-dimensional cavity extending from the level of the nipples to the anal sphincter. Despite my morning in DRD's clinic performing sixty rectal examinations, I had no moral authority to do this uncomfortable procedure on a casualty patient. I regretted the absence of potentially valuable information, perhaps essential in making a diagnosis. To insert a finger up the rectum is to gain access to knowledge about diseased organs within the abdominal cavity, for as the dictum goes, "If you don't insert a finger, you'll put your foot in later."

I soon became quite good at distinguishing diseases such as pneumonia and cardiac failure, which masqueraded as abdominal pain, from the conditions that might need urgent surgery, like perforated stomach ulcers, acute gallbladder disease, bowel obstruction, and torsion of the ovaries or a testicle. I learned that severe abdominal pain lasting more than four hours was most likely due to a condition requiring an operation. "Common things occur commonly," as the aphorism went.

Acute appendicitis was the most frequent inflammatory condition, remaining among the most challenging of diagnoses, primarily because it mimics almost every other inflammatory disease of the abdomen, such as pancreatitis, colitis, and inflammatory bowel disease. There was no definitive investigational test for it. I enjoyed examining acute abdomens and making the diagnosis of acute appendicitis. I envied the house surgeon who got to operate on the patient and always sought confirmation as to what was found. In the near future, I would be the one wielding the knife. I could not wait.

In my mind, I decided who needed an urgent operation, who should be admitted for observation, and who to send home. When Shirley could spare a few minutes from her busy workload, we would compare my diagnosis and disposition plans. Initially, my evaluated decision assessments score was poor—around twenty percent—but then, I had no authority to order the tests that might have refined my determinations.

Shirley suggested that I acquire and read the definitive book on diagnosing and treating abdominal pain—*The Early Diagnosis of the Acute Abdomen* by Zachary Cope. It was a delightful surgical classic full of sound knowledge and key diagrams. Gradually, the averages of my decision score rose to seventy percent or so—it was never perfect. The  enigma of abdominal pain was sufficiently subtle.

When in doubt, an exploratory laparotomy was done, which was considered the pen-ultimate test to figure out what was going on. If I was lucky, in the absence of the busy surgical house staff, I would be asked by the on-call surgeon to help as first assistant. The pathology I saw and the operations I witnessed never failed to awe me. I was, as the saying goes, like a kid in a candy shop, touching every organ and wondering with reverence about the Lord's most beautiful arrangement.

I made sure that I would be allowed to do a part of the operation: just something as simple as double clamping a vessel and dividing between it, holding the scalpel and excising part of an organ, or persuading the surgeon to let me close the abdominal incision. With each operation, I felt that I was becoming less awkward with the instruments and more familiar with the surgical culture.

A negative laparotomy—no abdominal causes for the pain —was perfectly acceptable, for it ruled out potential deadly diseases such as pancreatic, hepatic, and ovarian cancers. In these cases, I seldom got to bed before midnight. When I did, it was with a sense of contentment.

On slow nights, I hung out with the nurses, listening to their general chatter. I learned that they had a Rolodex with the names of frequent patients who came into Casualty feigning abdominal pain to get a shot of narcotics. Mostly, they were drug addicts who visited central London's eight different Casualty Departments on a rotating basis to get their fix. After ruling out a physical cause for their abdominal pain, recognizing their plight and name from the Rolodex, most nurses were sympathetic and obliged "the wreck of a human specimen," as one referred to them, giving a shot of either pethidine (Demerol) or morphine. There was a subset of nurses with less compassionate views who injected sterile water. In my opinion, this was preferable to the patients who received a 3H colonic enema —high, hot, and a hell of a lot of soapy water to discourage their future visits. I reflected on this approach for some time and concluded that such punitive measures were an abuse of power, even in the absence of a drug rehabilitation program. But there was nothing I could say. I was a mere student, and Casualty was not a sanctioned rotation.

On other nights, the head nurse asked me to sew up lacerations instead of calling the busy or tired surgical house officer. I loved it. Together with a staff nurse, I took the patient to one of the minor Casualty theaters. The nurse showed me how to done the sterile gloves and how to stay sterile throughout the procedure. After cleaning up the area with sterile saline then Hibiclens, she instructed me on the use of either 1% or 2% Lidocaine local anesthetic. This, she said, depended on how long I estimated the procedure was going to take—the higher concentration for a longer anesthesia time. The question of whether I should use with or without epinephrine that constricted blood flow to the wound's edges depended in part on the depth of the wound. On distal limbs or digits or patients who were elderly or had diabetes, she suggested not using epinephrine.

Wounds that were tears through tissues were highly contaminated. She showed me how to debride dead tissue using a scalpel, removing foreign bodies, thoroughly irrigating them with saline to obtain fresh bleeding, and loosely wrapping them. I was then to see the patient again in forty-eight hours and reassess the wound. If it looked clean, she suggested closely approximating the wound edges to prevent infection. For lesser wounds, the nurse taught me which to sew shut and which to steri-strip to get the best cosmetic result. I learned how to hold the suture instruments, how to place the suture material through the tissue, how to tie a knot using instruments, and how to hold a pair of scissors to cut above the knot. I witnessed the discharge instructions given for post-injury wound care and tried to see the patients when they came back for their follow-up.

After such one-on-one teaching, I felt I was proceeding in my journey to becoming versatile with operating procedure and instruments—particularly the scalpel. I felt the joy of being able to help a patient.

One evening, the head nurse told me to assist the new senior house officer who had replaced Shirley. He was a young Casualty officer who probably had graduated three years ahead of me and was assigned to sew up a nasty head laceration on a drunk in Minor Theater, Room 3. I loved to improve my shaky sewing ability. I was sure he would supervise me closing the wound.

I opened the door. The patient lay snoring on the treatment

table, covered from head to toe with sterile blue drapes. Behind the door, the senior house officer was passionately gorging himself on a nurse. While he was kissing her neck, she threw back her head; her body arched forward, eyes closed in divine bliss as he worked his way down her shoulders. His hands caressed her under her disarrayed uniform, skirt hitched up to her waist, his hand fumbling with her pink panties. Eros's silent show of ardor continued for what seemed like a fascinating forever. I gaped wordlessly, frozen in the doorway, too flabbergasted to speak. She slowly opened her eyes and saw me, gasped, and screamed silently. Pushing him away, she adjusted her clothes, and scurried out of the room.

The senior house officer turned on me and yelled, "Get the fuck out of here, you sod." The patient stirred under the drapes. "What? Me? Have you finished?"

# 28

## CUT & SEW

*Surgery is the red flower that blooms among*
*the leaves and thorns that are the rest of medicine.*
—Richard Selzer MD

W hen I was seven and living with my Oma and Opa in Germany, a newly arrived refugee from occupied Soviet East Germany challenged my authority as leader of my roaming street and forest gang. Despite him being eight years old—a year older than me—I was the gang leader by virtue of having lived there longer. I knew most neighbors and was very familiar with our neighborhood streets and the secrets of our woods. He disagreed, arguing that age was the criterion, which would make him the leader. An argument led to a fistfight, and we duked it out, surrounded by jeering boys. My right punch split his left eyebrow. Blood flowed down his face, and he started to cry as the other boys screamed, "He's bleeding! You've blinded him!" Terrified, I ran to Oma's and hid under her bed. Gulnar tried to coax me out by telling me that I had done the right thing, but I cried and felt guilty for hurting him. I retained leadership of the loosely connected neighborhood boys, for he wasn't allowed to play with us again. I was the king of my domain.

In my last year of grammar school, I became queasy in biology dissection and left the room. My classmates laughed at me, knowing I was hoping to become a surgeon. I next drew blood the summer before attending medical school when I shot a rabbit while hunting on a friend's farm in England. At nineteen, I was horrified to see the poor animal struggle and die, and I vomited. How would I handle operating on humans?

As a medical student, surgery gave me a sense of being—of worth and self-esteem—and it provided the very status mentioned by my headmaster when he told me: "You need a label . . . some professional title." Surgeons operated on the sick, healed them with decisive accomplishments, and often managed to perform great operative triumphs. They had intimate knowledge of the body's structure and pathophysiology and were motivated and compulsive people with a sense of accomplishment. The words "operating theater" said it all—wasn't that where the drama was?

The lottery system that established how students choose their surgical firm once more worked in my favor: I got my first three months with Professor Pilcher, as I'd hoped. He primarily operated on lung cancer and diseases of the esophagus. My second three months would be spent learning general surgery, working with Mr. Hart, a senior consultant and surgeon.

In England, a very formal distinction is made between physicians addressed as doctor and surgeons addressed as mister. Its evolution goes back to medieval times in the 1400s, when barbers were members of the Company of Barbers Guild. Although they did not have a medical degree or formal qualification, they were frequently called on to perform surgery. The symbolic red- and white-striped barber's pole still seen today signifies clean and bloody bandages.

The Barbers Guild eventually merged with the Fellowship

of Surgeons to form the Company of Barber-Surgeons, whose members retained the title of mister. Although members of the new guild were required to serve a surgical apprenticeship, their social standing in the class-conscious society remained firmly on the lower rungs. When summoned to a respectable home, they were obliged to use the tradesman's entrance. Physicians required university training to receive a medical degree and were thus titled doctor. When summoned, they used the front door.

In 1745, dropping the name barber, the surgeons formed the Company of Surgeons, which eventually became the distinguished Royal College of Surgeons in 1800. Surgeons were also required to receive university training to obtain a medical degree and their title of doctor. After surgical training and passing an examination, successful candidates become Fellows of the Royal College. The title of doctor is then dropped, and the surgeon reverts to the historically distinguishing label of mister.

In the academic world, Professor Pilcher, the chair of surgery, was the top dog of the surgical pyramid. Mr. Hart was the number two man. The house officer, who had just finished medical school, was at the bottom of the organizational chart. In between the top dogs and the house officer were a cadre of junior and senior house officers with one  or two years of experience and registrars-in-training like residents in the United States, along with six medical students who were greatly valued because of their hunger to learn and willingness to work endless hours.

Patients admitted to Professor Pilcher's surgical unit fell into two major groups. There were those with lung and esophageal cancer, who were primarily operated on by

Professor Pilcher, and then, there were others with general surgical problems—hernias, varicose veins and gastrointestinal diseases. These fell into the purview of Mr. Hart, who assigned them among his cadre of registrars.

The house officer "ran" the service, often referred to as the firm. He admitted all the patients, clerked them, knew everything about them, prepared them for surgery, assisted in as many operations as possible, allocated medical students to assist the registrars, cared for the patients post-operatively, and, somehow, found the time to eat and sleep. A good house officer was a diplomat. He did the bidding for and sorted out ego-related problems of the other house officers and registrars and smoothed over slights among them and the nurses. The medical students who rotated through the service every three months were invaluable to him, for they were his to use as personal servants to make his life easier, all in the glorious, altruistic name of surgical education. He organized us and weaved our daily chores into the structured routine of the firm. The discipline was a top-down deferential hierarchy.

The house officer on Professor Pilcher's firm appreciated me as one of the more dependable medical students, one who was enthusiastic to learn. My craving to be in the operating theater and to assist on cases provided him an excuse not to assist, giving him time to be on the ward and attend to the many issues that cropped up. I became a convenient substitute for him, but I accepted this role and loved every moment.

Alas, it left little free time to spend with Victoria, which we both lamented, particularly because surgery was of greater intensity than medicine. Fortunately, she was also quite busy with her second-year bookwork across the street at University College. Canterbury Hall was some distance away, preventing any spur of the moment quickies, because by the time she made her way to the hospital, my momentary slack time could have been filled with some urgent surgical issue. We managed to squeeze out sufficient time at the end of the day to nurture our deepening love and satiate our increasing physical cravings.

Professor Pilcher and Mr. Hart, along with their registrars, had designated the outpatient clinic and operating days. Predictably, a wave of patients came the day before surgery, usually appearing on the ward after lunch. The house officer assigned me first to clerk the professor's patients on the understanding that I would assist by relieving him during some of the professor's prolonged operations. I was thrilled at the prospect of scrubbing and being the second assistant instead of observing outside the immediate field, simply standing on a stool behind other surgeons, barely seeing the action over their shoulders.

When I finished clerking the professor's patients, I would clerk the general surgical cases, despite knowing they had been already worked up. I took my time to get a history and do a physical examination, focusing primarily on the system or organ attracting the knife. I was aware that time precluded a more intimate chat about their lives, jobs, and interests, as was typical during my six months of medicine. The more dependable and efficient I became, the more patients and tasks the house officer assigned to me.

Some of my fellow students did not savor the knife or the long hours and tended to disappear on the pretext they were attending the afternoon lecture, seminar, or clinic. This meant more patients for me to clerk and, consequently, to assist in the theater activities I relished. Post-operatively, I helped the house officer, learning by doing, caring for the patient with dressing changes and other minor tasks until they were discharged.

Professor Robin Pilcher was a tall, slender man with narrow lips, a thinning crop of white hair, and exuberant auburn fuzz growing from his ears. He was soft-spoken, warmed to people readily, and was well-versed in general and thoracic surgery.

His demeanor depended on whether he was operating or doing rounds. In theater, he was a quiet leader. There was no chitchat or bantering. He started his cases at 9 a.m., which meant the knife went into the patient at 9 a.m., and the surgical crew, including myself, had to come at 8 a.m. to get everything ready, although I mainly stood around observing—learning by seeing and through osmosis.

I was an enthusiastic sponge, absorbing every aspect of surgical culture: surgical behavior, traditions, and technique. I remembered a line in Mother's letter from Cairo to her parents in Hamburg that was written on my birth. She boasted about me as an infant, saying, ". . . he sees everything, nothing escapes him, he hears everything, he smells every-thing, loves every animal . . . in short he loves life and the world."

Professor Pilcher insisted that he alone would position the body on the table. He placed the patient pillowed comfortably on their side, with their arm in a special hang-retractor placed over their head. This "just so method," as I called it, afforded maximum exposure to the chest wall and the underlying diseased lung, providing full access to the operative field. Because of the critical function of lungs in providing air to the patient, when Professor Pilcher operated on one or the other, the anesthesiologist placed a double-lumen tube through the mouth, down the main windpipe and inserted one lumen into each lung, allowing separate ventilation. When Professor Pilcher operated on the left lung, the right was aerated. He could then deflate the left lung to remove it or cut out the diseased part.

When he heard of my interest in becoming a surgeon, he invited me to scrub. I joined him and his registrar in the ante-room. We scrubbed our hands and arms in silence, sharing soap and water. In the meantime, his circulating nurse quietly washed and painted the patient's chest wall with antiseptic pink chlorohexidine. Then, she widely draped off the operative field.

On entering the room, the gowned and gloved professor moved into the sterilized surgical field. He operated swiftly, with élan and assurance. He incised the chest wall from the armpit to the mid abdominal line in one swift, clean, curvilinear cut. Leonardo DaVinci would have admired the artistry. The registrar assisted him to control the skin bleeders, remove a rib, and insert the spreader to part the surrounding ribs.

My first view of a lung nearly made me heave. The deflated organ looked like a large, black, dried sponge. My thoughts went back to when I attended Birchfields County Primary School. As a member of Roy's gang, we smoked Woodbines in the back alleys, feeling empowered and like adults. It was difficult *then* to imagine how nicotine caused the lung cells to become cancerous, a notion too far into the future to even entertain. I was relieved that I had coughed and wretched with each puff, forcing me to stop. I could proudly state that I started smoking at nine and gave it up by ten—only flirting with smoking on special social occasions to appear sophisticated.

The gray-white neoplasm was solid and invaded the spongy black lung tissue in tendrils. As he explored the extent of the mass, Professor Pilcher looked up at the illuminated chest X-ray to correlate the findings as he began to cut out the cancer. His long-term scrub nurse, who had operated with him for years, stood by his side. She shared his view of the operative field and was one step ahead of him. She anticipated his every move, gently slapping the specific instrument into his outstretched hand at just the instant he needed it. He never had to ask for an instrument or draw his gaze from the depth of the wound.

I observed Professor Pilcher's skilled and seemingly effortless moves with wonder. I watched, mesmerized, as he cut out the lobe of the lung that contained the cancer and over-sewed the cuff of remaining normal tissue, tied off blood vessels and branches of the trachea with the help of his registrar, the first assistant who stood opposite him. His movements were graceful, never wasted or superfluous. I imagined that every surgeon was as dexterous and expert and hoped that one day I would be too.

Given the tight operative field, I stood next to the registrar —four engaged bodies surrounding an anesthetized one: the professor and his scrub nurse on one side and on the opposite side the registrar and me. As the second assistant, I had a front row seat to the action. I played a small part and felt needed and important. I held a retractor in one hand to keep the surrounding tissues from collapsing into the wound and obscuring my colleague's vision. In the other, I grasped a sucker, clearing pooled blood about the operative site or sucking up smoke from the Bovie burn that coagulated the bleeders. With my attention fixed on the operative field, I would try to guess Professor Pilcher's next move to avoid awkwardly disturbing their well-rehearsed routine.

A team of nurses hovered in the background during the three- to four-hour operation, each with a specific and essential task, contributing to the safety of the patient and the procedure. One kept track of the number of sponges used within the chest to confirm that an equal number were removed from the wound and that none were left in the patient. Once Professor Pilcher excised the diseased tissue, he retired from the table, and the registrar moved to the professor's position. I now stood opposite him, ready to assist in closing the long chest incision. Before we closed, we heard the circulating nurse's loud pronouncement: "Sponge count is correct." Only then did the scrub nurse hand us needle holders loaded with wire to bring together the ribs. We used a cotton thread to close the soft tissues of the chest wound, and then, the scrub nurse placed the dressing.

While we closed the chest incision, Professor Pilcher wrote a brief operative note, went for a cup of tea, and waited for his next patient, who was anesthetized in an anteroom. The turnover time between his cases was barely long enough for me to go and empty my bladder. Gradually, I became a familiar face at the operating table and was rewarded by closing the wound with the scrub nurse while the registrar attended to administrative duties. I found these long incisions tedious—they took forever to close. The boredom and my lack of patience precluded my becoming a thoracic surgeon; closing long wounds did not suit my temperament.

On rounds, Professor Pilcher always wore a starched long white coat, which matched his pale complexion and white hair. His demeanor was different from his top-dog performance in the theater, and he saw not only his own, but also every other patient on the surgical unit. Professor Pilcher's rounds contrasted in style from Sir Max's, seldom taking more than two hours. I began to understand that a distinct beginning and a definitive end characterized surgery, whether during an operation or on rounds. Instead of the Sister running the show, Professor Pilcher's house officer was the point man. His trailing entourage was smaller and much more compact, consisting of Mr. Hart, a mid-level registrar, occasionally a senior house officer, the unit's medical students, the Sister, the charge nurse, and a couple of student nurses. On rare instances, there were visiting professors.

The house officer presented the established or post-op patients, detailing their progress during the past twenty-four hours. Professor Pilcher listened intently, frequently nodding in agreement and asking a few insightful questions. He discussed each patient's overall condition, quietly addressing the group. The conversation occurred around the patient's bedside. I, together with the other students, listened intently and seldom contributed.

Each patient admitted to the surgical ward had an affliction and a predictable operative course. In contrast to my experience in medicine, surgery was more concrete, never nebulous. I felt very much a part of the team, like being a rowing crew member aiming for a common goal and outcome.

When the patient was a new general surgery admission, the student presented the case, giving a succinct history of symptoms and a proposed operative plan. Professor Pilcher turned to the patient sitting up in bed or in a bedside armchair and greeted them warmly, showing genuine concern for their well-being. He looked each patient straight in the eye and told them in his soft reassuring voice about their upcoming operation, their expected progress, and the anticipated date of discharge. The Sister stood close by with her notebook, marking down the instructions concerning their care, making these straightforward teaching and work rounds. With the new patient's permission, either Professor Pilcher or his senior registrar would show us how best to examine the pertinent surgical organ—enlarged thyroid gland, abdominal mass, inguinal hernia—with the curtains drawn about the bed.

When it came to showing the students how to examine the abdomen, he made a major show of it: He carefully asked the patient about the onset of the pain, its character—constant, waning, getting worse, foods that brought on the pain, area it was radiating to (back or abdomen)—what relieved it or made it worse, their appetite, their weight loss or gain history, last bowel movement, and, when relevant, the menstrual history as it related to the pain pattern. He listened to their lungs and heart to exclude pneumonia or an irregular heartbeat that may be referring pain to the abdomen. He started to talk to them about daily life to distract them while intently watching their face for signs of pain induced by his palpitations, which generally started in the opposite quadrant of the belly where he suspected the disease and pain was. In areas of high suspicion,

as suggested by a history such as the gallbladder, gastric/duo-
denal ulcer, diverticulitis of the colon, or appendix, he palpated
gently. In the area where the pain was greatest, he palpated the
quadrant progressively deeper and saw the grimace reflected
on their face. He'd suddenly release the pressure and hear
them groan from the pain. Satisfied with the exam, he would
exclaim this is where we will make our cut and remove the
disease, but only, he then reiterated, after we have done a rectal
examination. Once more, learning how to examine an
abdomen made me feel that I had taken another step toward
my goal of becoming a surgeon.

I learned a great deal of nuanced information. In the
evening, back in my dorm, I augmented the new practical
knowledge I had seen that day by reading about the disease
processes, its pathophysiology, and the proposed operation. My
fallback surgical books were my bibles: Bailey & Love's *Short
Practice of Surgery* and the two volumes of Maingot's *Abdominal
Operations,* while my prayer book was Zachary Cope's the *Early
Diagnosis of the Acute Abdomen.*

Quite often, when a woman facing a diagnosis of breast
cancer was upset or weepy, the professor would stop rounds
and perch on the edge of her bed. He gently held her hand to
reassure her and engaged her in hushed talk, out of our earshot
but in his Sister's presence, all the while stroking the patient's
arm. He only rose when he had calmed and settled the patient's
concerns. The scene reminded me of the pictures I saw as a
child in Germany during Sunday school of Jesus laying his
hands on the sick. The effect was similar—calming and reassuring—no matter how dire the message. It impressed me so
much that I subsequently adopted this "hands-on therapy."

I wondered if Professor Pilcher knew the 1880 poem by
Spencer Michael Free, "The Human Touch." A poster of it
hung on the back of the toilet door in the Annex. I read it every
day while I sat there, weather permitting. No one knew who

had hung up the placard. The author was an American surgeon at Johns Hopkins. Watching my newfound hero, I found myself reciting it in my head:

*Tis the human touch in this world that counts*
*The touch of your hand and mine,*
*Which means far more to the fainting heart*
*Than shelter and bread and wine.*
*For shelter is gone when the night is o'er,*
*And bread lasts only a day.*
*But the touch of the hand*
*And the sound of the voice*
*Sing on in the soul always.*

That poem and Professor Pilcher's stroking never failed to remind me of a rare pleasant memory associated with Mother. Occasionally, she told me that when I nursed as an infant, I sometimes stroked her arm. My pleasure came not from the story itself, but from understanding that Mother held a pleasant memory and took the time to recall it for me.

# 29

# MR. WINTERBERRY

*The only time you run out of chances is when you stop taking them.*
—Anonymous

During the initial week of my surgical rotation, I was assigned to Mr. Winterberry, my first surgical patient. I began with his chart, which I found unusually thick. Flicking through it, I read numerous consultations from urologists, pulmonary physicians, and cardiologists. The occasional surgeon's notes were brief and to the point, requesting that the patient be transferred from the surgical service to the radiation ward to complete his radiation therapy. The counterargument made by the radiology consultant was that he was a surgical patient by virtue of having had a biopsy of his rectal cancer. The consultant went on to argue "my service is merely providing *a therapy* . . . *a service* in the form of daily radiation and that by virtue of his cancer, he is a surgical patient and should stay on your service!"

There seemed no resolution. The surgeons saw his biopsy as *the operation* and his main therapy as *the radiation*. As such, in the surgical mindset, he was occupying a surgical bed and was not an acute case. A tug of war concerning his housing was being waged in the public chart, whereas I felt that a couple of minutes in a meeting—or even a phone call between Professor Pilcher and the head of radiation therapy—would have cleared up the confusion and made the patient more comfortable. The dictum I learned to apply throughout life is treat the patient and not the disease. Its corollary was administrative issues should not result in the patient being shunted between services. Take responsibility for a patient.

Although he was not considered a patient with a major surgical problem, I learned that there is no such thing as patients with minor problems. In my mind's eye, the same as the patient's, every operation is a major operation because all operations carry inherent complications that are considered major by the patient, even though the surgeon may dismiss them as minor.

Mr. Winterberry was deemed a chronic patient and, thus, was not seen regularly during rounds. Fearing I would have to present him at any moment, I made it my business to see him. His bed was the last one along the wall in a distant corner of the open surgical ward. He stared at the ceiling; his face unreadable. We made brief eye contact when I introduced myself, and he seemed mildly curious. I was another new medical student, emulating the tone and stance of the others who had treated him during the course of his long illness. He resumed his distant gaze, and I remained standing, my hands in the pockets of my short white coat. I asked to clerk him, and he agreed, remaining flat in bed with the covers drawn up to his chin.

He had rectal cancer; its biopsy was *the* operation, and the cancer had not been removed. I did not yet know that squamous cell cancer could be treated by radiation to preserve the anal function. To break the ice, I asked him his occupation.

"I'm a stockbroker, a trader."

To put him at ease, I said, "Oh! I spend each Sunday after-noon reading *Barron's,* following a couple of pretend investments."

He perked up. "What sectors are you interested in?"

"Mining—primarily Rio Tinto Zinc and DeBeers. To learn about market behavior, the best companies . . . I'd love to someday make a few pennies on the side."

"I can help you." As he raised himself onto his right elbow, the blanket slipped, revealing his pajama top. "How much would you like to invest?"

My £700 annual scholarship covered tuition, living expenses, books, and food. I had no spare cash. I tried to keep a sense of professional decorum, replying, "Five pounds."

"Well, I can't charge you a commission." Following a long pause, he added, "Are you willing to lose it all?"

Lose it? Was he kidding? I had put myself in an awkward position. Five pounds sterling represented my entire week's food allowance. I pictured myself going hungry or inviting myself to Victoria's place or to other friends to get meals throughout the week. What would I tell them? I had gambled away £5, not on the horses or the dogs—on the stock exchange! They would laugh. Lose it? Of course not!

But what I came out with was, "Yes," as if I lost £5 every day. To a surgeon, it would be small change.

"Well, come back tomorrow. I'll see what I can do."

The next afternoon, I reluctantly handed Mr. Winterberry a £5 note, wondering if I should ask for a receipt. He told me about several mining companies, none of which were familiar to me. Throughout his lively discourse, he took on facial expressions that probably approached his usual self and gestic-ulated broadly. In a sparkling, conspiratorial voice he asked, "Do you know of Hampton Gold Mining Area? It's an Australian mining company prospecting for gold in the Outback. Rumor has it that they've found uranium. They are listing at one shilling per share, currently selling at three pence. Your £5 would give you eighty shares. If the rumor is true, the shares will rise and you will make a tidy sum. If it's false, you'll probably lose your money."

I was following along until he mentioned the "R" word. Rumor? Did he say rumor? I dealt with facts. He slipped my £5 note into his pajama breast pocket, and with that, I lost one week's subsistence. I had acted foolishly, pretending to be nonchalant about the whole matter to save face. I excused myself to join teaching rounds. When I returned several hours later to perform my clerking, his bed was empty. Thinking he had gone to radiation therapy, I inquired at the nursing station.

"Discharged," was the reply.

Discharged? I had trusted my gut feelings based on five minutes of interaction. I had not clerked him or retrieved my £5!

A large manila envelope arrived two days later containing a multicolored certificate with a wide border of fancy curlicues, embossed with Hampton Gold Mining Area Company. I was the owner of eighty shares. I hid the envelope among my books, feeling acutely embarrassed at my folly.

# 30

# LOCUM HOUSE OFFICER

*Surgeons must be very careful, When they take the knife!*
*Underneath their fine incisions, Stirs the culprit—Life!*
—Emily Dickinson

A few weeks into the rotation, the house officer—the unit's Intern/"Man Friday"—took his two-week mandatory holiday. Professor Pilcher suggested I might wish to apply for the locum opening, temporarily performing the house officer's duties. Such an offer to be a locum—an acting intern—indicated to me that my hero thought I was sufficiently capable and knowledgeable to take on the extra surgical responsibility and to run his service. Surgically, I was moving up the ladder toward my ultimate goal of mastering the knife—it was a prestigious offer.

I accepted. It would be a great privilege and a wonderful learning opportunity, hard as hell, but a career booster. Would Victoria understand my loss of time with her? She understood that I'd be kissing life outside of the surgery world goodbye for the duration, and she supported my ambition.

The next morning, Professor Pilcher introduced me to the

ward's Sister and charge nurse now that I was a team member. I felt both regarded me with greater respect. After riding up the lift to the theater together, he assigned me a locker and introduced me to his operating nurse. The honor made me feel like a son.

Performing the house officer duties resulted in two changes. The first change of status involved acquiring the unit's pager. Now, all who wanted something done or had a logistic problem could get hold of me. I would be at everyone's disposal, at the cost of my freedom.

Because one of the surgical dictums was "shit flows downhill," I was paged almost constantly to solve all manner of problems related to my thirty patients. A slave to my pager, I answered to relatives, commands from nurses, and calls to outpatient clinics and to the operating theater. In between the pager squawking, I removed sutures, started IVs, inserted nasogastric tubes, discharged patients, digitally disimpacted constipated patients, and worked down the endless scud list of countless instructions given to me at rounds. I responded to calls to see an emergency patient in Casualty and calls by the night shift nurses. I prescribed meds for pain, sleep, and constipation, and I wrote daily progress notes. I waffled down dinner and lingered for a while on the toilet.

When the occasion allowed, I read up on new surgical procedures in preparation for the next day's surgery, hoping I'd be allowed to operate, not only assist, despite lacking my primary fellowship. On my "on-call" days, it wasn't unusual that I had to first-assist with an emergency operation late into the night, fighting hunger and fatigue, and then snatch some sleep before starting the next day's operating schedule and work routine. On slower days and slow weekends, I had the luxury of a cup of tea and a biscuit at 4 p.m. with a leisurely glance at the newspapers, fighting fatigue and resisting the temptation to nod off in the common room.

The second change involved moving into the house officers' quarters on University Street. My room put me in quick walking distance to the ward, theater, and Casualty via a connecting underground tunnel that surfaced in Casualty. The house officers' quarters adjoined the private wing of UCH and was located across an intersection from the Duke of Wellington, a cozy public house where doctors congregated for a ploughman's lunch and exchanged requests for consultation on patients while they drank a pint of the best bitter—the modest consumption of alcohol was socially accepted.

My comfortable on-call room on the fourth floor was small, with a sizable southeast window and a sink. I usually had an early bath or nap and then joined my fellow surgeons and physicians at eight for dinner, which was served in the all-male house officers' quarters. Rank and hierarchy were tradition, so there was a high table for senior house staff, who were served first, and then the remaining staff were served dinner by middle-aged Irish grandmother types who addressed everyone as "love." Small talk was the rule: "war stories" or requests for consultations to see other patients and render an opinion. Fearing an emergency would rob me of further sleep, I'd excuse myself and skip dessert, climb up to my room, and drop into bed, exhausted.

Wives, fiancées, and girlfriends were prohibited from entering the house officers' living quarters, nor were they allowed to partake in the communal dinner, could not have a cup of tea while reading the papers in the common room waiting for their man. Even wives were not allowed to spend the night with their husbands. That privilege was deferred to my off-duty night, when I generally returned to my dorm in the Annex, sleep-deprived, too exhausted and hungry to care about sex.

Tentative inquiries concerning the reason women were not allowed were met with astonished stares.

"Don't you know?"

"No."

"No one told you?"

"No!"

In whispered tones, the answer came. "Well, it's rumored it was Sir Max's decision. You see, his mama apparently wants her son to marry a nice Jewish girl. She doesn't approve of his companion, the Sister on the medical ward, who is Church of England." I understood the cultural and religious objections attributed to Sir Max's mother because they were similar to Egyptian or Muslim traditions. I was skeptical of the rumor, but short of asking either party, I had no way to verify this information.

The tunnels under London's busy streets conveniently connected UCH, house officers' quarters, and the hospital, and I suspected that the unusually dim lighting in the entrance hall at the University Street entrance to the doctor's quarters was no accident. An elderly beadle wearing bulky hearing aids stood guard at the entry. He had been deafened by a long night of thundering artillery barrage as a sapper during the battle of El-Alamein in Egypt. With his attention willfully focused on the lively goings-on at the Wellington, ahead of him, he deftly avoided seeing the estrogen-driven young women emerge like lemmings in waves from the tunnel behind him and quietly ascend the stairs to their waiting lovers as dusk transitioned into darkness. When I pressed him, pushing a refill of another pint while we propped up the bar once when I saw him at the Wellington after his "nth" pint of bitter, he confessed, "They pop up from the underground passages into the dimly lit entrance hall and disappear . . . behind my back. I swear I never see or hear them."

At 7 a.m., a cheerful maid would knock, saying through the closed door in her sweet Irish accent, "One or two teas?"

"Two teas, please" resulted in a cracked-open door through

which I received a tray with two cups of tea, a small pot of milk, and two biscuits. How thoughtful, except by then, most nurses and medical sweethearts had descended into London's subterranean tunnels, off to start their shifts—except Sundays, when the wonderfully convenient and considerate tradition of delivered tea lapsed.

Since I now ran the service, my duties increased, and my sleep decreased. Professor Pilcher's expectations were the same as when I was a student although my perspective as an insider had changed. In the morning before surgery, as we walked between beds, he chatted quietly in a convivial tone with his staff. His decisions were definitive yet conveyed an air of humility. He told me, "The more you see, the less black and white a case becomes." Unlike Sir Max, I suspected he did not seek eminence; his reward was the trust and privilege of operating on his patients.

I was responsible for all the admissions, and I made a point of clerking everyone so that I knew their problems before the operating schedule. I wrote up my notes, got the pre-op blood tests, chest X-ray, EKG, and obtained the operative consent. With the aid of a cheat sheet, I ordered the appropriate number of blood units to be cross-matched for the operation.

On Professor Pilcher's elective cases, he expected to find the chest X-rays on the viewing box for his review when he entered the operating room bright and early, so I retrieved these films from the radiology department the night before surgery. My habit irritated the radiologist, who could not find them to dictate a report the next morning. The professor took me aside to teach me a systematic way to read my patients' chest X-rays —a lifelong gift.

As Professor Pilcher's house officer, I routinely became the first assistant and learned to close chest incisions and to place underwater seals to help the collapsed residual lung tissue expand fully when the patient took his first post-operative breath. Once Professor Pilcher left the room, the nurses and the registrar helped me write the post-operative orders. I was the happiest when I was in the operating room and part of a surgical team—wanted and needed.

One day, halfway through the two-week locum, Professor Pilcher told me between operative cases, "I'm an old-time TB surgeon. I first started cutting in 1930. The advent of the anti-TB drug streptomycin means that medication rather than my scalpel will cure patients in the future." His face showed a moment of sadness. "I'm as dead as a dodo," he said, adding, as if talking to himself, "'Tis good timing, because I'm retiring." He did not say when.

I could not relate to what he said. To me, he was a surgeon despite the march of progress. The thought that medical advancement could make a highly skilled person obsolete seemed unfathomable. Would this happen to me someday?

I was beginning to grow into the role of a surgeon. I made rounds with the Sister, acquainted myself with the post-operative patients, listened to their complaints, attended to their dressing changes, and adjusted their medications. The value of the ward nurses was incalculable; they seemed to know every medical and social detail about each patient. They made my job—my harried life—more manageable.

When my fellow students met me, a new dynamic occurred: they greeted me with guarded respect. Had the ordained title of locum house officer changed me? Or had my conduct toward them changed? Yes, but not for the reason they might have thought. Although I remained the usual guy, courteous and friendly, my direct patient responsibility had uncovered my knowledge limitations as a physician and made me humble. My learning curve of diseases, medications, and operations and my skill for prioritizing tasks and patient care, including the diplomacy of interpersonal relationships, had risen exponentially.

We generally ate in the cafeteria but I discovered that lunchtime on the ward was a prized moment. When the food trolley appeared shortly before noon, able patients rose from their beds and took seats at the long dining table that was placed in the center of the  ward. The communal meal enhanced patients' appetites, encouraged them to socialize with one another, and quietly allowed them to compare their condition to their neighbor's— perhaps concluding that they were not that bad off after all.

After lunch, Professor Pilcher, the Sister, and I did work rounds. Professor Pilcher was kind and understanding, an excellent physician, an outstanding surgeon, and a man of compassion. We stood at the bed of a sick and emaciated patient who suffered from cancer. To ease his severe pain, he was regularly given an elixir called a Brompton Cocktail, a potent concoction consisting of morphine, heroin, cocaine, gin, and chloroform water—an English idiosyncrasy. I tried to impress the professor by saying that I had started the patient on penicillin because he had developed aspiration pneumonia. I was proud that I had showed some initiative.

As we moved toward the next bed, he stopped me and gently placed his hand on my arm. "Wouldn't it be kinder to let this patient slip quietly away due to his pneumonia, given that he has inoperable cancer of the esophagus?" I cancelled the order. Four days later, the elderly man died peacefully in his sleep. I never forgot the lesson: do not treat the disease. Instead, treat the patient with compassion and common sense in the context of the disease.

Professor Pilcher and I met twice in his modest office at the top of the medical school, where he addressed me with less formality. He insisted that as a surgeon, I view not only my X-ray films, but also the pathology slides of all the tissues removed from a patient. He told me not to rely on a written report—another valuable lesson. He then produced a few tissue slides of fixed lung cancer and a well-used microscope. Peering through the lens at the slide, he pointed out the characteristics of the "Indian file" arrangements of cells defining the most common type of lung cancer: squamous cell. A successful operation, he said, was one where the resected edge of the specimen—the surgical margins—were well clear of the disease. I peered down and appreciated what he was trying to teach me.

He familiarized me with the five criteria for measuring mistakes in surgery: an error in diagnosis; an error in procedure/or operative technique, when the wrong operation is performed; an error in management, when inappropriate treatment is given; an error in clinical judgment, when the surgeon misjudges the many aspects of surgical care; and the patient's disease—where no matter what treatment is given, the patient dies. He did not need to expand on the meaning and implications of each; I nodded in understanding.

"Have you heard of Professor Robert McWhirter's work?" he asked.

"No."

"He is a friend of mine, a very clever man. He is the Forbes Professor of Medical Radiology at the University of Edinburgh." He indicated a northerly direction with his hand. "He has some interesting results concerning women with breast cancer. Instead of the standard operation of radical mastectomy, where the woman's chest is grossly deformed, Professor McWhirter's results show an equal five-year survival rate for simple mastectomy and radiotherapy, a procedure that preserves the woman's breast, female form, and her dignity."

He paused to allow the effect of his statement to sink in and then added, "Many surgeons have refuted his methods and results, but they were published in the *British Medical Journal* and are convincing." He looked about and found a reprint. "It makes for interesting reading."

I took his offering, feeling he was sharing a secret instead of giving me a lesson. I had seen a radical mastectomy, which was akin to an amputation of a woman's chest wall. The procedure was grotesque: the diseased breast was removed, along with all the underlying muscles and lymph nodes. The surgical thinking at the time was that the more tissue that was removed, the greater the chance for a woman's survival. Professor Pilcher was telling me of a less-deforming approach. Through these informal surgical discussions, perhaps he was trying to take me under his wing. But at the time, I admired the man too much to presume he would be interested in mentoring me. He was "The Professor," holding the equivalent position in surgery as the famous Sir Max did in medicine.

I left his tiny office with McWhirter's reprint in hand. I read it. Professor Pilcher would never know how he had directed my future life. I found McWhirter's study and data sufficiently convincing that breast surgery became an important aspect of my later surgical career and the practice of lumpectomy, radiation, and chemotherapy the mainstays of my surgical practice. I abhorred more radical breast surgery that deformed women's bodies and negatively affected their psyche.

# 31

## CUT & GROW

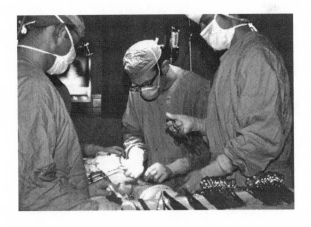

*Every surgeon carries within himself a small cemetery,*
*where from time to time he goes to pray.*
—Rene Leriche

D uring my second week of the locum, Mr. Hart
became the acting head of the unit. If there was a
reason for Professor Pilcher's sudden departure, it
did not trickle down to me. In one week, I would revert to my

lowly student status. I would lose the surgical house officers' privileges of carrying a pager, sleeping in a cozy bed, and being served tea in the morning and a free dinner at night. I would miss what I enjoyed most—the trappings of responsibility and the privilege of serving patients that accompanied the title of surgical house officer.

Mr. Hart was probably in his late forties, with fair thinning hair that he continually brushed off his forehead, revealing engaging blue eyes adding to his boyish good looks. He seemed friendly, was approachable to his patients, and enjoyed having students about him because he took each opportunity to teach at the bedside or while operating. After general surgery, his acquired specialty was vascular. His junior registrars and the house officer tended to avoid operating with him, assigning students to assist him for reasons I had yet to fathom.

Our first case together was a pneumonectomy, a left lung removal in a farmer admitted with extensive chronic, necrotizing aspergillosis—an unusual fungal infection that had failed to respond to medical treatment. We speculated that he had contracted it from dealing with hay. Although it was the same surgical team in the theater as with Professor Pilcher, the operator was Mr. Hart. I was the only assistant. The patient was perhaps a leftover from Professor Pilcher's list. This was the first time I saw Mr. Hart operate on the chest, and the procedure did not go as smoothly as when I was the second assistant to Professor Pilcher and the senior registrar.

We encountered a great deal of bleeding from adhesions of the diseased lung attacking the chest wall. Mr. Hart had to scrape the necrotic lung tissue off the diaphragm, the thin bellow that separates the chest from the abdominal cavity. Wherever Mr. Hart touched the tissue, it bled. Despite the chronic oozing, we managed to control it using pressure pads and electrocoagulation, though it never entirely stopped. I first heard the surgical dictum "all bleeding eventually stops" muttered by Mr. Hart.

Unlike Professor Pilcher, Mr. Hart constantly chatted away, making it difficult for me to concentrate on my tasks. Suddenly, he looked up at me and said, "Did you see *Darling* with Julie Christie? Wasn't she gorgeous? A well-earned award for Best Actress, don't you think?"

"Yes. She's a heartthrob."

"And wasn't her performance as Lara in *Doctor Zhivago* magnificent? He"—referring to Omar Sharif—"is Egyptian, like you."

"Yes." I took the remark as a compliment.

Then, he looked back down at the operative field, and our interlude ended. He removed the entire dark greenish diseased lung. It looked worse than any cancerous tissue I had previously seen, and it smelled putrid. We placed underwater seals and a suction drain to allow the remaining chest to expand. I helped close the long incision of the chest wall wound and, as before, found it tedious. After five hours, the bleeding had almost stopped although a persistent trickle came out of the drain—more than I was accustomed to seeing in Professor Pilcher's post-operative patients, which was probably due to the inflammatory nature of the disease.

Before he went home, Mr. Hart and I checked the patient, who had been moved to a modified room—the forerunner of a recovery room. A specialized nurse fussed over the patient as we stood together, opposite her. He was awake and physiologically stable but continued to ooze into the drain from his chest. Mr. Hart estimated the flow was at least the equivalent of one unit of blood, so he ordered a further transfusion. Turning to me, he said, "Keep an eye on him."

I could now use the lift with impunity, given my elevated status of locum house officer. I descended to the ward from the top floor and started to admit new patients, which took several hours. By late afternoon, the nurse paged me. "Can we give your patient another unit of blood?" With my admissions taken care of, I rode up to check on him. He sat propped up in bed, but to my dismay, he looked pale and continued to lose a significant amount of blood from his chest into the drain. With more experience, I would have ordered a coagulation panel to check if the patient had a deficiency of a clotting factor or if his platelets were low. In either case, he could have been given specific infusions to correct the deficit and assist in slowing or stopping the bleeding. As I was hanging the patient's fifth unit, Mr. Hart entered.

"Why haven't you telephoned me?" he said, clearly alarmed. "Can't you see he is actively bleeding? There is no use giving him more blood, is there? You should have called me. He needs reoperating to tie off some fucking bleeder."

He was right, of course. Not knowing better, I had been negligent. Had I been lulled into a false sense of security by the dictum that all bleeding eventually stops?

By 8 p.m., and without dinner, we operated again. Counter to our expectation of finding one major bleeding source, we found many small bleeding points on the inside of the chest wall, consistent with the inflammatory process. We electrocoagulated the sites extensively for more than an hour, such that the inner chest lining looked charcoaled. Indeed, my face and hair smelled as if I had been to a barbecue. We left a much drier operative field the second time around. We closed the patient's chest, and at about 11 p.m., we returned him to the makeshift recovery room with minimal oozing. It was another late night.

On my way through the tunnel to my sleeping quarters, I analyzed what had gone wrong. In looking at the situation critically and recalling Professor Pilcher's lesson, I had witnessed an error in judgment in accepting the amount of oozing blood and an error in management in waiting before reoperating. I was partly to blame because I became so absorbed with admissions that forgot to frequently check on the patient during the critical post-operative period. My take-home messages were to leave the operative field *dry*; in surgery, bleeding never resolves spontaneously, and nothing gets better on its own. And deflecting the blame on other team members was not endearing. I had a lot to learn, and Mr. Hart had much to teach me.

Mr. Hart was delighted to have me around and went out of his way to instruct and teach me, remembering that I was only an acting house officer—in reality, still a medical student. I wanted to look up to him and to believe he had surgical expertise I could admire. He had an air of silent bewilderment, which I first took to be a sign of scholarly thoughtfulness. As the week went by and I worked more consistently with him, my impression changed. I began to see his hesitancy to handle complex surgical conditions. I wondered if he was less experienced than his academic position suggested and worried that one day, I too might be in a situation beyond my operative capabilities.

Following the stormy chest case, we operated on patients with hernias and varicose veins. Hernia repair was among my favorite operations. The anatomy was agreeable, the results were pleasing, and the outcome was immediately gratifying. These cases went relatively smoothly.

Knowing that Professor Pilcher would retire and that Mr. Hart would most likely be the new chief when I would graduate in two years, I was determined to cement a bond between us during this locum. My strategy was that when Mr. Hart looked up from the wound during every operation while I was his locum, it would be my face he would see, my voice he would hear, and my assistance he would receive. The other surgeons at the firm would have others to assist them. If I could become his house officer on graduating, it would launch my surgical academic career beyond my wildest dreams.

I had to become accustomed to Mr. Hart's constant nervous nattering, masking his lack of what medical students sought in senior surgeons—silent confidence. He also occasionally made snide and unnecessary remarks to the younger nurses when they made a mistake. Senior nurses and registrars were visibly absent from his cases.

Late one afternoon, I accompanied Mr. Hart to an in-house surgical consultation on the medical ward. A fifty-four-year-old man presented with several weeks of constipation, although he could pass gas—indicative of an incomplete large bowel obstruction. After establishing his basic history, we examined the bloated abdomen and reviewed a recent barium enema X-ray. The patient had a long, partial narrowing, a three-inch segment, of his right colon extending to the transverse colon, the segment that crosses from the liver on the right to the patient's left side.

The tumor must have been a long-standing, slow-growing cancer partially constricting the gut wall—an obstruction akin to a dam. Inside the narrowed segment were several impressive cannon-ball-sized fecaliths—round masses of feces. Upstream, the colon was distended, and beyond the cancer, the downstream colon was collapsed, small in diameter, and empty of fecal material. Mr. Hart had the patient transferred to the surgical service with the diagnosis of partial large bowel obstruction. He pronounced that the patient needed an elective operation to remove the obstructing cancer.

After dinner, I read in my favorite textbook, *Abdominal Operations,* that given the extent of the tumor growth and its likelihood of developing a complete obstruction, an emergency right hemicolectomy was indicated to remove the cancer and the accumulated fecaliths—the size of which brought to mind elephant dung. The surgeon's mindset ought rightly to be one of "emergency operation." The primary indication implied by the text was the imminent threat of a complete blockage that would compromise the bowel's blood supply and lead to perforation, with spillage of stool into the abdominal cavity, resulting in sepsis and, eventually, death.

The surgery presented a number of challenges. Because the diameter of the colon—the lumen—was different on either side of the tumor, it was not recommended to join the two ends of the bowel after cutting out the tumor, particularly in the presence of uphill stool. Because of this, the right side of the colon up to the mid-transverse colon should be removed, requiring the surgeon to create an ileostomy on the right side and form a colostomy from the transverse colon. Six weeks later, when the emergency had passed and the patient had returned physiologically to normal, a second operation to sew together the two ends of the GI tract would restore bowel continuity. I read and reread the account, forming pictures in my mind. Abdominal surgery was fascinating, and this is what I wanted to do for the rest of my life. I volunteered to assist Mr. Hart.

Once the patient was asleep, I prepped and draped the huge dome of his belly. Mr. Hart pointed to it and said, "It's all that stool and gas accumulated behind the constricting cancer." I agreed. He made a small midline incision into the abdominal cavity and expressed his surprise to find a big apron of fat popping out. He cursed. The patient was fatter than we both had estimated. He extended the incision so that it went from the lower end of the chest to the pubic bone. Liberated from the confinement of the abdominal cavity, more fatty tissue, attached to loops of air-filled guts, floated and spilled out onto the field.

Even with my inexperience, I could see this was not going to be an easy operation. As the stress mounted, so did Mr. Hart's chatter. He cursed the patient for being so fat, for his greed, for his gluttony, and on and on, deflecting his surgical difficulties onto a sick person. Finally, he found the constricting tumor and resected it, including a cuff of the large bowel on either side. I assisted as best I could, all the while feeling that a more experienced helper, like one of his junior registrars, would have made his task easier.

To my surprise, he did not do a right hemicolectomy, which would have removed the accumulated fecaliths. I silently watched him sew the two ends of the large bowel together, thinking that he must know what he was doing. When he finished, he seemed pleased at the resulting doughnut-like ring where the two ends of the bowel joined. To my eyes, the junction of the two bowels was not that much larger than the original cancer-constricted channel. This was not the recommended operation.

Several large fecaliths remained on the right side and would have to pass through the narrow man-made junction. Pointing to the cannonballs of stool, I asked, "How are these going to pass through?" He looked up at me for a silent moment and in a very vexed tone said, "These are soft stool, they'll just slide through and stretch it." He did not attempt to test his assumption. I had my doubts. Annoyed with me, he asked, "Don't you have a 2 p.m. lecture to go to?"

Had he forgotten I was now his locum house officer and not a medical student? I did not argue. Feeling I had transgressed some line of authority, I broke scrub and left theater. The scrub nurse would assist him to close the incision. Full of shame, I felt like an idiot as I changed my clothes. I had embarrassed him by questioning his procedure. Maybe I had not read about the correct operation. Still, I remained concerned by what he had done. It defied common sense. I could not see how such large hunks of stool could squeeze through such a narrow and fresh connection. I had read that the standard operation called for the conventional two layers of sutures to join the hollow tubes, but he had used only one. I was ill at ease the rest of the day and felt no better at bedtime. It seemed an error in judgment, and I cursed myself for not making a stronger case and advocating for the patient and the commonsense operation.

For the next couple of days, I did not scrub with Mr. Hart, keeping myself busy with work on the wards. During rounds, I stood at the back of the student crowd and let the Sister take the lead. From time to time, Mr. Hart would glance at me.

Three days later, the patient died. As locum house officer, I had to present a thumbnail sketch of his illness to my peers and the other faculty surgeons on the firm who had assembled to watch the lunchtime post-mortem. Mr. Hart was absent. I limited myself to the patient's history and physical findings, avoiding my interpretation of the events during the operation.

Professor Smith, the professor of pathology who had done the post-mortem examination, pointed into the open abdomen of the corpse and addressed the assembled congregation. "The unusually large fecal accretions, bigger than any I've previously seen, could not possibly pass through. What I understand from the operative note was a primary anastomosis. Under such circumstances, perhaps in this situation, a standard operation, such as a right hemicolectomy, should have been considered." Hearing this brought me no comfort.

During the operation, I had worried about this very result and now was guilty for not pressing my point at the time. I was angry at Mr. Hart's dismissal of me. I ceased to hear Professor Smith and was seething with fury, feeling I was complicit in my patient's death. This case was an important one for me because my judgment had been correct. What would have been lost if Mr. Hart and I had discussed my question? He would have had a chance to reassess the situation, thereby preventing this unnecessary death. I came to understand that the hallmarks of a good surgeon were the three As: affability, availability, and ability. Surely, the latter point should have ranked higher.

My locum house officer stint ended with the return of the well-rested unit's house officer. I gladly relinquished care of my surgical patients to him. For a long time after that, while I was still a student on the surgical service, I avoided Mr. Hart, and perhaps, he avoided me. We parted on a less than satisfactory basis.

# 32

# THE CHRISTMAS BALL

*Any fool can cut off a leg—it takes a surgeon to save one.*
—George G. Ross

The surgical rotation spanned the Christmas holidays. Victoria and I joined a group of medical students, including Bowtie with his tuba, and went to the Euston and St. Pancras railway stations to sing carols on several evenings. Although I eyed him with suspicion as we stood around in a circle singing our hearts out, I wondered whether he was trying to atone for his hurtful comments. His tuba carried the tune; our weak voices were drowned out by the station's background noises. Finally, cold and unable to attract an audience, we disbanded.

Despite the cost, I bought two tickets to the Christmas Ball —my first. Not having a dinner jacket, I rented one with all the accessories. Decked out in my finery, I felt very much the conservative British surgeon, well worth the pretty penny I paid for the jacket. All I was missing was a gold watch and chain. Victoria and I would form a foursome with Rory McCloy and his girlfriend. We planned to dance through the night and then follow the tradition of breakfasting at 5 a.m. in Covent Garden, London's farmers' market.

The ball, held about a week before Christmas, was the hospital's premier annual social event. The enormous library, with its polished mahogany flooring, was transformed into a winter wonderland, complete with seasonal decorations, a huge Christmas tree, and a traditional swing band. Both a Caribbean steel drum group and a classic rock band, each in one squash court, took up residence in the basement, offering everyone dancing alternatives. An elegantly adorned refectory served a traditional Christmas meal with Champagne.

My plans matched those of most medical students attending the ball. I would quietly slough off the surgical service in the early afternoon, giving me a chance to clean up and sleep a few hours to get ready for the 8 p.m. evening festivities.

Before that, at around 11 a.m., Mr. Hart sought me out to ask if I would like to help him on a vascular case. He said that a patient had developed gangrene of his left toes and the operation would improve the inflow of blood to his foot by removing the atheromatous plaque. He added that he would be starting soon.

This put me in a quandary. I had not assisted him after the last surgical disaster, helping the junior registrars instead. He must have sensed my ambivalent feelings toward him. In about eighteen months, I planned to ask him for a recommendation to spend my elective period at Massachusetts General Hospital in Boston. Also, if he was the new professor of the surgical unit and replacing Professor Pilcher, I was hoping he would select me as the house officer.

I had never done a vascular case before so I agreed to assist, expecting the operation not to interfere with our plans for the ball. I assumed that Mr. Hart was going to the ball as well because he was applying for the professor's position, and it was a place to see and be seen.

Numerous delays in starting the case allowed me to read about vascular insufficiency to the limbs and the need for an angiogram X-ray with contrast medium to outline the entire arterial tree from the aorta downwards—the main artery going from the heart through the chest and the abdomen to just below the umbilicus, where it divided into two iliac arteries, each going down one leg as the femoral artery, branching out to supply oxygen and nutrients to the feet and toes.

The definitive surgical treatment to improve the inflow of blood to the threatened gangrenous toes was poorly described and beyond my comprehension. This was another reason for assisting that I justified to myself as the delays dragged on into the afternoon. Mr. Hart had spent time in Boston training in vascular surgery. I was venturing into unfamiliar territory, and here was my chance to learn. Inwardly, I was quite excited, although Victoria took the news less enthusiastically as the delays accrued.

Salvaging a threatened limb was an emergency. When I went to find out why there was a delay, I discovered the patient had yet to obtain an angiogram. The radiologist had left to prepare for the ball and was instructing Mr. Hart over the phone about how to get a view of the vessels by taking serial X-rays down the leg after injecting contrast. It was obvious that Mr. Hart had not persuaded him to return and perform this crucial test. The patient also had to be seen by a cardiologist because of the high frequency of arterial disease affecting the coronary arteries, making him a high-risk candidate for a heart attack while on the operating table. I failed to understand why Mr. Hart had not declared an emergency and mustered all the resources necessary to obtain prompt help. Was he a surgeon or a pushover?

To my dismay, the case finally started around 5 p.m. If I had not agreed to assist Mr. Hart, I would be back in my dorm, getting ready for the ball. Instead, I had arranged that Victoria would collect me from the operating theater around 8 p.m. and so took my tuxedo with me to the hospital.

My first surprise after we congregated in the operating room was that no angiogram had been obtained. How would Mr. Hart know the location of the obstruction and where to make the incision in the artery? Was it a narrowing of the artery causing insufficient blood flow to the toes, or was it a clot —thrombus—that had formed elsewhere and shot off down the leg's artery? What about the patient's cardiac status? Perhaps I had read too much, but I saw my surprise matched by the anesthetist's because she would not have put the patient to sleep had she known that X-rays still needed to be taken.

Neither Mr. Hart nor I had scrubbed as the X-ray technician maneuvered the heavy, portable machine over the anesthetized patient. The first shot was over the upper leg, taken a few seconds after Mr. Hart injected contrast medium into the femoral artery at the groin. The procedure was repeated several times, X-rays being taken down the leg to the ankle.

Armed with the plates, the technician left to develop the films in the basement. We hung around in silence, waiting for the results, listening to the beeping of the cardiac monitor, each lost in our thoughts. Twenty minutes later, the results were disappointing: on the first film, we saw the tail of the contrast medium, the second film missed the contrast, and in the third, the contrast left such a weak outline of the vessel that we could barely see it. More time passed as the whole process was repeated without improved results.

Since he saw no major constrictions in the faint and fuzzy images, Mr. Hart's hunch was that the obstruction was higher up. How had he determined this? I didn't dare ask, fearing a humiliating comment. We were going to operate on the vascular tree without a road map. Having examined the toes before the patient was anesthetized, I was not that impressed by the degree of dry gangrene on his left three toes. Could this operation not wait a day, even twelve hours, to ensure the necessary pre-op work-up had been done and that the patient was in an optimum condition? What was the hurry?

After scrubbing, prepping, and draping the lower abdomen and the limb, Mr. Hart made an abdominal incision to explore the left iliac artery in the pelvis. By now, it was well after 6 p.m.; my regrets were growing. When the iliac vessel was located and visualized, the anesthetist injected the patient with heparin, an anti-coagulant, to keep blood from clotting. Mr. Hart placed loops of silk ties above and below the section of the iliac artery that he planned to open, and I cinched them to prevent blood loss. I stood opposite him. My other task was to keep his visual field clear by sucking up the blood spilling out of the iliac incision.

He made an incision, an arteriotomy, into the top of the exposed vessel, through the three layers of its wall, and after I sucked out the spilled blood, we saw its lining. Instead of being smooth, as in a healthy artery, it was ragged, diseased with contiguous, soft, buttery yellow atheromatous plaques that extended circumferentially about the inner lining of the vessel, and for the entire exposed section. I could easily imagine how this revolting fatty stuff had narrowed the artery's lumen. Mr. Hart was pleased. "This is the site preventing adequate blood flow reaching the toes."

He dissected a plane below the cheesy plaques, working on the surface of the middle muscular layer, and scooped out the fatty intima. It was gratifying work because we were getting rid of the diseased lining, widening the lumen of the vessel so that more blood could eventually flow through it. Throughout, he chatted away, telling me—even though he mostly spoke to a scrub nurse—how he had learned this technique while doing his BTA (Been to America) in Boston. Finally, we were moving along with the operation and making up for lost time; the clock behind him read past 7 p.m. As we progressed, I could see that the disease process seemed to extend both above and below our cinched segment, and I began to worry about what would happen next. We had only cleaned and draped a small area of skin about the incision site, not allowing us to easily extend the skin incision.

Mr. Hart, too, began to recognize the seriousness of his predicament. The disease was a systemic process in reality, not a constricting lesion that could be tackled and remediated. Atheroma is a generalized systemic problem that, in this case, likely could have extended below the ankle into the small vessels of the foot or above into the aorta. As he pondered this predicament, the circulating nurse came in with the news that a medical student called Victoria was outside the operating room dressed for the Christmas Ball, inquiring how much longer we were going to be. It was the wrong moment and the wrong message, and Mr. Hart lost his cool. "Fuck the Christmas Ball!" he shouted. "We're trying to save a patient's leg. You can't just leave me here alone!"

We both knew that he required an experienced vascular assistant, and presumably, I was all that would be available on this night. Mr. Hart persisted in his bumbling about, searching for solutions to the surgical quandary. The anesthetist suggested several courses of action I did not understand and that Mr. Hart irritably dismissed. The lack of an angiogram delineating the extent of the disease in the leg vessels contributed to Mr. Hart's paralysis. At this stage, I felt equally frustrated because I was useless in this very complicated situation. We were both trapped. Despite his ongoing efforts, there was no visible improvement to the blood flow to the leg based on conventional clinical signs of pinking and warming of the foot or the finding of a bounding pulse at the ankle. The vessel kept clotting off beyond his dissection, aggravating the situation, despite the additional anti-coagulants reluctantly given by the anesthetist.

It was almost 10 p.m., and we were all fatigued. I would have loved to leave, but I could not. By now, I knew that even if he became the professor of surgery, I would not want to work for him. He was the antithesis of Professor Pilcher in character, confidence, and competence. Things seemed to go wrong with each complicated case. I now understood why the house officers avoided him.

The ball appeared to be a factor in his failing to secure adequate help, but based on my limited operating experience with him, I knew that he was disinclined to seek assistance or advice. Why had he not phoned a colleague and asked them to join him or requested an intraoperative consult, the need for which should override pride? For any number of reasons, he did not, and at the time, I did not know of this option.

The operation turned for the worse: the vessel he had explored began to clot once more when he tried to flush it with blood by loosening the top cinched silk on the iliac artery. In an irritated voice, he told the anesthetist to give the patient more heparin to prevent clotting.

"I've already given him the maximum for his body weight," came the young woman's reply. In a last-ditch effort, he passed an intravascular catheter down the leg artery, inflated the balloon with saline, and pulled it back into the arteriotomy wound, retrieving a lot of fresh clots. Next, he injected heparin directly down the vessel in an attempt to prevent further clotting and blockage. Discouraged, he closed the arteriotomy in the iliac artery. Shortly after 10 p.m., he started to close the incisions he had made.

I heard via the grapevine that the patient's toes were ultimately amputated. Vascular operations seemed to go on and on, precisely because blood vessels clotted, even when the patient was given adequate anti-coagulant medication. I much preferred abdominal operations—as the saying goes, "shit does not clot." Vascular surgery was not a field I would pursue.

I reluctantly left the theater when Mr. Hart dismissed me. He claimed he would complete the case. I was amazed that Victoria had waited and didn't chastise me. Her radiant face lifted my spirits, even through my exhaustion. I could have gone straight to bed but I wanted to be with her. I could not have had a better mate. I showered and quickly dressed.

We met up with Rory and his girlfriend in the library. Rory and I bought drinks for the four of us and ascended to the catwalk that wrapped around the upper parts of the library. We admired the beautiful decorations enhanced by falling snow outside and the graceful couples in holiday finery waltzing to the orchestra below. Too tired to consume alcohol, I pulled out two old books, slid my Champagne glass deep into the recess of the bookshelf, and replaced the volumes. I would have enjoyed going down to the basement to dance to the fast and loud beat of the guitar-shrieking youths mimicking the Beatles and Rolling Stones to vent my frustration at another failed operation, except I was weary and Victoria was too self-conscious for that kind of dancing.

In the early morning hours, the four of us walked to Covent Gardens in our finery. The produce workers were starting their shift by having their 5 a.m. breakfast. We joined them. Exhausted from our all-nighter, we joined the early morning commuters and took the tube back to our respective rooms, where we slept for a few hours before getting back onto the medical treadmill.

## 33

## BENEATH THE RAFTERS

*Illustration by Jonathan Marrow FRCS, FRCEM*

*Sex is hardly ever just about sex.*
—Shirley MacLaine

B y early June 1967, the next two major rotations were in obstetrics—eight weeks at University Hospital and the other at another hospital. I caught up with my first assigned patient, a Mrs. Coleman, on her way from the maternity ward to the labor room. Professor Brant, who looked unusually young for his position, settled her into the reclining labor chair, feet apart with knees partially in the air and covered with a sheet. The attending midwife held her hand and offered her sips of iced water, despite the slow IV drip in her left arm.

Mrs. Coleman was a 32-year-old American executive from New York who already had a three-year-old son delivered by C-section at an East Coast U.S. hospital. She and her family had recently transferred to London. The Professor of Obstetrics was a lean and indefatigable man, with a BTA to Yale, who took a particular interest in Mrs. Coleman's delivery. He had determined that Mrs. Coleman's dream of a vaginal birth was achievable. Mr. Coleman was at work, and in keeping with the customs of the time, he was not allowed or encouraged to be with her during childbirth. The portly registrar in scrubs and white Wellington boots kept his distance.

Back home, Mrs. Coleman explained, a vaginal delivery after a C-section was contra-indicated. The presence of a previous uterine scar was perhaps the weakest point of the contracting organ. The scar could not stretch and dilate in concordance with the rest of the uterus; it might rupture, endangering the fetus and mother and leading to an emergency salvage operation. "Once a cesarean, always a cesarean," was then the rule in the United States. Mr. Brant, who drew many plaudits from his patients, was standing next to Mrs. Coleman in his long white coat. He addressed me, saying, "There are several case reports in the obstetric literature of successful vaginal deliveries following a LSCS."

"LSCS?"

"Lower segment cesarean section," the midwife said.

"That's the horizontal incision placed between the top of the cervix and the uterus to extract the baby and placenta," he added in a lowered tone. The midwife nodded. It was now obvious to all that on my first day of this new rotation, I knew nothing about obstetrics. Continuing in his reassuring voice, Mr. Brant said to no one in particular, "We are going to proceed with each stage of Mrs. Coleman's labor with great care, aiming for a natural vaginal birth, although we will be ready to operate at a moment's notice to ensure a safe delivery." Mrs. Coleman anxiously agreed. In his clipped Queen's English, his eyes fixed on me, he added, "I want you to follow her progress and report any unexpected changes directly to me." Patting Mrs. Coleman's hand, he walked away.

Mrs. Coleman's cervix had dilated rapidly to three or four fingers. Each contraction was accompanied by loud groans and pleas for pain medication, more so than her stoic English sisters, who labored in the adjoining rooms. She even entreated to be "knocked out," despite knowing that the meds might diminish the force of the contractions. Between them, she complained of backache and rolled onto her side so that I could massage the point of greatest discomfort.

I felt helpless, merely timing the contractions, rubbing her back, and trying not to be in the midwife's way. Knowing I was a novice, Mrs. Coleman ignored me, apart from gripping my arm forcefully with each contraction, and instead pleaded for medication from the midwife. Her eyes lit up when she saw that her repeated entreaties stoked my anxiety. I was unaccustomed to patients in overt pain during my surgical rotations. She could see my sympathy and perhaps thought I was more likely to be her advocate despite my novice status.

"How many deliveries have you done?" she asked.

"This will be my first."

"Nurse Emma, stay with me," she shouted out immediately.

She was right. I was green behind the ears and on call on my first day. There had been no time to wade through the obstetric text before being summoned to the busy labor ward. I would also miss the afternoon O-B lecture.

Earlier that morning, after a refectory breakfast, knowing I was on call for the next twenty-four hours, I had gone up to my overnight cubicle in UCH's rafters. Just as I dropped off my bag with toiletries, a change of clothes, and a couple of obstetric textbooks I intended to read, my new pager whined and vibrated, dancing like a disoriented cockroach on my bedside table.

I telephoned the operator. "Yes, hello, this is . . ." I hesitated. Should I call myself Dr. or Mr. Meguid as a student on the unit?

An authoritative voice said: "Meguid. You're wanted in the labor room right now." It was the O-B registrar. We had not met, but I hoped we would get along. It was 9:15 a.m.—no time to open my books or to even find the toilets.

The midwife gloved and stepped forward, spread Mrs. Coleman's knees with her elbows, and inserted her goopy jelly-covered hand into Mrs. Coleman's vagina under the white sheet. Mrs. Coleman groaned.

"Good news. You're coming along nicely," the midwife said cheerily.

"Mr. Meguid, here," she continued, "will time your contractions and report to me. Your bladder is full and we'll drain it. Take some deep breaths and close your eyes for a while." With that, she too left the room but soon returned with a large kidney dish, a blob of lube, a sterile catheter, and a box of latex gloves. "Glove up and drain her bladder," she said to me.

"Have you done this before?" asked Mrs. Coleman.

The midwife jumped in. "He's done surgery . . . a very skilled student . . . you're lucky he's on today."

On seeing me sit before her knees, Mrs. Coleman reflexively snapped them together and placed her hand over the sheet, covering her crotch and thighs, crying out with an oncoming contraction. I waited while the midwife said, "Pant, pant, don't push." After it passed, I pried Mrs. Coleman's knees apart. She insisted on keeping the sheet, which covered her thighs and hung over her knees. I crawled under it like an old-time photographer, edging my way forward in the tight space and pale light. I could hardly breathe. Her pale inner thighs resembled cold wax, or the vertical white walls of the narrow Corinth Canal, as I moved toward my goal. Then, I stopped, confronted by a horrific, unexpected sight. Her labia were shaven, swollen, and marble-like; not a hair remained, only the semblance of black stubbles and a stark-naked ugliness. Was this the "thing" that James Laughlin described as "the altar of love, the sacred place, the locus of the sacrament where the ritual of the mysteries is enacted?" It looked obscene, irreverent, vulgar, and not one bit sexy.

The image was worse than a flash view I had of Mother after her bath years ago when I had pushed open the ajar door. Seeing me, she covered her front with a towel and turned about to pick up the bathmat, inadvertently giving me a full view of her private anatomy.

The stifling enclosure made me lightheaded.

"How are you doing down there?" came the midwife's voice.

"All right," I replied hesitantly and, with eyes closed, advanced the catheter between Mrs. Coleman's labia. I came up for air.

"How much urine came out?"

"Nothing."

"Let me see. Mrs. Coleman, try to relax and drop your knees further apart for me. Let's pull this sheet up a tad so we can see what's going on here."

Mrs. Coleman closed her eyes, turned her head away from us, clutched the bed railing, and obliged.

The midwife sat on the stool between Mrs. Coleman's thighs and exposed the labia. I had inserted the catheter into the vagina. She looked up at me, slowly raising her left eyebrow for a few seconds. "Get me a fresh catheter," she said.

"What's going on down there?" chirped in Mrs. Coleman nervously.

"Nothing much. You're doing fine. I'm familiarizing Mr.

Meguid with the anatomy. Don't worry. Let me know when a contraction is coming."

"This is all very embarrassing," said Mrs. Coleman.

"Keep taking deep breaths—in through your nose and out through your mouth, each time relaxing more. Now, Mr. Meguid, this is her clitoris, below that her urethral opening into which the catheter should go, and as you can see, below that is the gaping vagina. Somewhere up there is Mrs. Coleman's lovely baby about to come out."

I felt pale.

"Is it coming?" asked Mrs. Coleman.

"Very soon. Remember to pant when you get a contraction."

The midwife slickly inserted the catheter into the bladder and golden urine flowed immediately into the large kidney dish.

"Are you feeling better?" the midwife asked.

I nodded.

"Not you, you clod," she whispered, winking at me. "Mrs. Coleman? Are you feeling better?"

"Yes."

The midwife got up and removed her gloves. I sheepishly did the same.

"Now, Mrs. Coleman, close your eyes and try to rest. You'll need your energy. Your contractions will start again. I'm going to check on my other patients. Mr. Meguid will be staying with you."

I moved up to the railing, "Mrs. Coleman?" She opened her eyes. "Would you like some more water? Shall I refresh your facecloth?"

"OK."

The midwife returned with an IV bottle labeled oxytocin. "I'm going to piggyback this solution onto your regular drip."

"What is it? Oh no, not oxy, is it?" Mrs. Coleman concluded that her progress had stalled.

"Yes, this will stimulate your contractions and help you along."

"Does Mr. Brant know? I mean, am I failing at this attempt? Is it necessary? Perhaps I should have a C-section after all. I want to talk him."

"It's quite natural to help a patient along. I spoke to Mr. Brant, and he ordered this to strengthen your contractions. He's about to lecture the students, and then, he'll come and see you." The midwife turned to me and said, "Perhaps you should attend his talk. I'll take care of her."

I hesitated.

"Go on, I'll see you later," and with that she smiled, adding, "We have a long day ahead of us."

Mr. Brant's mid-day lecture in the auditorium was on abortion. I was glad I was there because there were only a handful of students. I had never given this subject much thought because I planned to become a surgeon.

He was an eloquent speaker, dropping a hint that he had returned from a sabbatical in America. He informed us that abortions in the United States were illegal, unlike in the United Kingdom. "Here," he said, "terminations are allowed during first trimester, pending an affidavit from the patient's physician and a psychiatrist." I took copious notes on the estimated number of deaths from back-alley abortions in countries that prohibited the procedure. The passion with which he delivered the case for legal abortion was extraordinary; he was a zealot on the issue. He argued it was a woman's right to control her body, and by the time she had made the painful decision to have an abortion, in his experience, she had gone through hell. Lastly, he emphasized that the patient was exercising her right and that a cluster of cells should not be confused with a living human.

The male side of the situation was not covered. I wondered, what if the male partner or husband was emotionally involved?

Did he always agree with the decision to abort? Were there post-abortion emotional consequences for the couple or the woman and even for the man? The more I thought about the topic, the more I realized the complexity of the issue.

The forcefulness of his message impressed me, while the lack of counter-arguments gave me pause. Overall, I assessed that he espoused progressive arguments, and I tended to agree with him.

The topic was a painful one for me to deal with. How would I adjust to this issue as a physician if I encountered it? Mother's close friend and confidant, Sister Röske, had revealed to me Mother had considered aborting me.

Had she discussed this with my father or only confided her thoughts with her closest friend?

Mr. Brant finished his lecture with a discussion of the traditional method of D&C to accomplish the task, along with its complications, such as uterine perforation. Despite the enlightening lecture, as a surgeon, I would not have use for the information since obstetricians did this operation and thought of the lecture as more of a break from my apprehensive patient back in the labor room.

Following the lecture, I took the opportunity to grab a quick lunch in the medical school's refectory. Choosing to sit alone, I reviewed what I had learned so far during that morning. First, confronting the uncamouflaged genitalia was a shock. The image put me off all thoughts of sex. Would I have reacted like this if Fred, my cadaver, had been a woman? Second, unlike in surgery, I was presently not a team participant, just a mere observer. Third, the midwife, like most nurses I had encountered, was doing a fantastic job. Fourth, I sensed some tension between the registrar and the rest of the staff. Fifth, the content of the lecture on abortion was most informative and educational. Professor Brant knew his stuff.

My pager interrupted my thoughts. Another delivery, one of

twenty-five babies I needed to deliver to pass the obstetric course. I returned to the ward and found that Mrs. Coleman had stalled. She looked exhausted seven hours into her labor. She once again begged for the pain medication, which was not dispensed since an opioid slowed the fetus's heart rate and masked potential uterine rupture. While I was joining Mr. Brant and the midwife at Mrs. Coleman's bedside, discussing the probability of a C-section, the registrar came up behind me and briskly said, "Get on and see the new patient. This one," he added, pointing at Mrs. Coleman, "is going to have a C-section over in the private wing, and I'm assisting." Before leaving he said, "Next time don't disappear without my permission. You are on call, and we have patients to take care of. Understand?" He strutted off like a peacock in his Wellington boots. I did not know his name, but he was an insensitive, arrogant bastard.

Mary, my new patient, was eighteen years old and well along in her labor. A new midwife followed in my wake, while in the background, the groaning Mrs. Coleman was wheeled out with her drip bottles clanging against the pole.

The midwife showed me how to do a thorough vaginal exam to assess Mary's progress. She had dilated well, and I could feel the fetus' crown. There had been no time to shave her or give her the traditional enema. She merely lay on her back—in her street clothes—looking away from me as I took a history between contractions. There was no trace of a boyfriend —neither in her story nor by his presence. In a low-key monotone, Mary said she was from Belfast. She seemed sad in what I saw as a happy event.

"When my membranes broke, I took the ferry across the Mersey and the train from Liverpool to London." Her contractions had become progressively stronger and closer together. She collapsed in Euston Station's toilet, and an ambulance brought her to UCH, where the Casualty nurses rushed her up to the maternity ward. Mary had no idea of her estimated due date, could not remember when she got pregnant, and had had no prenatal care. Not even her mother knew she was pregnant. Each month, Mary would cross off four days on the kitchen calendar, indicating that she had her period to hide her condition. She certainly did not look pregnant, and no one in her family suspected—they had no idea she was here. The midwife had drawn blood to measure various indices.

Mary was stoic as her baby crowned. Her tissues were supple and the baby small, and her vaginal opening was sufficient for the midwife and I to deliver the baby. Mary followed instructions when told to push down and when to pant. There was no need for an episiotomy because the shoulders came out with her final push. It was a girl.

I had delivered my first wonder—a healthy, vigorous, five-pound infant. Overcome with emotion, tears welled up in my eyes at the miracle. I wanted to dance about the room and pronounce to the world my achievement. The midwife saw my euphoria and smiled.

She brought me back to reality by showing me how to clamp the cord and divide it and then how to massage the lower abdomen to help deliver the placenta. It appeared in a gush of blood, mucus, and brown meconium.

I watched her examine the baby while it cried and shook its arms, eyes barely open, shocked at entering the cold world. After cleaning off the baby and placing silver nitrate drops into its eyes to protect against infection by syphilis, gonorrhea, or chlamydia, which are usually tested for during pregnancy, I inserted a small tube through its nose into the stomach to ensure the esophagus was intact. We swaddled the newborn and placed it into the incubator.

Feeling in high spirits, I presented her daughter to Mary, placing the baby on her chest. I was startled when she displayed no emotions—not even a triumphant smile. She supported it with one hand, looking down at the stranger. I was assigned to fill out the birth certificate while the midwife cleaned up and then left the room. I began my questions to complete the paperwork. "What's her name?"

Mary shrugged. After a few moments of silence, I suggested Victoria. Mary nodded. I wrote it down. Hello world, meet Victoria O'Rourke. When it came to the father's name, Mary remained expressionless and started to cry quietly.

UCH had probably as many social workers as midwives, perhaps because of the proximity of Euston Station, a terminal for the railway lines from the North and the Midlands. Concerned with Mary's apathy, I paged the social worker. "Sign the birth certificate and place it in the chart. I'll see her shortly when she comes up to the ward." Two aides moved Mary and baby Victoria, and that was the last I saw of them.

After the excitement, the cup of tea in the nurse's room was refreshing. I even welcomed the stale biscuit. The bully in his Wellingtons came in.

"Go to Bay 3 and sew up the episiotomy."

"I've never done that. Could you show me?"

"It's simple," he said without moving. "Use a 0-Chromic—a heavy thick thread. Start at the top of the wound, take full thickness bites, and approximate all the layers in one continuous running suture until you reach the edge of the introitus. I'm off to assist Mr. Brant." With that, he walked out. An episiotomy is an incision of the postero-lateral vaginal wall and the perineum that enlarges the vaginal opening, allowing the baby's head and the wide shoulders to pass easily through the birth canal without tearing the tissues. Large, heavy "mayo" scissors would be used to get a clean, straight cut, a few inches away from the urethra and anus.

I went to Bay 3, where a woman lay with her feet in stirrups, holding a midwife's hand as she waited. I drew back the covering, saw a medium-sized cut, and examined it. The muscle of the vaginal wall formed a sandwich; one side was the vaginal mucosa and on the other was the skin with its subcutaneous tissue in between. There was a modest amount of bleeding from the cut edges. Exploring the wound with my gloved fingers, I did not find any particular blood vessel, only oozing muscle. Based on my limited surgical experience, I decided to close each layer separately after anesthetizing the wound with local anesthesia. Using a more delicate 2-0 chromic stitch with a smaller needle, I approximated the vaginal mucosa wall first and then the skin with its subcutaneous layer, making sure the skin edges of the introitus, the outside of the vagina, met to re-establish the snugness of the vaginal opening, hence ensuring a clean scar. I left a gap at the edge to allow residual oozing to escape. Finally, I took the larger 0-chromic and placed some stitches through the mucosa-muscle-skin sandwich to approximate the muscle and stop further bleeding.

"Did you have a boy or a girl?'

"A lovely girl," came the reply.

"And is your husband pleased?'

"He's at work. He hasn't seen her yet. Probably tonight during visiting hours."

My closure took longer than what the registrar had suggested, and when I was about finished and admiring my work, the registrar walked in.

"What are you doing? Looking at it he said, "This is not plastic surgery. You're not doing it as I told you." He was fuming.

Apparently, Mr. Brant had not wanted his assistance, and he was shitting on me.

"I applied basic surgical principles of closing a wound in layers, after anesthetizing it."

"It's unnecessary and a waste of time. No one will see that incision. After birth and after an episiotomy, the nerves there are numb, so local anesthesia is unnecessary. Now go to Bay 7

and close the episiotomy in the way I told you. Understand?"
He turned around to leave.

"Wait. Wait," I said raising my voice. "The patient may not
see it, but she will feel it. She can *feel* it. I wouldn't want my
balls sewed together without anesthesia. Would you?"

Taken aback, he said, "You're a cheeky bastard. Do as I tell
you, or I'll fail you. There's lots of work to be done. Now get on
with it, you slacker."

He shuffled away in his Wellingtons. I wanted to shout after
him, "Prick! You're a bloody contemptible prick!" Yet I
controlled my temper. Rising, I looked at the patient. She was
wide-eyed. Had she seen the smoke blowing out of my ears? I
thanked the midwife, who supplied me with the local anesthesia and sutures, and had constantly adjusted the overhead
light so that I could work. I asked her if she minded cleaning up
after me.

"No, no, love, you run along. Don't worry, he is a difficult
man." The "prick," who had pulled rank by taking my case, had
prevented me from assisting in my first C-section. Mrs.
Coleman had been my patient. I was livid—he had cheated me
out of an operation.

UCH was not located in a residential area. Most of the deliveries came from further afield or arrived from distant locations
by train. The few local ones were referred to us because of
some complications. Either the fetus or the placenta was
malpositioned in the uterus or the patient had preeclampsia or
another life-threatening condition meriting careful monitoring.
We had an excellent state-of-the-art infant intensive care unit
and had our share of premature babies. The fluctuations of
deliveries increased almost in correlation to the arrivals of
distant trains into Euston and St. Pancras Stations during the
afternoon and early evening hours. Many had similar stories to
that of Mary. Sadly, these young women had not received
adequate prenatal care, if any, endangering their lives and that

of their babies. Most lived in a state of fear and psychological isolation. If only they could have confided their predicament to a family member.

By late evening of my first day, we entered a slack period. Usually, those who were free would gather informally with a registrar in the corner of the nurse's room, cup of tea in hand, to discuss an interesting patient or to field questions from the on-call students. Our registrar was not interested in teaching students and was not there.

While I was learning how women birth babies, the third Arab-Israeli conflict—the Six-Day War—revived passions between those Jewish students with staunch Zionist leanings and Arab students entangled in the plight of the displaced Palestinians, leading to rowdy brawls in the University Union. I remained out of the fray by choice, recognizing that the political problem was not as black and white as the press made it out to be and that the solution was complicated and not within my sphere of influence. Some fellow Arab students who wanted me to demonstrate in support of the Palestinians accosted me and mocked my lack of partisanship. Equally, the two fanatical Zionist students in my class, those who had hurled toilet-roll missiles at me a few years earlier, harassed me again. Making their index fingers into the shape of a gun and mimicking a shot, they'd fire imaginary bullets at me. I tried to ignore their hostile acts and wished they made an effort to get to know my views and not to assume I was a "hostile Arab."

My Cairo passion Magdalena was visiting London from Warsaw. Her father was posted to Brussels, and she was happy to be abroad again. She telephoned me in the morning, suggesting we have dinner together. It was wonderful to hear from an old flame and to think that although close friends had been scattered to the various corners of the world by Middle Eastern politics and war, an attempt was made to keep in touch, to recapture past pleasant moments, and to give meaning to our earlier lives.

I explained the type of rotation I was on, its time demands, and that I was on call that evening. Unless she wanted to eat early in the evening, in the hospital refectory, I would probably not be able to join her. She declined. I begged off her other off-campus meeting suggestions, sensing that she might be wanting to revive our Cairo mid-adolescent love.

I felt a pang of guilt, for I had never taken the opportunity to tell or write to her about Victoria, my profound new love, and how my life had moved on. Exhausted, I was relieved Magdalena had not telephoned again, and around 9 p.m., I went up to my cubicle. I fell into a deep sleep, vividly recalling the day's events in convoluted dreams. A serene baby with Victoria's adult, seductively alluring face floated across my vision, alarmingly replaced by a huge blimp of a repulsive-looking, pallid, naked vulva with green eyes and sharp teeth advancing toward me, roaring like a Chinese dragon, ready to devour me. In fear, I struggled, holding it at bay with outstretched hands, moaning and groaning so loudly that a fellow medical student bunked in the next cubicle banged on the plywood partition.

Disoriented, I awoke in the semi-darkness, my scrub shirt soaked with sweat. The neon strip light in the corridor shimmered through the frosted glass window set in the door. It was almost 11 p.m. I kicked off my shoes, took off my soiled scrubs, and fell back onto the bed naked. My body ached from the tension and toil of the day. Curled up child-like, I hoped it would be a while before the midwives or registrar telephoned me for the next delivery. I sank into a dream-free sleep.

Suddenly, somewhat roused, I became aware of a tall figure standing just inside the door, backlit by the corridor's glare.

"It took forever to find you . . . are you awake?" the disembodied voice whispered.

"Who are you?" I replied incoherently. Was this another dream, a hallucination? Was I talking to myself?

"The dinner went on for so long . . . are you awake?"

It was Magdalena.

"Oh, I'm bushed," I replied groggily, unable to focus or rise from the bed, wishing she had not come. The outline of her coat, followed by her skirt, dropped into a heap onto the floor. She pulled her sweater over her head, shaking her long hair free, and snapped off her bra. Liberated, her breasts bounced, throwing shadows against the glass. They swung loose as she bent to strip off her pantyhose. Befuddled, all thoughts of guilt and apprehension about Victoria vanished.

When I last saw her in Egypt six years ago, she had been a teenage tomboy—smart, bright-eyed, full of energy and life, with striking beautiful features and a charm brought out by her flirtations. Now, in the dim light, she appeared exotic—a breathtaking feminine transformation. As she came toward me, her womanly aroma flooded and saturated my nostrils, arousing me as her luxurious bush, striking even in the dimness of my cubicle, approached at eye level. Her faint perfume, mixed with stale cigarette smoke, wafted by as she bent over me, murmuring, "*Chcę cię*—I want you. *Kocham Cię*—I love you." I was alert and instantly responsive.

Her warm body slipped under the blanket, luscious, inviting, and hospitable. She engulfed me in whispers in a soothing in Polish tongue that conveyed comfort and solace, murmurs I wanted to hear and feel, murmurs I had fantasized about since I was a teenager. After a day living with pale, sterile, shaven lips, the whiff of her fragrance and the warm tenderness of her flesh reassured me that obstetrics had not dulled or killed off my appreciation of a woman's body or dulled my passion—I was still alive. Her hands expressed the urgency of her muttered needs, and her thighs were inviting and welcoming. We fell asleep, our legs entwined on the narrow bed. Our intimacies banished my ghoulish images of Mrs. Coleman's shaven muff.

Was it delayed gratification? Magdalena and I had become as close and familiar as awkward teenagers could be, though the opportunity to be intimate had never presented itself because her father's consular assignment suddenly changed and she abruptly left Cairo. At sixteen years of age, I found Magdalena attractive, gregarious, and vivacious. She was alive and caring, and our relationship developed rapidly into a physically aspiring and tormenting one as our mutual attraction grew. I admired and adored her coquettish air, her peculiar sense of humor, her endearing Polish accent, and life's viewpoint, which mirrored with my life in Germany. We had something for each other, preserved over the years by infrequent exchanges of letters and cards as we kept in touch always with the hope, even with the plan and intent, to meet for a long weekend while I was in England and she in Poland—but those were unrealistic dreams.

And tonight, we finally met again—pent-up fantasies finally acted out in a cubicle four floors above the labor rooms, where the product of such passion was delivered and began life. With our fusion, a profound confusion occurred in my mind.

She climaxed, and at that moment, with eyes closed, she softly murmured to herself as if in a dream "At last" . . . "forever." I heard her bare whisper—a soft muttering—near my right ear. Did the thoughts and words expressed during states of half-consciousness, states of emotional vulnerability akin to *la petite mort*—the brief loss or weakening of consciousness—reflect a deep hidden reality? Did "at last" mean an act long dreamed of but forestalled? And the "forever" a subtext of a bond lasting beyond eternity?

We slid into a blissful, deep slumber. I cherished our friendship. And the pangs of guilt stirred such that I resolved to tell Magdalena about my commitment to Victoria in the morning.

I jumped awake to the ringing of a phone coming from my neighbor's cubicle, who was next on the call roster for a delivery. Muffled by the partition, I heard a woman's voice say, "Ignore it." After several more rings, it stopped, and it then rang by my bed. Magdalena stirred and looked at me inquisitively through half-closed eyes. On the fifth ring, I answered.

"I have to leave."

"Must you?" she whispered. I nodded, bending over and brushing her hair from her face to kiss her goodbye. It wasn't a farewell kiss, but more one of gratitude that she had cared enough to track me down and that we had satisfied our mutual fantasy.

"Will you be long?" she asked, sleepily.

"I don't know."

"I'll stay a little longer in case you come back soon," adding, "Try to return to me. I have to go back to Brussels tomorrow. My parents are expecting me." Then, she added in an unhappy voice, "*Jestem pewien, ze rozumiesz,*" a phrase she had told me often in Egypt when the fire of our romance was at its height— meaning "I'm sure you understand."

With that, I whisked out the door, focusing on the delivery ahead of me and leaving the passing comet in my celestial sky.

We had spoken little, yet her presence was reassuring, reminiscent of familiar and happy times when, as teenagers, we had forged a sanctuary of togetherness, one so improbable during a period of political crisis, war, emotional turmoil and uncertainty in Cairo. Now, she was a mature woman in full bloom. She sensed the depth of my sexual desire, for she left her knickers behind—a memorable calling card—her sense of humor. Would she want to collect them one day? Picking them up later, they aroused me once more, and with the morning's light, reality set in: this would no doubt complicate my life. If there would be a next visit, I'd want to tell her about Victoria beforehand and hold Magdalena at bay.

Over the next eight weeks at University Hospital, I helped deliver fifty healthy babies—no complications. The sheer accomplishment of the happy moments, and seeing the delight on most mothers' faces, made me wonder if I should not become an obstetrician instead of a surgeon. I would still get to operate. The arc of an obstetrician seemed that early in their career, they did some cesarean sections, sewing up episiotomies of various lengths and complexities. Later in their career, they would do more gynecological-type operations, presumably on the same aging population.

I joined the other students during coffee breaks and became aware that I had butted into some whispered conversation. Had I heard that a nurse had a D&C in the private wing? She claimed she was sixteen weeks pregnant, but in fact, she was probably more than that because, rumor had it, the premature fetus had shown some brief signs of life. Apart from a sense of horror and disbelief, I wondered how I should process such whispers. Obviously, the metric of estimated delivery date was off by some factor. The gossip reminded me that medicine was a human endeavor.

At UCH, despite the "prick" bitching at me, I continued to close episiotomies in layers. It was the right thing to do. After our words, he left me alone, and I wondered if the midwives had said something to him. Three weeks later, he disappeared, moving on to his next rotation. A collective sigh of relief was felt as the work environment became less tense and more convivial. I thanked God. His replacement was his antithesis, one who taught and encouraged the students. We learned from the midwives too, and we taught each other.

Every baby I delivered, from my first to the fiftieth, was a wondrous miracle. However, thinking of poor, young, unhappy Mary, I recognize that not every mother welcomed an infant into her life. In 1967, an unwed mother bore a stigma, and an accidental pregnancy might break up a marriage. I saw mothers, both young and old, look with distant eyes—sometimes bewilderment—at the bundle I presented them. I observed a kaleidoscope of emotions as these tiny strangers appeared. Some babies were loved at first sight, nursed, comforted, and welcomed, while others were received without joy and were less well accepted.

From the many ways Mother repeatedly recounted my arrival to her friends, I got the impression that I fell into the latter category.

# 34

# VD-101
JULY 1967

*Only Bishops and liars get VD from toilet seats*
—Shirley Perfect

Before I could finish my obstetrical rotation at UCH, and move to my next experience at a district hospital in London's East End, the Clinical Dean's letter reminded of my delinquency in attending the Dermatology and Venereal Disease Clinic. It was not an oversight—I had gone twice, loathing each visit.

UCH sat on the periphery of Soho, London's red-light district, which provided plenty of patients for the clinic. It was in the basement, accessed from Gower Street via metal stairs. Climbing down surreptitiously was like descending into the Underworld. Despising the unsavory Victorian-era clinical setting, I reluctantly went to fulfill my course requirement.

I dashed down the stairs, fearing who may have seen me, thinking that a casual passerby or, worse, a fellow medical student might think I had some venereal disease, with its insalubrious implications. The dimly lit clinic had a dozen cubicles filled with women who sat in tilt-back barber-style chairs. A half curtain hid their faces and upper bodies, making this into a surreal picture. Their feet rested on metal stirrups planted and placed apart, separating their knees with their legs wide open, exposing their bare thighs, a shock of pubic hair with exposed genitals. Patients separated their labia providing a full anatomical view, often colored with the creamy yellow discharge of gonorrhea. Standing near the consultant and his nurse, I felt a great sense of discomfort at the situation. The humiliation of the patients was palpable.

The consultant was a tall, thin, middle-aged physician, resembling my image of Hades. He wore a white coat, had a scraggly beard and heavy horn-rimmed glasses with thick lenses, which framed his beady eyes. He avoided eye contact with all the students including myself, as he stood in front of each cubicle observing exposed female genitalia while mumbling into a Dictaphone. I could barely hear him as he quizzed his patients and listened to their disembodied replies. He muttered his diagnosis and treatment using Latin terms that I did not understand, but which his nurse noted. At the end of an hour, after he had walked down the line of exposed women, we persuaded the Consultant Physician to sign our attendance cards. Sometimes we managed to convince him we had attended on other days so he would initial for additional visits. We had to attend 12 sessions to pass the course.

It was the most abhorrent clinic I attended. Patients with a medical condition were denigrated by the implication of their disease in a seedy environment of anonymity, contrary to the gravity and dignity of the usual physician-to-patient relationship. I was too disturbed by the situation to learn anything about venereal diseases. After all, I rationalized, syphilis, gonorrhea and chlamydia could be relegated to the historic waste heap of diseases, thanks to the discovery of penicillin and other drugs such as erythromycin. It was like what Professor Pilcher had said about TB and streptomycin.

I was cornered by a question on our final pathology exam: "Describe a disease transmitted during intercourse, its pathological progression and treatment." My rudimentary knowledge of the stages of syphilis would reveal my total ignorance, while knowledge of other venereal conditions was, at that time, non-existent. Thinking for a while, I came up with three potential answers. If the patient wore 1. A condom, then no disease was transmitted. If I elected this topic, my answer would constitute a very short essay—too short. 2. Unwanted pregnancy—I would write about my recently acquired knowledge concerning termination. However, a pregnancy was technically not a disease. 3. I decided to write about the contagious virus that led to the misery of a cold. I wrote an elegant and comprehensive essay about the common cold, even adding a paragraph on herpes simplex, which caused the wretched cold sore.

I thought it was a rather brilliant treatise. The examiner was neither impressed nor amused. He scored me a zero out of ten. That unkind, humorless sod had seen through my deception. He could at least have given me a mark for ingenuity. After all, how many times did humans develop a cold after a good fuck, or any fuck for that matter, relative to contacting a venereal disease?

I had done sufficiently well in the rest of the exam to squeak by with a pass. Nevertheless, I was annoyed at his closed mind. There was no point in challenging the examiner, suggesting that next time he should be more specific in phrasing his question. I cursed him and hoped he would get an almighty debilitating cold when he next shagged his wife. He would certainly think of me while lying in bed, weak and aching in every bone as the virus ravished him.

# 35

# THE SPARKLE OF BEAUTY

*People are like stained-glass windows. They sparkle and shine when the sun is out, but when the darkness sets in, their true beauty is revealed only if there is a light from within.*
—Elisabeth Kubler-Ross

W hen I had saved enough money to buy the antique diamond ring for Victoria, we went to have it sized, and it was clear that she loved it. It fit perfectly. The stone glittered and sparkled, and Victoria glowed with radiant beauty. Mrs. Goldberg was happy to meet my beloved. She beamed her asymmetrical smile without drooling; she had obviously seen the neurologist that I had arranged for her.

As we stepped out into Woburn Place, Mrs. Goldberg called after us, "When is the happy date?" We both shrugged. We had not thought that far ahead. It made more sense to plan and see if we qualified as physicians first.

With its exquisite Victorian setting and multifaceted, brilliant stone, the ring looked gorgeous on Victoria's finger. The news that we were betrothed spread like wildfire. Lacking better options as students, Victoria and I decided to have a small engagement party at Mother's place. Claiming she moved from Manchester to London "to be closer to her son," Mother had recently bought a flat south of the Thames in Blackheath on the top floor of a newly built complex situated at the edge of Blackheath Common, a public expanse of green fields to the south, and Greenwich Park, with the Royal Observatory and the Old Royal Naval Hospital to its west. The Thames ambled past the park at its northern edge.

We had not allotted a budget, and our ideas of an engagement party turned out to be quite different. Victoria envisioned an archetypical British affair with canapés, Scottish smoked salmon, and Champagne, while I pictured a continental tea with sandwiches, sausages, and lovely cakes. We bumbled through the friction between us, disconcerted by each other's plans, never stopping to discuss our expectations and never agreeing on an overall concept. This became the pattern of our relationship—her ideas agreeable to me, my ideas often appealing to her, or together muddling through our misunderstandings to an interesting, if puzzling, cultural hybrid.

Mother generously helped with the provisions. She was curious to meet our friends, a mixture of my classmates at UCH and Victoria's from Westminster Hospital. Regrettably, none of

Victoria's family could come; Tim was at university in Birmingham, and Shirley was feeling down. Had we invited Uncle John and Aunt Joan or the cousins? Obviously, I had not expected my Egyptian family members to join us, given the distance and expense.

Mother had ceased telling me that Victoria was not a suitable match although she continued to express her feelings to John Rackey. Because he was a decade older than me and had once been married, Mother assumed he would side with her.

I basked in the congratulations of my colleagues, despite the tension that arose between Victoria and me concerning the sequencing of refreshments for our guests. Still, it appeared that everyone had a wonderful time. Victoria showed off her ring, and I took pleasure in her joy and beamed in the glow of her beauty.

We had no definitive plans for the next step although Shirley intimated that she dreamed of a grandiose wedding for her daughter. She pictured a cathedral, a princess dress with a long train, a tiara, and hundreds of guests with fancy hats, flowers, and bubbly. The mother-of-the-bride would be the center of attention. As she spoke, I could hear organ music reaching its crescendo in the background and imagined a choir of a thousand singing "Gloria in excelsis Deo." I could not imagine squeezing such an event onto the conveyor belt of medical school studies and exams. Victoria and I could not foresee a date, so I teased her that we would marry on Thursday.

I considered myself the luckiest man for having Victoria love me. She was the most beautiful, intelligent, and intellectually mature woman I had ever known. She made me feel deserving of her and worthy of myself. I adored her and our relationship. She did not see me as a "fucking foreigner," but as a unique person with an international background, in reasonable command of three languages, and with the personality traits of determination and the drive to excel. She made me feel accepted by my peers, for a true English girl loved me, and what's more, she declared a desire to have *my* "brown babies."

Yet the true meaning of love and commitment was scary—a feeling of vulnerability. Perhaps love was not permanent, as we always liked to think of it. Victoria's father had a wife before marrying Shirley, and after his demise, she had boyfriends. Mother looked through my father's photo album after his death and speculated idly aloud if a particular woman who appeared with my father in a photo had been his mistress. I hated her in that instant for doubting my father's faithfulness. The issue was all very bewildering, and I had no confidant to counsel or guide me.

Commitment? Certainly. Victoria was committed to me, and her devotion gave me strength. Yes, I could commit; I vowed to commit to Victoria, forsaking tenuous earlier romances. Come what may, she would always be first in my life. I would take care of her and any "little brown babies." Despite this, I feared her bond to me might weaken, leading her to desert me, as had the others whom I desperately loved. Had she not been momentarily tempted by a Valentine invitation?

I confessed my gripping, obsessive fear to Victoria, that like my father, I would be dead at fifty and that my time with her would be short. I could not see beyond that barrier. Everything I wanted to achieve *had to be accomplished* in the next twenty-six years, giving my entire existence a sense of urgency. My father became a full professor by the age of forty-five, so I aimed for age forty. Yes, I was going to love Victoria, hopefully with her by my side as an equal partner with equal ambition. Our love had evolved into a comfortable routine—she did not like kissing as much as I did or dancing—but one of mutual desire, dependency, security, and comfort. Although we had our small differences, as a life partner, she was the bedrock of my existence.

# 36

## HELL'S CRUCIBLE

*Thou shalt not be a victim,*
*Thou shalt not be a perpetrator,*
*Above all, thou shalt not be a bystander.*
—Yahuda Bauer

My second obstetrical rotation at a district hospital in London's East End was a nightmare. The registrar of the obstetrical unit turned out to be that "prick" I thought I would never see again. He strutted about in his green scrubs and white boots like a puffed-up army general, intimidating the midwives, bossing around the students, and ignoring the patients. My fellow medical students and I could not tolerate the registrar's arrogance and lack of compassion. The midwives did all the work and most of the teaching, too.

The East End of London was the district where new immigrants tended to settle. Naively, I was stunned to discover that the "prick" was also a racist. A large percentage of the patients admitted to the unit were from India, Pakistan, and Bangladesh —patients we seldom saw at UCH. He would not encourage midwives to perform episiotomies when a baby passed through the birth canal and out the vagina, instead letting mothers birthing their first, or who had large babies, tear. He should have repaired these, but he left them for the students to suture, doing little except exhorting the three students to sew quickly without due concern to prevent future urinary or fecal leaks. I saw some horrific tears that I knew would leave women with varying degrees of incontinence.

I spent most of my days judiciously sewing up complicated tears. I was enraged by his callousness and disrespect for women yet secretly delighted I could do surgery and was becoming more skillful with practice.

That heinous registrar was in the habit of doing end-of-day rounds at 8 p.m. We would follow him, hoping to be taught, but we were ignored. He would stop and ask the midwives about the status of their patient's delivery. On one occasion, a young Indian woman had been in labor for more than twelve hours and looked drained. Without examining her, he said, "If she hasn't delivered in another eight hours, we'll section her." Why did he not examine her to determine the cause of the slow or obstructed labor? How did he decide on eight hours? From where did this magic number originate? I had been chastised for questioning him. Before I could muster the courage to be rebuked again, he saw the next patient and left the delivery room.

At three in the morning, it was clear that the only way to deliver the baby was to perform a C-section. They moved the patient into the operating theater. An on-call anesthetist regis-trar appeared. She was from the Indian subcontinent, looked very sleepy, and saw the patient for the first time to familiarize herself with her medical-obstetrical problems. Her consultant, her attending, did not appear. The operating room personnel dragged out of bed looked tired and were unenthusiastic. I was tired too, but adrenaline was pumping through my veins.

By 4 a.m., the "prick" appeared, looking around with an air

of satisfaction. He had used the power of his authority to assemble this tired crew for the ill-timed operation. He asked the scrub nurse to assist him, indicating by default that we were to watch. The operating lights shone harshly on the woman lying on the table, her distended belly covered with a sheet. Her chest and breasts were immodestly exposed so the anesthetist could observe her breathing.

The "prick" and his nurse scrubbed, gowned, and stood on either side of the table, waiting for the patient to be anesthetized. A sedative was intravenously administered, and when the patient started to slump, the anesthetist placed a gas mask over her nose and mouth. I watched apprehensively. I had never seen a cesarean section before, and the lack of monitoring of mother and baby surprised me. The circulating nurse began to wash and drape the belly, and the anesthetist fussed about with the dials of her machine. I did not see the patient's chest rise or fall. Suddenly, the circulating nurse noticed that the exhausted and dehydrated mother wasn't responding—lifeless. Half-hearted attempts to resuscitate her followed. It failed. The "prick" didn't do a crash C-section to haul out the baby and save it. He stood there frozen. Inactive. Ineffective. He de-gowned and walked out of the theater. It was 4:20 a.m. Stunned silence. The silence of the grave.

This tragedy, the first death I'd observed on the table, was a horrific event. Avoidable. Shocking. Disheartening. An incredible calamity. I left the room distraught. I expected detailed deliberations would ensue in the next few days. Where were the consultant obstetrician and anesthetist whose job it was to supervise the training of registrars? The blame for the disaster, and the grievous loss of two lives imposed on a husband and family, lay at the feet of the "prick" for a critical error of judgment. Yes, murder due to neglect. There was a need for an open and honest discussion of the mistakes committed so everyone could learn from them and prevent this from ever happening again. No such review occurred.

I thought that this death would become a teachable moment and that students would be given a chance to express their shock, anxieties, and concerns—to mourn. And yet there was no mechanism to complain or discuss the appalling lack of care and attention. It was as if the lowest man in the food chain had no observational powers or point of view. No one asked us for our opinions. The coroner ruled the deaths as a "misadventure." Two deaths had occurred on the table, and it was a "misadventure?" My God.

I lived with the agony of what I had seen. It would never have happened at UCH because of a culture of supervision and accountability. My already low estimation of the "prick" descended further, to one of dangerous, even criminal incompetence—from purgatory to hell. He did not seem to recognize his failings, and his behavior and attitude did not change. If he felt any remorse or humility, he did not show it. He continued to ignore the students. By avoiding him, I could focus on sewing up tears and performing episiotomies in contempt of his decisions not to do them on Indian, Pakistani, and Bangladeshi women.

As if to distract me, I received word I should go to a theater where a gynecological procedure was about to start. Thinking I was wanted to scrub and assist, I rushed down from my on-call room to an extraordinarily Dantean sight, one not the *Paradiso* of surgery. The room was dark. Two blinding, overhead operating bulbs harshly pierced the blackness, illuminating the open lower abdomen of a woman. I could hear the anesthetic machine bellow rhythmically, ventilating the patient.

The sole operator was the new surgical house officer, who stood on the patient's left with forceps in one hand and dissecting scissors in the other, both hands trembling. From out of the dark, a disembodied voice said, "Now pick up the fallopian tube. No, that is the small bowel. The other tubular structure next to it. Tie it off using the silk thread the nurse is passing to you." As my eyes adjusted to the dark, I saw a man in scrubs, hands behind his back—the body to the voice.

"What is going on?" I whispered to a fellow student.

"He's Catholic, and she is having her tubes tied."

"Why is the registrar not scrubbing and doing the operation?"

"Some Catholic surgeons refuse to perform a tubal ligation solely for birth control to comply with the ethical and religious directives of the Catholic Church."

"Didn't he take the Hippocratic Oath? What did he tell the patient?" As my voice rose from a whisper, the instructions ceased, and the registrar stared at me. I got the message and walked out, feeling I had transgressed.

The situation posed an ethical dilemma for me. My loyalty lay in my commitment to the patient. I had a bond to treat them, a covenant—a signed consent form. Surgery was a hands-on profession. They had violated medical and moral ethics. Did the registrar think that if he stood a foot from the table, he was innocent—that the darkness could hide him?

I stepped out and peeked into the next room. In the bright light, I saw my first D&C—dilation and curettage. The patient had retained part of the placenta after birth, which bled profusely. Anesthetized, she was lying down with her legs in stirrups. Sitting on a stool between her legs was the gynecologist, while the scrub nurse hovered next to him. He inserted a thin metal probe through the opening of the cervix, through which blood was steadily oozing out. He advanced it for 8 cm to the apex of the uterus, muttering under his voice that he detected a retained spongy placenta, the cause of the ongoing blood loss.

Taking a series of shiny Hagar metal dilators that increased sequentially in width from 3 mm upward to 10 mm, he slowly and methodically dilated the cervix. The procedure went smoothly because the patient was postpartum and the cervix was softer than usual. When the cervix was fully open, he inserted a curette and systematically scraped out the inside of the uterine cavity. Initially, some unidentifiable bloody tissue was scraped out. He continued until there were no returns. With a pad placed over the vaginal opening, a nurse took down the patient's legs, placed them together, and covered her before they woke her up from anesthesia.

Even after witnessing successful operations and procedures like the D&C, I remained haunted by the death of the young Indian woman and her baby. Would I be responsible for an operating table death some day? After what I had seen, my flirtation with becoming an obstetrician died. In dismay and protest, I packed my bag and left Hell's crucible well before the official end of the rotation.

# 37

# THE APPENDECTOMY THIEF

*If you want others to be happy, practice compassion.*
*If you want to be happy, practice compassion.*
—Dalai Lama

A few days after walking prematurely out of a district hospital in London's East End, I weaseled myself into the ongoing obstetric rotation back at UCH. I responded to an advertisement urgently seeking a Surgical Locum House Officer for one week on a Mr. Simon's general surgical service at the Whittington, a district general hospital in Archway, Islington, in north London, a solidly lower middle-class district. The Whittington was one of UCH's affiliated teaching hospitals. I applied to enhance my surgical skills and quench my thirst to operate, but above all to bury my frustrations at the unbelievable crimes I had witnessed.

My friends told me that Mr. Simon had a busy service, serving a large white population, many of whom were originally from Central Europe. The Census showed an influx of new immigrants from Africa.

The position became vacant on a Thursday and being a

student, I would not receive any recompense. I telephoned Victoria and told her about my coming absence. "It's good experience for me. I'll be operating on types of cases not seen at UCH. I'm sorry my limited free time and the distance from your flat in Notting Hill doesn't allow for me to come and visit you despite my ongoing and deep love for you my darling."

She graciously accepted the situation, perhaps because she too was busy and my locum was only for one week. A day later I received a wonderfully warm letter from her. I read and re-read it for it characterized her so much. And, it brought out my feeling of love for her.

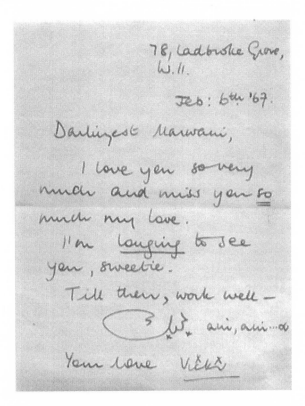

When I turned up at 11 a.m., as instructed by a secretary, Mr. Simon looked me up and down. "Where have you been? You're late." Then he added, "Where are you from?" without making eye contact. He was a stocky, square-shouldered, hard-faced man of middle height, probably in his mid-fifties.

"University College Hospital."

"No man. What country?"

"Egypt, Sir."

He grunted, and rolled his eyes. "Go change, I'm about to start a case." That was my first inkling of his dour attitude—one I was going to try to live with as best as I could. Eventually I understood that his well of misery was bottomless.

Once in theater, we embarked on a gastrectomy. The upper end of the stomach where he was working was somewhat obscured by the left lobe of the liver. I diligently retracted it out of his way, fearing that if I pulled too hard the edge of the retractor would crack open the liver's lining, causing a lot of bleeding.

"Pull, man, retract the liver. Be careful. Can't you see I am struggling?" I adjusted the retractor and gently did as instructed. His field lay in semi-darkness. Addressing the circulating nurse, he barked, "I can't see properly. Will you adjust the light to shine into the field?" The circulator grabbed the edge of the operative light above his head and tried to move it to illuminate the area where Mr. Simon was working. "No, no, that's no good. It's worse now. Fix it so I can see." She tried several times to move the overhead fixture so that the beam of light hit the area under the liver. Each time he complained more irascibly. Another nurse nudged her aside and tried for a few moments. It was obvious to me that the mechanics of the overhead light required grabbing the light handle and adjusting the beam straight down into the operative area.

"You are both useless. Give me a sterile glove." He slipped the fresh glove over his bloodstained one and, stretching overhead, took the handle, and adjusted the light to his liking. Slipping the contaminated glove off, he resumed operating.

I had never seen such behavior or contemptuous demeanor toward the operating room nurses, who were from Ghana and Kenya. Throughout the procedure, he constantly berated them about their inadequacies, no matter how hard they tried to assist or please him. I was mortified, noting that they distanced themselves from his vicinity while remaining in the room. He was a bigot.

At the time his disposition was common among certain upper-class English who were still living in the heyday of a glorious Great Britain. They wore an air of fashionable superiority. To add insult to injury, they would claim England was now being "invaded" by a flood of ex-colonial foreigners from Africa and India. Winston Churchill clearly expressed such an attitude in his writings, particularly in *The English-Speaking Nations.* I had encountered this attitude on occasion in Shirley Perfect's utterances and tolerated them good-humoredly since she and her sister, Bunt, had come to Great Britain from New Zealand in the 1930s, and I loved her daughter.

It had been an exhausting day. I was surprised by a phone call to Casualty my first night. "You are on take and there is a patient here with appendicitis," said an ethereal voice over the telephone.

Unfamiliar with the hospital complex, it took a while to find where I needed to go in the maze of corridors that must have once been a sprawling, Dickensonian workhouse. I had felt confident about making the diagnosis, having encountered several cases of appendicitis during the nights I had spent in Casualty at UCH. However, when I met the seventeen-year-old young man, his symptoms were anything but typical. Perhaps it was my fatigue after dealing with Mr. Simon, or that bewitching early night hour, that made me too fearful to be sure.

Hopeful that he would come to my rescue, I called him and related to him my concerns. Noticing the uncertainty in my voice, he barked down the phone, "Do you know what time it is? Call your registrar!" He hung up. I got the message that he was well into his third scotch and certainly did not want to be bothered with minor procedures such as an appendectomy. I cursed him silently under my breath. I should have realized that he would be no nicer to this novice than he was to the other staff that attempted to help him all day long.

The registrar was also a locum and had arrived in the early evening, although we had not yet met. It was somewhat jarring when I called him. "I will be there in a while." I retreated to my on-call room where I fell asleep waiting for him.

"Where the hell are you?" the registrar's irritated voice streamed across the line. In the background, I heard the clang of surgical instruments. This time I knew which corridors to take to find the Theater. The patient was already asleep and without introductions, my registrar indicated that he had not expected to be doing a house officers job getting the patient into the operating room. I was too tired to respond that I had expected to meet him in Casualty, while the young man was awake. Instead, I scrubbed, gowned, and painted the patient's abdomen with an antiseptic solution, before he moved in and without a word performed the appendectomy. I assisted. He removed a normal lily-white appendix.

An examination and a mutual discussion may have prevented exposing this patient to an anesthetic and an opera-tion; both had inherent complications. Not a day went by while I was on that locum that I did not reflect on the dynamics of the situation. I had a bigot for a consultant, and an irate locum registrar who missed every opportunity to teach a novice. Was this the environment I wanted to practice in?

In contrast to Professor Pilcher, Mr. Simon never wore a white coat, not even on rounds. Instead, he wore a fine tweed suit with a vest. Since he did not address the ward Sister, his registrar, and me directly, we took our cues about a patient's management and dispositions from the surrounding air into which he spoke.

I was surprised how his attitude toward different patients varied. He was curt to the point of rudeness when dealing with elderly females who appeared to originate from central Europe, and indifferent to patients who barely spoke English. His unfriendly interpersonal relations with the staff also dismayed the Sister who ran his ward. His demeanor differed sharply from that of Professor Pilcher who was charming and kind to all his patients, and to his staff. Despite feeling uncomfortable in Mr. Simon's presence, my philosophy was that I could learn from everyone—both positive and negative lessons—what to do and what not to do.

Mr. Simon seemed to operate mainly during the day, on a stream of elective and emergency cases. I had difficulty keeping up with his activity. At the Whittington, the surgical caseload was much greater and more varied than at UCH. I admitted and worked up patients with a wide array of common surgical diagnoses, not seen at a primary teaching facility where consultants had specialty interests and expertise. Mr. Simon operated on a selection of abdominal cases including diseases of the liver and biliary system, such as retained gallstones in the duct.

Through it all, I relished the surgical immersion this locum afforded me. It clearly revealed my previous limited exposure and the paucity of my surgical knowledge. I had no time to eat a proper dinner, merely scoffing down food in the cafeteria, before returning to the ward to prepare my patients for the next day's operations.

I would assist during surgery and care for the patients during their post-operative period. I barely slept four to six hours a night, if I was lucky. It was exhausting. The tension and stress level rose dramatically when Mr. Simon was in theater. He was always in a hurry and appeared agitated, barking orders to whoever stood near. He was a clumsy surgeon—like a ballet dance in worker's boots. He was competent but burned out, laying blame all around him.

On my last day, there was a moment of pernicious joy. During afternoon rounds, we came to a patient from central Europe on whom he had not operated. She complained of constant abdominal pain. Her belly was thin and scaphoid, sunken with a concave rather than the normal convex contour. I saw the crosshatches of numerous surgical incisions. She was a diagnostic enigma to Mr. Simon and since all routine tests including blood, urine, barium enema, and upper GI x-rays were normal, he was convinced she had Münchausen syndrome. This is where a patient had a psychiatric disorder, seeking attention by being operated on and then cared for— manipulating her environment to be a constant patient.

Standing beside her bed, briefly glancing at my shoulder before looking into space somewhere between the Sister and his registrar, he mumbled under his breath, "Never operate on pain. You'll find nothing, and you'll leave the patient with a scar. Pain alone in the absence of other findings is a perception in the head and not a disease in the abdomen—not a surgical disease." Yet each day the patient insisted, in her heavy accent, that she suffered from abdominal pain and could not even sit up or get out of bed or eat.

A standoff followed. He said to her, "There is nothing wrong with you," and to the Sister, "She should be discharged." She lay apparently helpless, with her abdomen exposed, and wailed insistently.

Each stared at the other. What was going to happen? My heart pounded as we all must have wondered how he would resolve the confrontation. Turning to the Sister, he demanded, in an irritated voice, a glove and some lubrication. He knelt on the floor, while the Sister positioned the patient onto her left side in the traditional knee-chest position, and with a gloved finger, he did an incredibly forceful rectal exam. The patient howled with the discomfort that he was causing her. I took a step back, appalled at the unnecessarily vigorous exam. Was he a sadist, too?

As he withdrew his finger with a smug expression on his face, a huge squirt of liquid stool sprayed all over his vest, shirt, tie, and suit jacket. We all would have cheered if we had dared. A shit-covered Mr. Simon rapidly retreated. That was my last and enduring picture of him for I left that evening. The image of this patient in pain remains imprinted on my brain.

So, what did I learn in one week? A surgeon has to overcome the internal barrier of ego, recognizing his limitations and fallibility. Had it occurred to Mr. Simon to obtain a medical consult or even a second opinion? A fresh pair of eyes may have evaluated the situation differently. Had he thought that the patient might have had angina of the gut, a condition similar to cardiac angina? An angiogram of her gut vessels might have shown a constricting arterial plaque in the main artery to the small bowel. A Teflon jump graft, bypassing the stricture, would have cured her. Another lesson I learned was that even crazy patients become sick—never dismiss them. Professor Pilcher wisely said, "Treat the patient."

# 38

# THE LISTER PRIZE

*If the love of surgery is a proof of a person's being adapted for it, then certainly I am fitted to be a surgeon; thou can'st hardly conceive what a high degree of enjoyment I am from day to day experiencing in this bloody and butchering department of the healing art. I am more and more delighted with my profession.*

—Lord Joseph Lister

To be among the best is an identity that surpasses any circumstances, national or ethnic—Sir Max proved it. Although I thought I had left my father's ghost behind after my second MB, I realized that I was still driven by his omnipresence to excel, to accumulate accolades and accomplishments by putting in extra hours seeing patients and studying, and then take the internal prize exams—junior and senior medical, junior and senior surgical, surgical pathology, surgical instruments, and obstetrics. This included the prestigious Lister Surgical Award—*the* prime one I desired and that I was determined to get during the three years of my clinical training.

These extracurricular prize exams were established in tribute to prematurely deceased or famous faculty members, in the names of past students, or in memorial to distinguished old boys such as Lord Lister, the surgeon who discovered carbolic acid's antiseptic properties. The annual exams were competitive, and usually, no more than a handful of ambitious students applied. They involved extra reading and the acquisition of a more profound depth of knowledge than was typically acquired during medical school. I wanted an award badly.

The thirty-minute oral tests were standardized. First, the candidates clerked and examined a patient who had an unusual disease, an odd manifestation of one, or presented with a very complicated scenario. After clerking them, the student presented the case to a couple of examiners. Blood work and X-rays were not included. The candidate's ability to relate a comprehensive clinical story of a patient's disease process, a sound treatment plan, and the patient's overall prognosis was assessed. The highest scoring candidate receiving *cum laude* and won the named award—seldom cash, only academic recognition. The others were rated as having achieved a first-, second-, or third-class rank of merit.

During the medical rotations, I participated in the Junior

Medicine Award. The patient, a woman, presented with the physical signs of folic acid deficiency, a diagnosis that I managed to make. However, I failed to connect the unusual "pins and needles" in her feet to the deficiency because she did not have similar findings in her hands—the classical neurological involvement of the "stocking and glove" presentation. I did not win the medal; instead, I received a first-class award. I was disappointed and rued the fact that I had not picked up the clues my examiner was giving me.

A few months later, I took the Senior Medical Award exam. This case was even more complex. I did not come as close as I had hoped to provide the examiner with a comprehensive diagnosis, and I got only an upper second class. I consoled myself, for by then, I knew I wanted to become a surgeon.

During the surgical rotations I focused on the surgical awards because these would help my chances of getting my first house surgeon's internship at my teaching hospital. There were four different awards in surgery, and to my irritation, I received a second-class award in both the junior and senior categories. I chided myself that I just was not good enough. I would have to try harder.

The Erichsen exam in surgery involved knowing the name and history of surgical instruments *randomly* presented to the candidate. I spent hours after the main operating day poring over the entire array of instruments, learning their names and utility. At last, I was recognized with a first-class award. I knew the names of the instruments I would be using for the rest of my surgical life. And then, there was the Magrath exam in obstetrics and the Alexander Bruce exam in pathology. In both, I was recognized by receiving a second-class award.

The last competition was the most prestigious. I really, really wanted to win it. I was in the final months of being a medical student before graduating and embarking on a surgical career. I was confident that I would be able to tackle most of the problems referred to our teaching hospital, particularly since I had done a locum for Professor Pilcher on the surgical unit, had spent most free evenings examining patients in Casualty, and had done a locum in general surgery at Whittington Hospital.

At the assigned time, I was to examine a patient on the surgical ward. As I entered his screened-off bed, I was surprised to recognize him as a patient who I had already clerked and whose operation I was to assist at the next day. I knew him and his disease well. The patient recognized me.

He had a peptic ulcer. I had read extensively about the disease and prognosis. I would have made a good showing with him, able to give an eloquent, dazzling, surgically focused presentation, and then discuss his differential diagnosis and how I would conservatively manage him. If egged on by the examiner about what other therapy I would propose, I would recommend an operation, but not just any operation, a definitive one. I would be able to discuss the reasons why I would not recommend the other surgical options, their failure rates, and their short- and long-term prognoses for the recurrence of the ulcer. In fact, in preparation for his operation the following day, I had even read about the surgical management of stomach cancer just in case the ulcer was cancerous. I could see myself walking away with the prize.

I stood for a brief moment considering my options. My desire to win was *so* overwhelming that I would re-examine him, pretend I had never seen him before, and then present him to my examiners.

A little voice—my wretched super-ego—pricked my conscious: *that is cheating.*

*So what?* I replied indignantly. *Who the hell are you to dictate to me? Who would know?*

*Would you want this on your conscience? Could you live with yourself? Do you want to be known as a cheat? Are you strong enough for the dean's wrath, for potential expulsion and a stained career prospect?*

I rationalized I would probably do equally well with a new patient since I had immersed myself in surgery. Returning to the examiners, I confessed that I already knew the patient. They were flabbergasted that I had come clean.

Hastily, they assigned me an elderly female who was not on the surgical ward but the medical cancer ward—a medical patient with a surgical problem rather than a surgical patient with a surgical disease. By now, it was late afternoon. The jaundiced patient had missed her tea, was fed up at seeing yet another medical student, and was reluctant to give me her history. I had to extract every answer as if pulling teeth.

The effort of this exercise gave me a sinking feeling in my stomach that I was not going to win the most coveted prize. The reality of the unforeseen situation displaced my hope of walking away clutching that award and crowing, "And they said it couldn't be done," in front of my fellow students. I began to lose focus and concentration, overcome by negative thoughts.

I returned to the matter at hand, fearing—knowing—that the prize would elude me. It was clear the patient had had enough. She grudgingly let me examine her abdomen, where I found an enlarged, tender liver, but no additional signs of liver disease. Apart from her visible jaundice, she had no other pathology. She had a dressing covering an ulcer on the tibia, the main bone in her left leg, just below her knee. She refused to let me remove the dressing to examine it. This was crucial because each ulcer has characteristics of specific diagnoses. In my desperation, I nearly pulled the dressing off. I had to know, I had to see, I had to feel. Even with my hands on her dressing, she refused and placed hers protectively over it.

I tried in the remaining minutes to persuade her, to coax her, even to charm her to let me peek under her dressing. Recognizing my progressive frustration and growing irritation, she grabbed the bedspread, yanked it up, and covered her legs. I was shut out.

Confused and angry, I stood in front of my examiners. I was unable to put together a cogent clinical picture connecting her ulcer with her jaundice. I performed poorly, scored dismally, and was humiliated. I had lost.

I finally understood that my eyes had been on the prize, not the patient, and that I had let my ambition overrule my love of humanity. Years later, I saw this patient's stern and disapproving face float by me as I examined and operated on a Polish miner who had a cancerous ulcer of the leg. By now I had the knowledge and experience to realize it had the potential of spreading to the liver and causing jaundice.

# 39

# SMALL AND VULNERABLE

*A baby is an inestimable blessing and bother.*
—Mark Twain

After my experience at the Whittington, I followed the official learning schedule of three months' rotation on Professor Leonard Strang's pediatric unit at UCH. The ward had a few hospital beds interspersed among open cribs and tent-like cribs covered with zippered plastic hoods for children with severe upper respiratory tract infections—mostly croup. The misty atmosphere facilitated the patients' breathing and coughing up their clogs of phlegm.

I felt a great empathy for my small and vulnerable new patients and could relate to their helplessness. My mind went back to a time when Gulnar attended pre-kindergarten and brought home whooping cough. I was not quite three, so my illness was more severe and prolonged than hers. One afternoon, I awoke from my nap in my darkened room, panicked with a heightened sensation of asphyxiation, unable to cough up the thick plug of phlegm. Fighting for breath, I stood up in my crib, rattling the bars, powerless to cry for help. Mother finally came to pick me up and banged on my back to loosen my congestion. Whooping repeatedly for air, I started to cry, incensed at her tardiness and my frightening inability to catch my breath, I lashed out at her. She dropped me into my crib and walked away, slamming the door while I kept struggling for air. It seemed a very long time before she returned. First, she rebuked me for striking her. I could still see her wagging finger and hear the displeasure in her voice. Only after admonishing me did she pick me up and bang on my back, finally clearing my airway.

Now, I stood beside a hooded crib, listening to the rush of the mist entering the tent. How medicine had advanced since my childhood. In the dry Cairo air, I could not cough up the globs of thick viscous mucous that built up in my windpipe, resulting in the terrifying and prolonged sensation of suffocation. Because of that experience, I disliked attending Burnage Grammar School's swimming program at the Manchester public baths, fearing the water and drowning in it. It took many trips to London's University Union pool during the first term to overcome my innate apprehension while learning to swim underwater. Before that, the "smoggy" days of Manchester were also difficult for me, generating a sense of anxiety about getting sufficient air. These children in their misty environment would not have that lasting sensation nor a fear of asphyxiation.

Pediatric patients admitted from Casualty with a high fever of unknown origin, which tended to be frequently associated with seizures, also drew me back to my childhood in Wedel, where the treatment for my very high fever involved thick warm socks and heated rooms, piles of blankets, a hot mustard poultice, and spoonfuls of purple stuff that tasted chalky, sweet, and of raspberry. In the pediatric ward, nurses sponged down patients admitted with fever of an unknown origin, giving aspirin to lower their temperature and barbiturates to prevent a seizure. The house officer worked them up, attempting to determine the cause of their temperature rise, the most common conditions being a urinary tract infection or bronchiolitis. In most cases, the event was benign, not recurring.

I was assigned to a two-year-old boy with hydrocephaly. In this condition, cerebrospinal fluid accumulates in the brain, preventing the bones of the skull from fusing together, resulting in an enlarged head and making him look like a Martian from my childhood comic strip Dan Dare in the *Eagle*. I measured the head circumference daily; if it exceeded 42 cm, I was to insert a long sterile needle attached to a syringe between the unfused skull bones, advance it directly into the ventricle, and suck out 20 cc of fluid. Because the brain does not have pain sensors, the infant sat in his crib and let me perform my task, which Professor Strang initially supervised. After washing off the puncture area with alcohol, I proceeded as instructed. I felt queasy but did not show any emotions, having learned to suppress these during my surgical rotations and electives.

"My concern, professor, is that while inserting the hollow needle, I pass through a great deal of brain tissue and remove a core of white matter when drawing up the fluid. Does that have a long-term detrimental effect on the patient?"

"You mean removing a block of some hundred-thousand brain cells in your needle?"

"Yes."

"The brain has redundant tissue, so as far as we know, we do no harm."

After seeing me place a plaster Band-Aid on the needle insertion site, Professor Strang looked pleased and turned away. Perhaps that is when I should have vomited. *Give me a belly to examine anytime*, I thought.

I spent a great deal of time on the ward getting to know the patients, many of whom had been there for extended periods of time because of chronic conditions. Apart from the seizures associated with a fever of unknown origin, there were few admissions with acute problems, perhaps because UCH was in the shadow of London's prime pediatric hospital at Great Ormand Street.

In the evenings, I retreated to my dorm and read about the various pediatric conditions until Victoria and I would meet. Children fascinated her, and I believe our discussions of my various patients may have increased her interest in a career as a pediatrician. What a pair we would make—a surgeon and a pediatrician.

Professor Strang developed sufficient confidence in my proficiency to ask if I would be interested in doing a two-week locum rotation. I accepted, and once more, I moved into the house officer/doctor quarters, had meals served to me, and welcomed the customary morning cup of tea passed blindly through a half open door. Victoria, by now a veteran tunnel tripper, would sneak up to join me at night whenever her student on-call schedule permitted. Since the pediatric rotation was a less-demanding locum relative to a surgical one, we were seldom disturbed at night. She was now doing her clinical rotations at Westminster Hospital and had left Canterbury Hall, sharing a flat with another girl in the Notting Hill area of London at the early stages of its colorful Jamaican invasion.

Drawing blood from infants and youngsters was an unsettling event. Their fear of needles was, in many cases, worse than the actual prick. My dread of causing pain interfered with my attempts to obtain blood because I was not bold enough to pursue the goal of seeking and hitting a tiny vein in their subcutaneous tissues.

The solution for struggling infants was that a nurse and I immobilized the patient on a papoose board. Linen wraps attached to the board, including straps across the forehead, firmly swaddled the body. By the time the infant was secured, the superficial vein in the neck budged from the crying, facilitating the blood sampling. Thank God that the new sharp, disposable needles and plastic syringes were in common use. The children must have dreaded seeing me when I made my rounds. It was always a traumatic experience for both of us.

The most challenging task was obtaining a reliable, long-term venous access for a drip. Selecting the antecubital vein that we learned about in our introductory course was not a smart choice in children, whose activity would displace the needle. I tried to place the IV in the forearm—a more secure site—coiling the tubing around the access site before taping it down. In the event the tubing was tugged, the coil would take the tension, not the needle. However, children pick on their IV dressings. To conserve the integrity, I fashioned a paper cup to cover the IV site and taped the cup onto the arm. It looked strange and amused the nurses, who appreciated the practicality of the arrangement.

On this pediatric rotation, I did not have to deal with death; thankfully, my resilient little patients recovered quickly, despite the severity of their illnesses. Although I enjoyed pediatrics, I remained confident that surgery was going to be my game. Also, pediatrics reminded me too often of my painful and insular childhood in Germany.

After two final rotations, infectious disease and psychiatry, by early autumn 1967, I had completed all the mandatory courses offered by the medical school to make me eligible for the final General Medical Council (GMC) exam. If passed, the title of "doctor" would be bestowed on me.

# 40

# THE AUTUMN OF HER YEARS

*Our lives are rivers, gliding free to that unfathomed,*
*boundless sea, the silent grave.*
—Jorge Manrique

W hen Asad and I were nearing the end of our medical educations, we learned that Miss Freemantle, the fourth-grade teacher we had much admired in Cairo, now lived nearby in Haslemere, a town in Surrey. One Friday evening we invited her to dinner, along with Armenag, who now lived and worked in London. We planned to meet outside the London Hilton, Park Lane, in Mayfair.

I set off from Gower Street tube station in a buoyant mood. As I travelled under the streets of London, hanging on to a strap, Miss Freemantle occupied my thoughts. Ah, Miss Freemantle—could I call her Patricia?

*Patricia will you sit opposite me in the candlelight; lean forward; stare into my soul? You will see that I have continued to love you devotedly . . . well, sort of. You were my first mistress—albeit class mistress—my ideal beauty, I, your faithful philanderer. You, dear Patricia, are still the woman I have adored all these years. Would*

*you be my naughty mistress? I am a vigorous man. Forget Woolf.
Think of ME, oh my Aphrodite; be my cougar.*

Such were my euphoric fantasies at the prospect of seeing
her again. How could I forget her figure with those mighty,
high-riding breasts? They had jiggled, wiggled, and wobbled
me to distraction. How would they fare on this Tube ride, with
the carriage swaying from side to side? Up in her room I had
buried my face into her bra. Was that the bouquet of her skin's
oils mingled with her perfume? Whether in class or during
recess I made every effort to intrude into the cloud of body
scent that enveloped her like the stratosphere. Despite the
stuffy air in the carriage, remembering her feminine fragrance
still evoked my desire. Her voice? Had I forgotten? How strange,
I could not recall it. I loved her when I was an impotent little
boy. This mature man could love her, and adore her—placing
her on the pedestal she deserved. However, would I? Exiting at
Green Park I had reservations about my fantasies. True, I was 12
years older—she would be, too. I was about to start my career
—she had recently retired. How would our paths intertwine at
this stage of life?

I arrived a few minutes early. Approaching our rendezvous
point in the dimming glow of an evening sunset, I perceived
the silhouette of a woman in a suit, carrying a handbag, on
the corner of Park Lane outside the bright lights of the
majestic Hilton Hotel. She was much too small to fit the
memory of my class mistress. No one else was waiting. I
slowly advanced, thinking it could only be her. On approaching, her signature scent, faintly mixed with mothballs,
confirmed my suspicion.

"Miss Freemantle?"

She turned around, smiling. "Hello, Marwan. How nice to
see you?" Her voice was subdued. "You've grown, dear boy." She
added, "I suppose you would have."

We shook hands. Was this the paragon of beauty I had once

known. Why had she called me "boy" when I was nearly a doctor?

The others arrived, followed by the general chatter of all-around greetings. I stepped back. I was taller than she was. I looked down at her once flaming red hair, which had thinned and grayed. The formally erect posture that had radiated such confidence was now slightly stooped. Only twelve years had passed. She must have been older than I had appreciated back in my school days.

My suggestion that we go to a modestly priced bistro in Kensington High Street, more of a student-type eatery than the upscale restaurant in the Hilton, seemed agreeable. The gathering wondered how we would get there. I hailed a cab and we piled in. I sat opposite her on the taxi's jump seat, silently scrutinizing her. Since I had eaten at The Bistro previously, I led the way into the establishment. She sat opposite me at a table with a red-checkered cloth. I watched her in the flickering light of a candle stuck in an old wine bottle. We ordered.

Between bites, we continued to chat. Asad told her of visiting his father, the Indian Ambassador to Yugoslavia, and meeting President Tito after the Suez War. She gazed at him in admiration, shutting the rest of us out, confirming my earlier suspicion—he was her favorite. While she ate, I noted her narrow lips, wondering how I could have missed this feature. Or was my recollection faulty?

She told us of her teaching life following the evacuation from Egypt. Together with Miss Collins, a Cairo School colleague, she had spent several years working in Iranian oil company schools as headmistress. She supervised four other schools, allowing her to retire early.

"Did you get all the letters I sent you?" she asked? I had received the letters, the ones she had sent me in Manchester, encouraging me to continue to apply myself despite my loneliness. Her letters had touched me for she showed concern when

Mother did not write. In our correspondence, she emphasized that she had cared greatly about all her students. It was obvious that her vocation—her life—centered on them. I felt sure she knew each one well, following some with interest, observing their growth, maturity, and their first steps into their professions.

I observed her throughout the conversation, my mood subdued. I could not reconcile the vibrant Miss Freemantle with the woman who sat opposite me. She had aged. This fact alone disturbed me immensely. How was it that when I saw her twelve years later, time had made such a difference? She looked less robust. It was more than the effect of the shifting candle-light on her face. Gone was the joie de vivre she had projected. Her once majestic breasts now obeyed the laws of gravity. I wondered if she had endured a debilitating illness. The vision of her made me sad. *Media vita in morte sumus*—In the midst of life, we are in death. Perhaps I was more afraid of aging than dying. What would the march of the decades do to me?

She had probably closed the chapter on Egypt—the pain of eviction—the necessity of abandoning her students, for it never cropped up in our evening's chat, although it lingered under the surface, a collective trauma that had profoundly changed our lives. She was glad we had turned out to be the confident young men she had predicted when she had invested her all in teaching us. Miss Freemantle volunteered that she now lived with Miss Collins in a cottage in a genteel part of the country.

There were so many questions to ask. Did she know she had been my Venus? Did she suspect we had rummaged through and admired her underwear? Was she aware she had taught us much more than what she offered in class? Was Mr. Woolf really her lover? Why had she never married? Was she perhaps gay? The idea of asking even one of them constricted my throat.

The image I had long held—that grandiose pre-adolescent

fantasy of the glamorous Miss Freemantle—had fossilized. And yet, the woman before me was the real woman—kind, compassionate and understanding—just as we had once been the immature boys. I was pleased to see her again for it affirmed love, respect, and friendship.

Above all, she was satisfied, indeed contented with life—while I, for one, had yet to resolve my many conflicts and contradictions. Contentment was one more lesson I could learn from her—to strive for a state of equanimity in my life. I wondered if I would ever achieve the wonderful gift, a lesson she stealthily was transmitting.

# 41

# THE ELECTIVE

*I'm a surgeon. I make an incision, do what needs to be done and sew up the wound.*
—Richard Selzer

In late August 1967, Mr. Hart's office sent me a note. He was now the academic dean, and he thought I might benefit from more intense and varied exposure to surgery at Massachusetts General Hospital in Boston. He suggested I address a letter of inquiry to Dr. Gerald Austen, the chief of the surgical service, asking if I could do my elective there.

His letter supporting my career choice and sponsoring me came as a surprise. I didn't think he thought highly of me, particularly since I had questioned his intra-operative judgment on the patient who eventually died and later expressed my frustration at his futile attempt to salvage a patient's leg. Had my attitude toward him embarrassed him? At the time I received the letter, the thought did cross my mind that perhaps he was sending me away—out of sight, out of mind—because I hadn't seen him as a great surgeon. Years later, when I needed a copy of the medical school transcripts, I discovered he had given me an "above average" grade; if only I had known that at the time. The revelation astonished and pleased me. Although I had expressed criticism of his operative abilities through my body language, I remained loyal and did not speak of him in a negative way; I detested gossip and considered it destructive. Now, he was proposing to advocate for me.

The response from Dr. Austen came within a week, on crisp stationery elegantly embossed with the crimson Harvard shield stating VERITAS. Dr. Austen invited me to participate in the fourth year Harvard medical students' graduating class of 1967, who were starting their elective surgical rotation on the first of November. He wrote that a place was reserved for me at the Vanderbilt dorms on Longwood Avenue, Brookline, which was opposite the medical school quadrant. The letter instructed me to register at the Harvard Medical School's student office upon my arrival. In his final sentence, Dr. Austen said that he looked forward to meeting me and to my full participation on the surgical service. Maps of the school quadrant and Vanderbilt Hall were enclosed.

I was amazed at his generosity, filled with pride and gratitude to receive such a gracious letter, not to mention grateful to Mr. Hart who, despite our misadventures, appeared to promote my interests. Maybe he had not judged me as severely as I had feared or as harshly as I had judged him. The letter gave me confidence, lifted my spirits, and increased my options. Soon after, Form I-20—a Certificate of Eligibility for Nonimmigrant (F-1) Student Status—arrived. With this document, I could apply for a visa.

As a foreigner in England, I could probably get an elective in many of England's less-prestigious backwaters, but my BTA would give me a competitive edge when it came to finding jobs in London—certainly at UCH with Sir Max for a medical house job or with Mr. Hart for a surgical one.

Around this time, in early August, I came across an advertisement in the back pages of the *British Medical Journal* offering a British Medical Association Medical Students' Travel Scholarship. It seemed to have been crafted just for me because it would support a more unusual request for travel to an elective. I wrote a brief application and enclosed a photocopy of the letter from Harvard, sealed the envelope, kissed it, hoping it would bring me good luck, and dropped it into the mailbox.

My euphoria slowly ebbed with the realization of one major insurmountable obstacle: I was a prisoner of my Egyptian passport, which did not include permission to travel to the United States of America.

Whatever my medical preoccupations, we lived in a political world. It was barely a year since the humiliating Six-Day War when the Arabs were crushed by the Israeli forces who were saved only by the Americans pouring weapons in from Europe to replace their battlefield losses. The defeat stung the Arab psyche into anguish and shame—even those living in England.

Nasser broke off diplomatic ties with the United States. Throughout the Arab world, an intense hatred arose toward America for their pro-Israeli, anti-Palestinian, anti-Arab bias. Although cocooned in my medical studies, I could not avoid feeling dejected. Here I was holding the Harvard letter in my right hand, and in my left, my Egyptian passport, which would prevent me from traveling to Boston.

Egyptian students studying in England were technically under the supervision of the Egyptian Education Office, which occupied an old Edwardian house on Curzon Street, in the Mayfair District of London. Its effeminate, red-haired Scottish secretary, Hamish Erskine, was a long-time fixture. He was the Education Office's institutional memory, probably assuring his tenure, and had probably worked for a dozen directors over the years. He was the interface between the Egyptian director and the various British colleges, not to mention the cadre of

Egyptian students studying in United Kingdom universities. Mr. Erskine was a bubbly, colorfully dressed man in his mid-fifties who spoke with a lisp and on occasion stuttered in a stream of well-enunciated Classical Arabic. He had been an Arabic scholar at Oxford and could read and write Standard Modern Arabic, was well versed in Islamic history and the Qur'an, and often quoted from it in the midst of his English prose. It struck me that after all the years of interacting with Egyptian students, he had not picked up any colloquial Egyptian Arabic, which most of us spoke.

I often wondered who his real paymasters were; was he also a British agent? He would have been right at home as a character in a Graham Greene, Ian Fleming, or John le Carré novel. Hamish Erskine had been the secretary of the Education Office for thirty-two years and knew my father when he had been a student at University College in the 1930s. On the rare occasions I visited, he greeted me with great pomp and affection, and after offering me tea and would introduce me as the son of the famous Professor Abdel Aziz to anyone who hung around his open office door. He regaled me with stories about my father in his student days. He always asked about my "dear Ma'ma," and he would tell me what a handsome couple they were and how my dad's eyes always sparkled in her presence.

Shortly after I arrived in London in 1963 to start medical school, I had visited the education office. Mr. Erskine told me the reason my father had named me Marwan. "Your father, the wise man, chose the name Marwan," which he enunciated correctly, "because he admired the progressive scientist Caliph of Damascus, Marwan." He smiled, pleased at the revelation. This disclosure was news to me.

The Egyptian Education Office was a mechanism for Egypt's government to monitor its students in London who were not familiar with British culture and, therefore, might conflict with the law or to look after those who had problems academically. Most successful students seemed to avoid going to the office and did not participate in its student activities.

On this occasion, I saw him with a grave problem. My Egyptian passport limited me to traveling only to Italy, Austria, Switzerland, Germany, Holland, France, and England. This allowed me to take a ship from Alexandria to a port in Italy or France and then a train across Europe to England since international flying was in its infancy and very costly.

In fact, when my passport was issued in Cairo in the summer of 1960, the clerk at the passport office had only listed England. I cajoled him to add the other countries because I didn't know which way the train would travel from Italy or France to get to the Hook of Holland or Calais in France, the port of embarkation on the Channel Ferry to England. He sarcastically asked me if "His Highness was going on a grand tour of Europe?" I smiled. Was he aware that even if I wanted to go on a grand tour, with the national shortage of hard currency, I could only take E£12 or $72 out of the country? I was satisfied with all the countries he had finally written into my passport, including Germany, where my Oma and Opa lived. Alas, the one country I had not imagined I would need or travel to at the time was the United States.

Armed with the Harvard letter, I skipped the Friday afternoon pharmacology lab and walked from Gower Street through parts of London I had never seen because I generally traveled by the Underground. I hoped to meet the Egyptian director, dazzle him with my letter, and gain permission to travel to Boston. When I arrived in the early afternoon, communal Friday prayers were over, and most students and the director had left for the day. Only the affable Hamish Erskine remained.

After he saw the Harvard letter, he was carried away by all the beautiful places I could visit when I was in America. In his joviality, he did not seem to notice my solemn mood. Finally, when I could get a word in, I asked if the director could permit me to go. The question stopped his wandering imagination. He told me that the director did not have such authority and that it had to come from the Minister of Education in Cairo. However, he felt sure that the minister had probably been one of my father's students, and permission would be granted immediately.

"Yes, yes, but when would I get this green light," I pressed him, "because . . . because I must leave by the end of October."

"Oh, well," he said. "All you have to do is send a petition of application to the Minister in the Mogamma, and I'm sure he will reply right away. After all, this is Harvard!"

At the sound of the dreaded name of that monstrous building in Tahrir Square, my heart sank. I knew what happened to petitions in the Mogamma. More than likely, it would take forever to reach Egypt, and then, it would lie on the minister's desk for another forever. The secretary saw my despondency and offered to send the petition by diplomatic pouch after I paid the appropriate tax. He tried to convince me that I would hear within a couple of weeks. I did not feel like asking him my odds of getting permission given the bad blood between Egypt and the United States.

I wrote out the petition while he obtained a Xerox copy of the letter and my passport, and by 4 p.m., I left the office feeling wretched, emotionally drained, and unconvinced that I would ever hear anything more on the matter. I was sure that I had wasted an afternoon, not to mention missed a pharmacology lab that I would have to repeat in the future.

Retracing my steps north in the direction of Oxford Street, I crossed an unfamiliar square. Looking to one end I saw a vast, white fortress. As I neared, I saw that there was an impressive golden eagle over the front façade. A passing bobby told me it was the Embassy of the United States of America. I stopped to gaze at the impressive edifice gleaming in the afternoon sun. "If you're looking for the consulate, its entrance was around the side," the police officer added. I was curious and made my way to where the bobby had pointed. Sure enough, a placard above the door said Consular Section, and it was open until 5 p.m.

Venturing in, I found myself in a long, narrow, vacant room. At its end was a counter with a window. I tapped on the glass, and a woman appeared. She slid open the window.

"What's your number?" she asked brusquely.

"What number?"

"You have to take a number and wait until you're called," she said, pointing to a red dispenser. She snapped shut the window, disappearing from view.

It was fourteen minutes to five on a Friday afternoon, and no one else was in sight. Why did I need a number since I was the only person in the room? In trepidation, I tapped on the glass again. She reappeared, partially slid open the window, and took my number. "What do you want?" she asked. I produced my Egyptian passport, the letter from Harvard, and Form I-20. She read the letter and looked at my passport photograph. I started to explain that I did not have the United States of America listed when she cut me off. "Do you want a visa?"

I nodded.

She inserted the letter and Form I-20 into my passport. "Come back Monday afternoon," and started to close the window.

I was horrified. "I need my passport," I insisted and stuck out my hand. It was my only identification. Holding my passport almost over her left shoulder out of my reach, she repeated in an irritable tone, "Do you want a visa or not?"

My face fell. "Yes."

"Come back on Monday and take a number."

She closed the window quite forcefully, barely missing my fingers. I watched her vanish into a side room with my passport.

In Egypt, bureaucrats engaged in polite small talk, and if they knew you or your family, they might even offer you a cup of tea or coffee. Even British officials were less brusque than what I had just experienced. I was stunned, convinced I might never see my passport again, sure that no visa would be forthcoming. Wearily, I walked out into the afternoon sun. It was almost 5 p.m. I was not sure what was going to happen. When I passed the same bobby, he smiled. *This is no smiling matter,* I thought.

As I made my way back to my dorm in Gower Street, I sank once more into a despondent mood. The woman had no idea how incredibly difficult that passport had been to obtain. What's more, I felt naked without it and did not even have a receipt to prove she had taken it. I worried all weekend.

On Monday afternoon, the consulate was crowded and resembled a bazaar, with people jostling each other and small groups huddling in conversation. I shoved my way through the densely packed multitude to get to the dispenser. When my number was called, I went to the now-familiar window and handed it to a clerk, who smartly closed the glass, once more barely missing my fingers. It was not too long before they called my number again. The glass slid open and my passport with the Harvard letter was handed to me without a word before the window shut forcefully once more. I fully expected, on opening my passport, that a three-dimensional red "DENIED" would pop up—for such was the bureaucracy in Egypt.

Instead, a colored visa occupied a full page, stating that I had multiple-entrances to the United States. I nearly cheered with delight and shed a tear of gratitude to Mr. Hart for my good fortune. I quickly made my way through the crowds and out of the building before some bureaucrat could change his mind and reverse my astonishing good luck.

A week later, on returning to my room from afternoon lectures, a letter addressed to me, with a return address of the British Medical Association, Tavistock Square, London WC1, lay in the entrance hall. It simply read:

```
Sir,
We are pleased to inform you that you
are a recipient of the British Medical
Association Medical Students Travel
Scholarship. Enclosed please find a
cheque.
Congratulations.
Your obedient servant,
The Secretary
```

Wow! I could not believe my luck. Images of my sitting in a Boeing 707 at 30,000 feet, eating a shrimp cocktail followed by a delicious American steak, perhaps even sipping an Old Fashioned—decorated with a fresh slice of orange, just as John Rackey had described—floated through my head. I would then have a snooze, and on waking, I would be served a cup of tea with delicious finger sandwiches and cakes as we headed to Boston. I visualized the temple to modern surgery, Massachusetts General Hospital. As I picked up the check, which had slipped out of the envelope, I stared in disbelief. It was for £15.

Surely, this must be the first installment of funds for my extraordinary trip to Boston. Fortified with pride at being the awardee and at getting an American visa against all the odds, I scurried around, mustering sufficient coins for a cordial telephone call. The secretary's name was at the top of the letterhead. He picked up the phone as I fed coins into the telephone box at my end. I told him how very honored I was at being selected and that I was looking forward to going to America for my elective period and wondered when the next installment check would arrive since I wanted to buy an airline ticket.

There was a long silence as I fed more coins into the telephone. "Hello? Hello?"

"Young man, you are very ungrateful. You have the *honor* of winning the award," and with that, he hung up.

This check was it? I could not believe it. How did anyone think I could get to America on this puny sum? Had I not emphasized my elective plan by enclosing a copy of the letter of invitation from Harvard Medical School? Was I the butt of a practical joke? Of what use was an award of £15 to anyone wishing to travel beyond the fringes of greater London by Tube? Nonplussed, I climbed the stairs to my room, picking up last week's issue of *Barron's*. An article on the phenomenon of Hampton Gold Mining Area caught my eye. I blinked a few times. They found uranium? What were the chances?

The quoted price for each share was £34; my £5 investment amounted to £2,720. Dear Mr. Winterberry. I telephoned Mr. Winterberry's office, only to hear with sad regret that he'd died of metastatic rectal cancer. I expressed my deepest condolences. They would be happy to help me trade the certificates.

I decided £500 would go into my bank account for my working capital to go to the United States. The rest was invested into three companies. To preserve the capital: DeBeers. For growth: Rio Tinto Zinc. And the smallest amount, for income, I invested in Marks and Spencer, where I always bought my yearly supply of socks and underwear. I then bought my round-trip ticket.

*Boston, here I come.*

———

Victoria and I had discussed how we would survive our prolonged separation. Although we would both be immersed in our studies, we planned to chat weekly by telephone. The possibility of her coming to visit, since we were now engaged, hung in the air, for surely, we would miss each other immensely.

I left on October 31, which I found out was Halloween, celebrated at the time only in America, which explained why the flight attendants wore fancy costumes. I had to get used to new cultural customs! Flicking through the flight magazine before falling asleep as we cruised over the Atlantic, an advertisement to vacation on the Caribbean island of Antigua caught my attention. It was not the £60 excursion fare from New York to Antigua that caught my eye but the accompanying artwork. It showed an aerial view of green palm trees, their branches hanging over a yellow beach lapped by a turquoise blue sea. A romantic young couple lay sunbathing on a large red towel. Mesmerized by the scene, hearing the waves and feeling the sun's warmth radiating off the page, I wondered, *Could this be Victoria and me?*

Completing the immigration form in Boston was a challenge. There was little room to write my full name: Amin Marwan Abdel Aziz Abdel Meguid. The questions that followed were date of birth, sex, and color. Color? It followed the same first three questions on the British driver's license, so I dutifully wrote down the color of my eyes: gray-green. Then came some arcane personal questions, among them asking if had had syphilis.

The line nudged forward toward immigration. Finally, I faced a uniformed female officer. She projected an impression of bulk, both bureaucratic and physical. She wore thick horn-rimmed glasses, no lipstick, and the faint shadow of a mustache. Her rolled up-sleeves exposed substantially muscular arms, and from a side view, I glimpsed mid-calf woolen socks over thick nylon stockings. In a deep voice, she read aloud all my answers, checking each off with her red grease pencil.

"Is this your full name?"

"Yes."

She glanced over to my Egyptian passport, where my name was written in both Arabic and English. According to Egyptian tradition, my name is a combination of my grandfather's, my given name, my father's, followed by the family name.

"It's too long to fit on a credit card."

"Credit card?"

"Yes." Looking up at me she said, "Michael. Yes, Michael, that's a good name. Michael." With that she crossed out most of my name with her red wax pencil and wrote "Michael," leaving my Arabic name Marwan and my last name Meguid. She placed a red check behind the name.

"Date of birth? Next time put the month first." Red check.

"Male." Red check.

She did a double take, peered at me, and faltered, "Gray-green? Gray-green! Are you being funny, son?" Red X crossing out what I had written.

"You're either black or white." With that, she cursorily viewed the rest of the form and stamped my passport.

With pride she announced, "Welcome to America."

## ACKNOWLEDGMENTS

I am deeply grateful to many people for their help and support in taking a manuscript and making it into a book. I'm thankful for all those who provided reading, editing, psychological insights, and to those who offered suggestions when I was struggling with English when I might be crafting my thoughts in Arabic or German.

Thanks to my friends from the English School Cairo for your ongoing friendship. At every reunion I have had the privilege of clarifying memories and moments of truth.

I can't begin to thank my fellow medical students including UCH's medical, surgical, and nursing colleagues with whom I had the pleasure of learning. I am particularly sad that Jonathan Marrow, my close friend and dissection companion, who proofread the manuscript and offered valuable insight, is not with us to see the final product.

I am indebted to Carolyn Ring for her masterful help in patiently bringing this book into being.

And lastly, I appreciate my dear Jo-Ann's unwavering support. Her devotion and reassurance as we talked through the ideas and stories cheered me to the final pages. Lucy, my faithful Chihuahua sat by my side throughout the years of writing.

# ABOUT THE AUTHOR

Born in Egypt, Michael M. Meguid spent his childhood in Egypt, Germany and England, and attended University College Hospital Medical School in London followed by a surgical residency at Harvard Medical School. A surgeon and a Fellow of the American College of Surgery, he studied human nutrition at MIT to benefit cancer patients and was awarded a PhD. He is the recipient of numerous national and international honors. In addition to his demanding operative schedule, he ran a research laboratory which was funded by the National Institutes of Health for twenty-five years, and his research has won awards and continues to be cited.

Michael M. Meguid is a Professor Emeritus of Surgery, Nutrition, and Neuroscience in Syracuse, New York, and an Editor Emeritus of *Nutrition: The International Journal of Applied and Basic Nutritional Sciences.* On his retirement he earned an MFA from Bennington Writing Seminars in Vermont, and attended workshops at Queens University of Charlotte, North Carolina, and Non-fiction Seminars at Goucher College, Maryland.

Meguid's short stories have been published in *Bennington Review*, *Stone Canoe*, *Columbia Medical Review*, and *Hektoen International*. He has given readings in Florida and London and has a thirty-episode podcast entitled "Making the Cut" currently subscribed in thirty-eight countries.

You can find a video trailer for his first biographic memoir *Roots & Branches: A Family Saga Like No Other*, on his YouTube Channel: http://bit.ly/3oND7iV, and the print, Kindle and audio books are available at https://bit.ly/Roots-Branches.

*Roots & Branches* is the first in a series of books entitled, *A Surgeon's Tale. Mastering the Knife: Seeking Identity & Finding Belonging* is the second installment in the Surgical Quartet. The series is a historical biography that spans five decades and reaches beyond the mere personal to convey something of the cultures, people, politics, and places that touch the inscrutable heart of human nature. This multifaceted immigrant's story percolates with tales of intrigue, scientific dishonesty, medical discoveries, illicit romance, unspeakable scoundrels, and murder all the while disclosing the rites, rituals, rules and language of surgery. It is a story of life with all its warts, love and affection—or lack of it, but ultimately, it is a story of triumph and passion.

Meguid reads, writes and lives on Marco Island, Florida with his four-legged muse, Lucy. He welcomes hearing from his readers directly at meguidm@gmail.com or via his website https://michaelmeguid.com/.

# SURGEON & LOVER
## FULFILMENT & FOLLY

Please enjoy an excerpt from Michael M. Meguid's third biographical novel, Surgeon & Lover: Fulfilment & Folly, which will be released in 2021.

Surgeon & Lover is dedicated with gratitude to:

Robin S. Pilcher FRCS FRCP (1902–1994) Professor of Surgery at University College Hospital, London, who inspired me and encouraged me to pursue my dream of becoming a surgeon.

and

WG Austen MD FACS, Chief of the Surgical Services at Massachusetts General Hospital, Boston, who enabled my surgical training in the U.S. which changed the course of my life.

# 1

## TEMPLE ON FRUIT STREET

*Massachusetts General Hospital is hardly general.*
Aphorism

The Harvard residence, Vanderbilt Hall, was a two-story building, partly covered by creeping ivy, stretched along Longwood Avenue. It housed students from Harvard Medical School, as well as visiting students. I reached my second-floor corner room at the farthest end of the hallway by late afternoon.

I plunked my suitcase on the unmade bed by the window, surprised to see another bed in the corner, with baggage slipped under its metal frame. Exhausted and jet lagged, I made my bed and gladly fell into it. There was no last thought as I escaped into a deep sleep.

The Vanderbilt door monitor told me, with a heavy German accent, to catch the Green Line's first tram at 5 a.m. He kindly gave me change for a dollar bill, instructing me to feed the coins into the machine inside the first car and to get a transfer ticket.

I waited in the semi-darkness along the track. When the half-empty train came, I was surprised to find it a two-car tram. On entering, I noticed people were dozing in their seats. I had expected an underground similar to London's. The cars rocked back and forth along the open track, eventually sliding underground as we approached the high-rise offices of downtown Boston. At Park Street, I disembarked and waited by the track for the red line. At last, a light emerged from around a corner, and a single tramcar wobbled down the track toward me, stopping some distance down the line. The car was crowded with women and men wearing white. I followed them off the train at the next stop, the Charles/MGH station, reasoning they were heading to the hospital entrance on Fruit Street. In the early morning mist, crews worked their skiffs on the Charles. It was 5:45 a.m., an unearthly time to start rounds, but a sign that surgery was serious business here.

I joined the surgical team, a group of about twenty people, outside the emergency room (ER). I was quite conspicuous in my gray suit among the others in white. There were two teams of residents: the white service for private patients, and the ward service for indigents. The senior resident, who introduced himself as Everett Sugarbaker, directed me to the second group. The medical students introduced themselves, as did Dr. Levin, the chief resident, who explained the routine we would follow. The welcoming friendliness and my immediate inclusion were entirely different to the reserved, hierarchical British system.

Rounds began in the emergency room, where we identified overnight surgical patients awaiting a semi-urgent operation. Dr. Levin added their names and the procedures to the daily operative schedule—the "add-ons." These patients came to the ER with surgical problems and were subsequently worked up during the night after they were seen and deemed in need of an operation.

From the ER, we rode up the elevator to the intensive care unit (ICU). The ICU concept was entirely new to me. About sixteen bays distinct from the nearby operating suites were staffed with specially trained and dedicated nurses for the most seriously ill surgical patients who needed specialized care and close monitoring "24/7"—an American idiom I immediately understood. The concept made immense sense to me when I thought back to Mr. Hart's lung patient that I inadvertently neglected working up newly admitted patients such that he nearly died from ongoing post-operative blood loss.

Finally, we started rounds on the ward service. These patients did not have an attending surgeon and often lacked insurance; they were the responsibility of the chief resident, who was in his fifth year of general surgical training. A student would present their patient's progress during the night, with the intern chiming in to provide the latest developments or additional data, such as the results of tests ordered during the night. I noticed a professional camaraderie, an attitude of mutual help, regardless of the level of training. The stress of the surgical situation and the common goal of wanting to help patients survive forged solidarity among the different levels of staff, nurses, and students. The sicker the patient, the more the common concern among the group, and the more the individual group members expressed the emotional responsibility, all of which was strikingly different from the pecking order in England to which I was accustomed.

Another glaring distinction from rounds back home was that the nurses did not accompany us. Orders were written into a book, flagged by patient name, which a secretary transcribed, freeing the nurses from administrative work. I had my doubts as to the efficiency of this system, for I much preferred the nurse's presence on rounds. The advantage was that one could hear the nurses' professional opinions concerning patient progress and communicate directly to them the changes that were wanted.

One of my lasting impressions from my first day of ICU rounds was of a recent Italian immigrant, a Mr. Renaldo, who was unconscious and suffered from hemorrhagic pancreatitis —a condition I had never encountered. Intubated and paralyzed, the relatively young patient had an open abdominal wound extending from the xiphoid at the lower sternum to the pubis, covered by moist, large gauze pads to keep his guts from spilling out. There was a tube in every orifice—an endotracheal tube via a tracheostomy attached to a respirator to breath him, a nasogastric to drain stomach, bile, and GI juices, a Foley to empty the bladder, an arterial catheter to monitor blood pressure, a central venous catheter to draw blood, one to input saline into the abdominal cavity, with a sump suction to drain fluid output and the patient tethered to monitors.

The chief resident must have seen me grow pale. He explained that in hemorrhagic pancreatitis, the digestive juices were attacking its organ. There was no definitive or curative treatment; they washed out the destructive enzymes in the hopes of ending the cycle. Earlier, the chief resident had used a sterile teaspoon to scrape out dead pancreatic tissue. I learned that binge drinking had caused the patient's condition.

The effort, energy, and cost invested in trying to save one human being with a self-inflicted illness amazed me. I realized that in America, medical care and treatment decisions were not influenced by moral judgment or hopelessness. These complicated and challenging surgical problems were approached with a hopeful resolve to overcome them. The overwhelmingly upbeat attitude impressed me tremendously. Such a work ethos was pervasive and infectious, and I felt free of the constraints of tradition and was thriving in this positive atmosphere—the eagerness, the can-do approach to surgical problems, and life in the department.

Mr. Renaldo consumed an enormous amount of our time. I was not sure if he would recover, but he did serve to draw together my disparate physiological knowledge. I began to appreciate that in this unconscious man, who was covered only with a cotton sheet and surrounded by life-support machinery, the sum of the physiological parameters—temperature, pulse, respiration, blood pressure, fluid status, stable blood-metabolic chemistry and level of consciousness—painted the picture of his condition. Standing by his bedside, I understood that God had to be here in his fullest presence for Mr. Renaldo to make it —an awareness or prayer I would revisit many times in my career.

One duty on the medical student's scud list was to calculate Mr. Renaldo's daily fluid status because with him being uncon- scious, he could not compensate for his losses by drinking water. The patient's twenty-four-hour fluid intake had to equal his output, with additional fluid to offset losses from the skin, increased evaporation occurring with each one-degree of temperature rise, and losses from the open abdominal cavity. The change in daily body weight, although crude, was an inte- grator of these calculations. The details made my head spin. A summary of these figures was part of the daily presentation of the patient's status during morning and evening rounds. Despite such fine-tuning of patient care, over time, Mr. Renaldo developed anasarca—the general bloating of his body with swelling of his brain. I was overwhelmed by the complexity of managing such patients, the likes of which I had never seen at the Whittington or even at UCH.

A separate, specialty-trained trauma team managed the ICU's trauma patients, whose all-encompassing care was beyond my grasp in my initial days for lack of exposure to this discipline during my training. Despite my "greenness" doing rounds and being available at all times to assist on operative cases, trauma gave me the opportunity to integrate my basic science knowledge and begin to apply this to pre- and post-operative care, an aspect poorly emphasized in my training up to then. Operating was a skill that improved with time, but it had to stand on a solid foundation and understanding of basic science—the knowledge of how the body worked.

From the ICU, we visited the pre-operative patients on the wards to ensure that nothing was overlooked in preparing the patient before surgery. At this stage, either Dr. Levin or the chief resident assigned the residents who were to assist on the two to three simultaneously functioning operating rooms; usually, the student who worked up or followed the care of a patient joined the team. Throughout rounds, the intern made scud lists of tasks for those students not assigned to the OR that day. After the group dispersed usually around 6:30 a.m., we went to the cafeteria. We sat together dividing up the workload of the items on the scud lists. I had my first meal since arriving in America.

Sitting next to me was Tom Sos, who lived near Vanderbilt Hall. He invited me to ride with him to and from the hospital. On the days when the operation where I was assisting went into the late evening, he suggested I could sleep in the on-call room. He was interested in becoming a radiologist, like his father working in New York City. The other students eating their breakfast were very welcoming, friendly, and helpful. I was unaccustomed to being on a first name basis from the moment I met someone, let alone to their nicknames. A jovial student introduced himself as Stu, which I assumed was short for Stuart. You would never call anyone Stu in London! Jan Breslow was a tall, broad-shouldered, and handsome fellow with a particular interest in the hyperlipidemias; he was planning to be a pediatrician and had previously done some research with the hope of heading up a cholesterol-lipid research unit in New York. Lastly, there was Edith, a quiet, friendly student who planned to become an internist or psychiatrist. I was the only one seriously committed to surgery and could assist in as many operations as I wanted since the others gladly relinquished assisting in a case—an operative feast for me. Both Jan and Edith were married. They did not hang around much after taking care of their chores and learning obligations, which included admitting and working up their assigned patients and, like in London, attending mandatory morning and afternoon teaching seminars for those not scrubbed.

I was impressed by their visionary paths for the future. Mine was relatively ambiguous. I wanted to become a surgeon but had no idea how I would make this happen. At that time in England, training and upward mobility depended in part on which attending one knew—a more hit-or-miss approach. Promotion to consultant or professor took longer to achieve, more due to the filling of "dead man's shoes"—a subtler process. Did this fit in with my imagined short life expectancy of fifty years based on my Dad dying? —for as George Herbert said, "Death keeps no calendar."

The American system of surgical residency was more straightforward. After completing medical school, graduates entered a residency program of their choice and underwent systematic training for a specific number of years. On completing residency, one sat for the specialty exam to get a certificate, following which one started a practice in their specialty. The concept was appealing to me—a bit like being back at school: there were measurable landmarks. In practice, I could be a professor a year sooner—and with more certainty— than if I trained in England.

Despite my jet lag, I went to Dr. Gerald Austen's office to sign in and announce my presence. His friendly secretary welcomed me and gave me a key to an on-call room and food coupons—limited to $2 per day—usually used for breakfast. Dinner was free after the refectory formally closed at 11 p.m., when we could eat whatever leftovers were available.

The secretary told me that one of the professors, Dr. George Nardi, had invited me to his home for Thanksgiving dinner in three weeks—a very kindly gesture that I accepted. She added that I could participate in the students' oral surgical test, which was done in early December. She further suggested that I should read Dr. Nardi's surgical textbook and added that the end of the rotation would be December 15, 1967. The news was a shocker. My return ticket was December 30. What would I do in freezing Boston, alone for two weeks, and where would I live? It would cost a pretty penny to change to an earlier return flight, even if I could get a seat during the Christmas season on my inexpensive London-Boston round-trip ticket.

My thoughts went to Victoria, wanting her company and the security of our relationship. I could see us lying under the coconut trees on the red blanket set on the yellow beach, lapped by the warm, azure Caribbean. I wondered if such a holiday would interest her, for she, too, had time off at Christmas. We could fly to Antigua from New York for a mere £60 round trip—a bargain, although we would have to depend on her mother for some of the funds. I was concerned that it might not seem proper to Victoria's mother to have her unmarried daughter gallivanting about a Caribbean playground with a man. The rumor would fly around the very conservative village of Sea View—a Peyton Place if ever there was one. Of course, Shirley had a good idea that we were sleeping together, if not at 95 Gower Street, then when I spent nights with her daughter in her flat at Ladbroke Grove, Notting Hill; that is what young lovers did. My German family would probably frown upon it, too, and it was surely taboo in Egypt.

Despite the cultural shift in American sexual attitudes happening in this time, I wanted the semblance of decency and respectability, perhaps because I now felt the responsibility that came with working in the highbrow surgical world in Boston. Some of the medical students were already married, and my newfound friends, who were probably four years older, saw me as a colleague. Victoria and I had discussed marriage before I left. Perhaps, we could get married in Boston; the last two weeks were a perfect time to honeymoon before returning to London when our busy schedules would restart. Shirley could always have her fancy wedding reception after I graduated in May.

The rest of the ward rounds that first day were a blur, given my jet lag and difficulty in understanding the numerous American medical acronyms. The patients here were sicker than I was accustomed to seeing and presented with more advanced stages of their illnesses; not to mention, the operations performed were more complex and sophisticated. I had difficulty understanding the various stages of a disease and found myself drawing on my physiological knowledge to follow the proposed therapy. The acronyms were so different from the ones I had learned in London. It would take me a few days of intense attention to catch onto the new lingo and still longer before I found myself using it with confidence.

The next day, we were finishing rounds when all the residents' pagers went off simultaneously. "Code Blue ER" squawked repeatedly from an overhead intercom. The team took off like a stampeding herd down the stairway. I was not sure what was happening but followed to catch up with them on the pavement outside the ER door. A blur of white-dressed bodies stooped over a man on a gurney. One of the physicians was pumping the patient's corpulent chest with vigor, shouting out orders for meds. With focused intensity, a nurse drew them up from her cardiac cart dragged out from the ER into the street. She handed a syringe to the team leader, who stuck the long needle straight through the undershirt into the patient's heart. As the resuscitation continued, the body lifted an inch off the gurney with each forceful thrust. Another resident frantically tried to start an intravenous line. Nurses attempted to cut off the man's trousers, while others pushed the gurney into the building. I was a helpless bystander, never having witnessed or learned to participate in a cardiac arrest, which made me acutely aware of how little I knew and how much I had to learn. An ambulance, a fire engine with flashing lights, and two police cars surrounded the scene. I noticed that all the first responders spoke with a peculiar Boston accent—or was it an Irish brogue? The firefighters refused to leave their colleague on the gurney.

The effort continued in the ER, with the patient surrounded by police, nurses, and residents. They intubated and oxygenated him. They stripped him naked and hooked him up to monitors. After thirty minutes, the enthusiastic effort ebbed. With no response from the patient to drugs, external cardiac massage, intra-cardiac stimulant, and defibrillation, the attempt ended, and they pronounced him dead. He looked so pale and young, with waxen facial features.

The nurses pieced together the story. The deceased had visited his girlfriend while her husband was attending church. During intercourse, he experienced chest pain and lightheadedness. Fearing a scandal, she dressed him, which explained the misaligned buttons on his shirt and his poorly fitting trousers. She clothed him in his winter coat while he was floating in and out of consciousness, losing valuable time before she telephoned his friends at the fire station, trying to keep matters confidential instead of dialing 911.

The resident team drifted away from the lifeless body. We left a chaotic scene of syringes, blood, catheters, and clothes strewn on the floor, presumably for the nurses to pick up. The mood was a somber one of reflection and defeat. Our usually upbeat, can-do spirits were slowly draining like water out of a sink. I wondered about the effect of repeated patient failure on our psyches over a lifetime. I was, then, unfamiliar with the term "burn-out."

In general, when faced with patient failure, I would first target myself, internalizing disappointment, hating myself and becoming depressed before scolding myself—it should not have happened—even if the odds were stacked against recovery from the outset. Illogically, my surgical self-confidence diminished. The haunting anxiety and baffling perplexities of losing a fellow human would persist. It was at such times that I tried to recall Professor Pilcher's comment that some deaths were due to "patient disease."

The low energy level among our team lasted only until the chief resident called us to order and reminded us of our tasks for the day—some to assist in the OR, others to the wards. I was to help Dr. Hermes Grillo, who, like Pilcher, was a thoracic surgeon. I met him at the scrub sink where he introduced himself. Immediately after scrubbing, we dipped our arms into a vat of alcohol up to our elbows—a sterility method I was sure would soon catch on in England. We toweled off, and the nurses dressed us in sterile paper gowns and gloved us, all while Dr. Grillo was relating pleasant memories of the various times he had spent in England. Unlike in London, the patient was rolled into the OR awake and only after Dr. Grillo greeted him was he put to sleep. My London brain imagined that this practice extended the turnover time between cases.

Dr. Grillo was reconstructing a man's trachea—the windpipe—located at a high level in the neck between the jaw and the sternal notch above the thyroid gland. The tracheal rings had previously been damaged during an emergency tracheostomy several months earlier when a tube for an emergency tracheostomy had been inserted during an emergency resuscitation. It saved the patient's life. As it healed, it narrowed the main airway, making it progressively more strenuous for the patient to breath.

After washing down the patient's neck and draping it, Dr. Grillo handed me the scalpel. I made a skin crease neck incision above the old scar with the intent to dissect out the old craggy scar. Grasping the scar tissue with a clamp, he raised it to assist my continued resection of the skin and its underlying fibrous tissue. A fresh bleeding plane of the neck tissue was entered. I could see what had to be done next: dissect down to the tracheal rings, resect the damaged old ring, and mobilize the entire trachea to obtain vertical mobility such that the new trachea could be sewn together again. This was beyond my current surgical skill. But watching Dr. Grillo do it would allow me to emulate the operative procedure.

"You did that elegantly." Taking a new scalpel, he proceeded. I felt a sense of usefulness and pride in my ability to assist him.

He opened the neck, exposed the trachea with its endotracheal tube through which the patient was being oxygenated. The damaged ring was excised, giving a quiet blow-by-blow description of what he was doing while he mobilized the rest of the trachea in the chest, freeing it from its attachments to the surrounding lung tissues. He reconstructed the continuity of the windpipe by sewing together the upper and lower sections. I held the skin retractors to give him the exposure he required and ensured his operative field was as free of blood as possible. Despite being a medical student, he sensed I was not a novice at the operating table. He told the scrub to give me the needle holder, which was preloaded with a small size chromic suture for closing the deep layer of the skin, telling me to start in the middle of the wound and to divide the remaining wound sections in half. This ensured that the wound would be closed evenly. He cut the suture above the knots and then showed me how to close the subcuticular layer of the wound with a single running stitch that approximated this layer, closing the shin with steri-strips to result in a fine-looking hairline incision. The nurse then placed a firm dressing.

While we were closing, he told me that he had built a career on reconstructing tracheas and excising tumors involving the windpipe. He had trained generations of surgeons in his techniques and had designed several surgical instruments specifically for these operations. I marveled at the strategy: learn a specialty, such as thoracic surgery, while focusing narrowly on an organ and becoming an expert in its care. I was awed by the proficiency needed to reconstruct a human windpipe—to restore normality for the patient.

Another professor I frequently scrubbed with was Dr. Paul Russell, who performed kidney transplants. Once more, the very concept of extending a person's existence and restoring their normal life through surgical intervention greatly impressed me. My horizons were expanding.

Reluctantly, I was drawn into a vascular emergency procedure. The vascular service's chief resident, a man with seven years of surgical training, and his crew of fellow residents wheeled in a middle-aged patient with an embolus that had lodged in the main artery of the leg. There were no measurable pulses in the foot by Doppler ultrasound, and the appendage was cold and white—*phlegmasia alba dolens*. I had nightmarish flashbacks of the evening of the UCH Christmas Ball, when I was stuck in theater assisting Mr. Hart on my first vascular case, which had been poorly worked up and lacked adequate radiological support. Here the operating room was well equipped for vascular surgery, having overhead X-ray equipment worked by a radiology technician, who was in the room. The appropriate instruments and specific sutures were available, stocked in the vascular room. Once the patient was asleep with his groin prepped and draped, the femoral artery was dissected out. Despite my dread, this operation was different.

The chief resident placed special vascular clamps above the

artery to prevent hemorrhaging when he made a small cut into it. He passed a vascular catheter down the leg. Once the overhead X-ray scan showed its opaque tip was beyond the suspected clot, he inflated a small balloon and slowly pulled back the catheter into the incision, returning clotted red blood and a denser white embolus. I could hear the echo of blood flowing in the distal arteries, as measured by the Doppler, and the leg almost immediately pinked up.

He placed the embolus on a green towel that covered a side table, and there was a general "ah ha" and joyful buzz among the residents. I missed the significance of this crucial piece of evidence. There was an air of satisfaction in the room as the chief resident carried the specimen off to the lab, leaving his juniors to close the wound. And leaving the patient with a viable pink leg. The pathology report, ready that evening, showed the white embolus to be myxoma tissue. It could only have originated from a tumor of the heart because 75% of myxoma tumors occur in the left atrium, the small chamber sitting on the ventricle. I now understood the triumphant "ah ha." I spent time reading about the condition in the library, waiting for the cafeteria to close to the public so that I could freely gorge myself on the day's leftovers for I was famished.

A few days later, the heart-lung pump team stood by, ready to help divert the blood from the heart after they cracked open the patient's chest. The uniqueness of the case drew a crowd of spectators, who stood three-deep to watch the operation. On walking in, I first met my benefactor, Dr. Gerald Austen. After a very gracious and welcoming introduction, he placed me on a stack of stools to observe the procedure over the heads of the crowd. Once the patient was on the heart-lung machine and the heartbeat had stopped, the tension in the room rose as his resident opened the right atrium and cleared it of blood. A beautiful, delicate, sea anemone-type tumor, a few millimeters in size, grew on the cusp of the mitral valve. There were no other tumors. With the élan of a perfect golf swing, the surgeon swiftly cut the tumor off the mitral valve cusp to a crescendo of cheers. It was my first time observing open-heart surgery. I felt faint, stumbled off the stools into Dr. Austen's arms, and blacked out.

Lying in bed that night, I reflected on events of the previous few days. The level of eagerness among the residents and my fellow medical students was astonishing. Their dedication to surgery and teaching was impressive, and their resolve for patient care was like nothing I had seen before. There was an atmosphere of enthusiasm and a willingness to extend the boundaries of surgical knowledge, free of the constraints of tradition or rank. Massachusetts General Hospital was the Mecca of surgery in the Northeast and drew difficult cases. The complexity and spectrum of surgical diseases and the numerous feats of operative skill left me in awe.

I felt that America was equivalent to a tempestuous teenager, full of energy and vigor, while Britain was the sedated grandparent straightjacketed by customs. Despite my admiration and respect for tradition, my admiration of the British, I was fast becoming addicted to the vitality, the "can-do" attitude, that surrounded me in Boston.

# 2

# LIFE AS A SURGICAL STUDENT

A chance to cut is a chance to cure.

—Anonymous

The wind was biting, and the heavy clouds spat snow nearly every day. Initially, the sight of white magic floating down from a heavily laden sky captivated me, reminding me of the enchanting time I first saw snow in Wedel when I was four years old. This mid-November snowfall did not let up. Huge snowplows with flashing lights barreled past the hospital, shoving snow to one side and spraying salt behind them.

Outside, the world grew eerily quiet, and in the muted night, there was a smattering of traffic and a twinkling of streetlights. It took me a while to realize that veterans of prior snowstorms had melted away. I felt alone in the warm hospital and was stranded when a state of emergency was declared and public transportation ceased. I lived three days and nights at Massachusetts General Hospital, seeing the same staff faces on the wards and in the corridors. Patient admissions for routine operations dried up, as did the supply of blood to the blood bank. The cafeteria didn't serve fresh fruit.

Emergency admissions increased. Ambulances deposited critically ill, elderly patients in the ER starting at around 5 p.m. I assisted in operations for perforated gastric and duodenal ulcers. Driving was hazardous, and a deluge of trauma patients from motor vehicle accidents appeared—which was new to my surgical experience. By 8 or 9 p.m., motor vehicle accidents were replaced by a wave of patients with gunshot wound, which ended sometime after midnight. I had not previously experienced such disruption of human anatomy—blunt or penetrating. Certainly, guns were not a part of the British social fabric.

The staff in the cafeteria, too, was stuck in the hospital. They soon recognized me—pale, tired, unshaven, and starving, wandering in between cases. I questioned how fresh the food was because they allowed me to choose dishes, even at lunch, without asking for a meal ticket. What I missed the most was a decent cup of British tea: boiling water poured over loose-leaf black tea in a teapot which after steeping for a while was served with milk. By early afternoon the next day, the sun came out, converting the snow and slush into thin layers of black ice. Unaccustomed to this degree of frigid weather, I set foot outside the building only to get the experience of the cold.

During a quiet period, I was told that once, a Boston mafia bigwig was shot. He had survived an all-night operation to patch him up. In the early morning, a presumed mafia gangster had walked into the lightly staffed ICU in a white coat and shot him at close range, finishing the initial assassination attempt. There was more excitement than indignation at the event. I wondered at the cost of time and supplies that had been squandered during the initial operation, bringing to mind Sister W. at UCH, who complained about the cost of my wanting to use an "American fandangle" syringe.

Amidst all the winter mayhem, I was electrified by the surgical discipline and seduced by the dynamic and systematic approach to the early management of a trauma patient. I was in awe of what could be and was done to save patients' lives. Since I was not part of the trauma team, I did not assist with operation or postoperative care and was merely an observer. Many of the techniques were developed during the war in Vietnam to save the lives of soldiers. Although I had no time to read the paper, the deaths and casualties of the war were a daily discussion among the residents and young faculty at meals. I remembered my anxious time in Cairo during the battles with Israel, and my aversion to meaningless death and destruction.

The residents and faculty appreciated my zest for work, encouraging and reinforcing that element of my personality. Unlike in England, where eagerness is understated and matters were approached with an air of reserve and subtlety, expressing enthusiasm in America was not disdained. I the last time I had enjoyed such euphoria, such a feeling of being alive, was when I was learning to glide in Egypt.

Each week, every complication and death were reviewed in front of the entire surgical faculty at the morbidity and mortality conference. During these meetings, a resident presented a synopsis of the patient's illness, the operative techniques used, and the complications encountered. The faculty discussed different aspects of the case with the intent of learning from any mistakes made. If the patient died, the pathologist projected the post-mortem findings. General discussions followed. The five categories of complications Professor Pilcher had mentioned to me a couple of years ago— errors in diagnosis, in operative technique, in patient management, in clinical judgment, and those due to patient's disease— were assigned and now became meaningful, given the context of the general discussions at what was simply known as M & M conference.

This conference expanded my surgical education immensely because I was hearing the opinions of the most senior faculty—the voices of experts who often didn't agree on the issue at hand. Most of the complications discussed were of low-frequency and high-impact. One such case was a poorly constructed anastomosis where loops of bowel were sewn together and leaked, leading to an intra-abdominal abscess or a catastrophic bacterial infection—both requiring re-operation.

I learned more than surgery, for I saw grown men—surgical residents—reduced to a state of regret and even self-deprecation when things went wrong. I also witnessed redemption and human growth, as regret grew into a second chance—magnanimously part of the American psyche.

Finally, more like the traditional tutorial format in London, there were regular teaching meetings on general surgical topics, where I found I had an edge on the clinical knowledge of disease and its pathophysiology. Surely, here I could develop into the person I was destined to become. The ambitious drive I inherited from my father could be fulfilled, unencumbered by the accident of my birth and buttressed by my acceptance as a human being and surgeon; here, my zebra stripes were not visible. Among these fellow medical students, I was an equal. I thrived in this atmosphere and wondered if getting my surgical training in Boston might be possible. First, though, I'd have to qualify as a doctor at my medical school in England.

Made in the USA
Middletown, DE
17 February 2021

33166222R00220